Defamation
and Related Actions
in Scots Law

Sticks and stone may break my bones,
but names will never harm me

Defamation
and Related Actions
in Scots Law

Kenneth McK Norrie LLB, PhD
Senior Lecturer in Law at
the University of Strathclyde

Butterworths
Edinburgh
1995

United Kingdom	Butterworths a Division of Reed Elsevier (UK) Ltd, 4 Hill Street, EDINBURGH EH2 3JZ and Halsbury House, 35 Chancery Lane, LONDON WC2A 1 EL
Australia	Butterworths, SYDNEY, MELBOURNE, BRISBANE, ADELAIDE, PERTH, CANBERRA and HOBART
Canada	Butterworths Canada Ltd, TORONTO and VANCOUVER
Ireland	Butterworth (Ireland) Ltd, DUBLIN
Malaysia	Malayan Law Journal Sdn Bhd, KUALA LUMPUR
New Zealand	Butterworths of New Zealand Ltd, WELLINGTON and AUCKLAND
Puerto Rico	Butterworth of Puerto Rico, Inc, SAN JUAN
Singapore	Butterworths Asia, SINGAPORE
South Africa	Butterworth Publishers (Pty) Ltd, DURBAN
USA	Butterworth Legal Publishers, CARLSBAD, California and SALEM, New Hampshire

A CIP Catalogue record for this book is available from the British Library

ISBN 0 406 054592

Typeset by Phoenix Photosetting, Chatham, Kent
Printed by Mackays of Chatham PLC, Chatham, Kent

To Amish Amin

Preface

It is almost 90 years since the last textbook devoted to the subject of defamation and verbal injury in Scotland was published. The second edition of Cooper's *Defamation and Verbal Injury*, by D Oswald Dykes, appeared right in the middle of the Edwardian decade and, while the law therein described has remained relatively stable, the society for which it was designed – and which it reflected – has little in common with that which exists in Scotland today. Notions of honour and dignity no longer have quite the social significance that they once did, and though personal reputation remains emotionally important to many individuals, few regard it as so important that it must be protected no matter the cost. It is precisely one hundred years ago that Oscar Wilde destroyed himself by the foolhardy raising of an action for libel in England. The warning remains good today. But actions for defamation are today raised primarily in order to recover direct economic loss that the wrong has caused, and the continuing necessity for the law to provide such redress cannot be denied. When Cooper wrote redress for affront was a major motivation in raising the action, but today it is difficult to feel sympathy with the pursuer who seeks damages only for the affront he or she decides to suffer. I am affronted by many things in life, such as wars, starvation, governmental destruction of the environment, institutionalised discrimination against homosexuals; yet I do not expect compensation for my affront. Affront is a healthy reaction that motivates us to action and ought not, in my view, to give rise to a claim in damages. Economic loss is quite different. If someone deliberately or negligently causes me economic loss then I should certainly be able to reclaim that loss by legal action, whether the loss is caused by words or by deeds. This book is concerned with redress for loss caused by false words. There is place for a book on the modern Scots law of defamation and related actions because of the increased economic value of reputations in business and commerce, in journalism and in most job markets. In addition, a textbook setting out the correct principles of liability in our law is long overdue. Throughout the twentieth century there has been a growing misunderstanding about the nature and purpose – and even the rules – of the Scottish action for defamation, and this book is an attempt to prevent these misunderstandings from becoming embedded into the law by judicial decision or even legislation. (The statutory reference to the non-existent concept of *convicium* is but one example of how error can become apparently established law.) The lack of a modern textbook has led to undue reliance, particularly amongst practitioners, on English commentaries and English authorities, which is unfortunate not only because it runs the risk of further distorting our law but also because the English law of libel and slander is hardly the part of their system that English lawyers are most proud of. I have used English authorities only in those rare instances where there is no Scottish case in point, and wherever possible Scottish authority is given preference even when substantially older than available English cases.

Many people have assisted me in various ways in the compilation of this book, and thanks are due to them all, including Professor G Maher and Professor JM Thomson for reading and commenting upon sections of the manuscript, Ms Eilidh Scobbie and Mr Gordon Brough for giving me access to (then) unpublished material and, in particular, Mr Alistair Bonnington for reading and making valuable comment upon the whole manuscript. Special thanks are also due to Professor JWG Blackie for giving his time to discuss numerous points of law and legal history. Thanks are also due to Mrs Jean McFadden and to my research assistants Mr Craig Harvie and Ms Karen Shaw. Amish Amin provides, as always, much needed support.

I have stated my view of the law as at 1 January 1995.

Kenneth McK Norrie
January 1995

Contents

Table of statutes

Table of cases

The page numbers in brackets refer to the page of the Scots Law Times (vols 1–16) on which the case is reported.

Abbreviations

Law reports

AC	Law Reports, Appeal Cases (House of Lords and Privy Council) (England)
Ad & E	Adolphus and Ellis's Reports (English Reports)
All ER	All England Law Reports
App Cas	Law Reports, Appeal Cases (House of Lords) (England)
B & S	Best and Smith (English Reports)
CLY	Current Law Year Book
D	Dunlop's Session Cases
DLR	Dominion Law Reports (Canada)
ECR	European Court of Justice Reports
EHRR	European Human Rights Reports
F	Fraser's Session Cases
GWD	Green's Weekly Digest
HL Cas	House of Lords Cases (England)
IR	Irish Reports
IRLR	Industrial Relations Law Reports
KB	Law Reports, King's Bench Division (England)
M	Macpherson's Session Cases
Mor	Morison's Dictionary of Decisions (Court of Session)
Mur	Murray's Jury Court Cases
NZLR	New Zealand Law Reports
QB	Law Reports, Queen's Bench Division (England)
R	Rettie's Session Cases
S	Shaw's Session Cases
SCLR	Scottish Civil Law Reports
SLR	Scottish Law Reporter
SLT	Scots Law Times
SN	Session Notes
Sc Jur	Scottish Jurist
Sh App	P Shaw's Scotch Appeals (House of Lords)
Sh Ct Rep	Sheriff Court Reports (in Scottish Law Review)
Sol Jo	Solicitors' Journal (England)
TLR	Times Law Reports (England)
WLR	Weekly Law Reports (England)

Journals

JLS	Journal of the Law Society of Scotland
JR	Juridical Review
LS	Legal Studies

Textbooks

Anton & Beaumont	*Private International Law* (2nd edn, 1990)
Carter-Ruck	*Libel and Slander* (4th edn, 1992)
Cooper	*Defamation and Verbal Injury* (2nd edn,1906)
Erskine	*Institute of the Law of Scotland* (2 vols, 1773)
Glegg	*Reparation* (4th edn, 1955)
Hume Lect	Hume, *Lectures on the Law of Scotland*, Stair Society
Smith	*A Short Commentary on the Laws of Scotland* (1963)
Stair	*Institutions of the Law of Scotland*
Stewart	*Delict* (2nd edn, 1993)
Thomson	*Delictual Liability* (1994)
Walker	*Delict* (2nd edn, 1981)

CHAPTER ONE

Historical introduction

Introduction

The law of Scotland has always placed high regard on a person's right to reputation. Stair, listing the important interests that are protected by the law, puts 'fame, reputation, and honour' third to 'life, members and health' and 'liberty'[1]. If character, honour and reputation is unjustly attacked the law provides remedies through the actions for defamation, verbal injury, and even negligence. As a society, we (rightly) pay less heed today to notions of honour than we used to, for name-calling no longer has the socially destructive potency that it once did. Yet attacks on character, honour and reputation remain actionable, not only because reputation retains emotional significance for a lot of people but also because its destruction can result in clear and substantial economic loss. A bad reference from an ex-employer that destroys one's reputation can render a person unemployable. A businessperson accused of untrustworthiness or dishonesty can have his or her business ruined. In today's society we might well be unsympathetic to claims for damages based solely on insult to honour, but destruction of a person's character as an economic asset is clearly as worthy of redress as physical destruction of his or her property. How and when that redress can be achieved is the subject of this book.

Attacks on character, honour and reputation are normally dealt with today through the action for defamation, which is, literally, the taking away of a person's fame, and it is this action that we will be primarily concerned with. But there are, as we will see, other forms of action too that achieve the same end. Before examining the different actions, this chapter will be devoted to a short history of the law in this area and will end with a speculative prediction on how the law may develop in the future.

The development of the law

A compensation given as solace for suffering, loss or injured feelings.

In Roman law insult, or affront to dignity, was actionable under the *actio injuriarum* and damages in the form of *solatium* could be obtained if the pursuer proved that the insult had been committed intentionally (that is with *animus*

1 *Institutions of the Law of Scotland*, I, 4, 4.

injuriandi). Patrimonial loss suffered as a result of injurious words was also actionable, under the *Lex Aquilia*, and damages in the form of reparation could be obtained on proof of *culpa*, or fault (which might or might not be constituted by intention to injure). The two elements of insult on the one hand and patrimonial loss on the other hand have always been recognised in Scots law[1], though the strict Roman law dichotomy between the two was never fully received. The logic of the Roman law position commends itself to common sense, though the two elements always overlapped to a certain extent: today they have clearly coalesced in Scots law into one action for which both solatium for affront and reparation for economic loss can be claimed. According to Smith[2], in the older Scottish practice insult was dealt with mainly in the Commissary courts which sought palinode (that is, a public retraction of the allegation made) and imposed solatium, while damage to reputation as an economic asset was dealt with mainly in the sheriff court or the Court of Session, which awarded damages for loss. In other words, he saw traces in Scottish procedure of the Roman law distinction between *animus injuriandi* (founding liability for insult) and *culpa* (founding liability for patrimonial loss). These jurisdictions were never, however, as exclusive as Smith suggests and the distinction between *animus injuriandi* and *culpa*, in so far as it existed in practice rather than law, disappeared completely with the establishment of the Jury Court. Smith criticises the Jury Court for imposing onto Scots law the English notion of malice as the basis for liability, but it has to be noted that malice was and is used as a convenient and more readily understandable term for *animus injuriandi*. The truly significant change brought about by the Jury Court was to recognise that malice (or *animus injuriandi*) was the basis of liability for both insult and patrimonial loss and that this was to be presumed from the harmful nature of the words themselves[3]. It is now malice rather than *culpa* that founds all actions for defamation and verbal injury (though, as we will see, *culpa* remains as an alternative basis for an action raised in negligence rather than defamation[4]).

Insulting words have always been seen in terms of attacks on a person's honour, and as such they originally came within the jurisdiction of the church courts, which jurisdiction came to be exercised by the Commissaries. Though originally the primary purpose of the action was to restore the pursuer's reputation (achieved by means of palinode), the church courts were wont to regard attacks on honour as ecclesiastical offences for which the penalty of fine was appropriate. The fine was frequently diverted to the injured party as compensation when patrimonial loss had been caused and in that way the civil remedy of damages evolved. Defamation therefore was before the Reformation both a criminal and a civil wrong, and when the Commissary courts were statutorily recognised after the Reformation as possessing the jurisdiction previously

1 Unlike English law where insult alone does not found an action.
2 *A Short Commentary on the Law of Scotland* (1962) pp 724–730.
3 Previously both *animus injuriandi* and *culpa* had to be proved by the pursuer, but this is not surprising at a time when defamation remained partly criminal.
4 Below at pp 5–6.

exercised by the church courts[1] the dual nature of the (relatively common[2]) wrong continued. The criminal aspect of defamation may well have predominated in the century or so after the Reformation, and it is worthy of note that Mackenzie deals with verbal injuries in his *Laws and Customs of Scotland on Matters Criminal*[3] rather than in his *Institutions*[4].

Jurisdiction did not lie exclusively with the Commissaries however[5] and the Court of Session, the High Court of Justiciary and even Justices of the Peace were used to hearing actions for defamation in the eighteenth century. However, it was not until the case of *Auchenleck v Gordon*[6] that the Inner House affirmed the jurisdiction of the Court of Session as a court of first instance in such actions, but of course penal sanctions were unavailable to the Court of Session. The continuing predominance of the criminal law element may well explain the paucity of decisions on defamation in the Court of Session in the years following *Auchenleck*. Though never formally abolished, the criminal aspect of defamation withered with the withering of the importance of the Commissaries[7] and had disappeared completely by the time the Jury Court was established in 1816[8]. This court took over actions for defamation from the higher courts though it was (and is) still possible to raise an action in the sheriff court. The Jury Court was absorbed into the Court of Session in 1830[9], which thereby acquired jurisdiction to try cases of defamation by jury as well as by proof before a judge alone[10]. The sheriff court never had the power to try defamation cases by jury but it retains the right to hear cases before the sheriff alone.

Since the abolition of the Jury Court, the state of the law of defamation has been remarkably stable and cases in the first half of the nineteenth century read with noticeable modernity. Most of the principles which are applied today had been laid down by 1850, though there has been the major development since then of the recognition of verbal injury as a separate, though related, action. Statute has impinged on the law of defamation only to a minimal extent. The Defamation Act 1952 introduced the defence of offer of amends for innocent defamation[11] and made some other minor adjustments, but has seldom figured in the law reports. Perhaps one of the most interesting features in the history of this branch of the law has been the fluctuating popularity

---

1 Stair Society vol 20, pp 369–371.
2 Ibid, p 370.
3 (1678) Book II, title 20.
4 (1684).
5 But see *Mackenzie*, above.
6 (1755) Mor 7348. The pleadings of the defender in this case contain an illuminating history of the jurisdiction of the Commissaries.
7 The inferior Commissaries were abolished in 1823 and the Commissary Court of Edinburgh abolished in 1836.
8 Jury Trials (Scotland) Act 1815. Defamation remains a crime in some circumstances in England: see Carter-Ruck, *Libel and Slander* (4th edn, 1992) pp 182–195. There is no possibility of defamation being revived as a crime in Scotland today.
9 Court of Session Act 1830.
10 Which process is today to be used in the Court of Session will be examined below at pp 160–164.
11 See below at pp 83–87.

of the action. In Stair's time actions for defamation were rare, certainly in comparison with England[1], and this continued throughout the eighteenth century. However, by the first half of the nineteenth century actions had become relatively common, though not outrageously so. By the mid-1880s numbers were substantially increasing and the heyday of the Scottish defamation action was the 20-year period between 1890 and 1910 in which there are over 250 reported cases[2]. Numbers declined thereafter and substantially so after the end of the First World War. Between then and 1990 no decade averaged more than two reported cases a year and some decades averaged substantially less than that. This decline in popularity of the action was doubtless the result of a combination of factors: the demise of the late Victorian ideal of honour, the unavailability of legal aid (and the poor roll), the fact that juries were almost unknown for much of the twentieth century, and the modest level of Scottish defamation damages, being amongst the most important. Possibly due to the publicity generated by massive awards in England in the late 1980s, the Scottish courts have recently seen an increase in the number of reported defamation cases. Whether this increase is sustained remains to be seen.

Development of the related actions

While the law of defamation itself has remained, as pointed out above, fairly stable since about 1830, there have been significant developments in related fields. As we will see more fully in Chapter 3, it came to be recognised in the middle of the nineteenth century that defamation was not the only way in which a person's character, honour and reputation could be attacked and suffer loss. As early as 1855[3] it was recognised that non-defamatory statements which were made with the intent to injure the pursuer and which did so injure could be actionable, and by the turn of the century such actions were being referred to as cases of 'verbal injury'[4]. It may well be, as Walker has pointed out[4] that the use of that nomenclature was unfortunate since 'verbal injury' had previously been understood to mean the genus of actions which contained defamation and other related actions based on character attacks. However that may be, the term has been consistently used throughout this century to refer to cases based on non-defamatory injurious communications and there is indeed now statutory sanction for this usage[5]; it is too late to attempt to return

1 At I, 4, 4 he says 'Such actions upon injurious words, as they may relate to damages in means, are frequent and curious amongst the English; but with us there is little of it accustomed to be pursued'.
2 The graph in the appendix shows the distribution of reported Scottish cases of defamation and verbal injury identified by the author between 1860 and 1994. The author is grateful to Mrs Jean McFadden for suggesting the creation of this graph.
3 *Sheriff v Wilson* (1855) 17 D 528. See further, below at p 51.
4 As Walker points out in *Delict* (2nd edn, 1981) pp 732–734 the judges were a little slower than the commentators and law reporters in using the phrase 'verbal injury'. The first edition of Cooper's book *Defamation and Verbal Injury* was published in 1894, though it was some years after that before judges were commonly referring to the other action as verbal injury.
5 Defamation Act 1952, s 3; Legal Aid (Scotland) Act 1986, Sch 2. And see further, below at pp 32–35.

the understanding of the phrase back to its old meaning. The categories of verbal injury have been recognised to include slander of property, title or business, holding up of the pursuer to public hatred, contempt and ridicule, third party slander, and other malicious falsehoods[1]. The defining feature of all of these cases, and the distinction from defamation, is that neither falsity nor malice will be presumed and will therefore require to be proved by the pursuer.

Actions for verbal injury remain rare in Scotland. A much more recent, and potentially far-reaching, development occurred in 1994 with the House of Lords decision in the English case of *Spring v Guardian Assurance plc*[2]. Here, the plaintiff had worked for the defendant insurance company and was seeking employment with another insurance company: his ex-employers gave him a very derogatory reference which effectively destroyed his hopes of working anywhere in the insurance industry. Now, the statements contained in the reference were admittedly defamatory and false and a successful claim for defamation would have entitled the plaintiff to substantial damages. However, notwithstanding the admission that the reference was defamatory and false, the plaintiff could not raise a successful action for defamation, for he would have been met with the defence of qualified privilege which, as we will see[3], imposes upon the plaintiff, in situations in which it applies, the extra onus of proving malice. This the plaintiff could not do. So instead of raising the action in defamation the plaintiff pleaded negligence on the part of his ex-employers, founding upon the case of *Hedley Byrne v Heller & Partners*[4]. The defendants admitted negligence but pleaded that the law did not allow an action for negligence upon defamatory words since this would obviate the defences available in defamation but not negligence and go against the policy upon which these defences (in particular qualified privilege) is based. While the Court of Appeal[5] accepted that argument[6], the House of Lords, by a majority of four to one, did not. Their Lordships did not accept that it could be a defence to an action for negligence that the defendants would have a defence had the case been one of defamation. They saw the case rather in terms of liability for economic loss and as a small extension of the principles laid down in *Hedley Byrne*, which allowed recovery to the recipient of a negligent misstatement who relied upon it. In *Spring* recovery was allowed to the subject of a negligent misstatement which was unjustly bad rather than, as in *Hedley Byrne*, unjustly good. The significant extension came in the notion of reliance, for in *Hedley Byrne* the plaintiffs had relied on the statement to their loss, while in *Spring* all the plaintiff had relied upon (ie expected) was that the defendants would take reasonable care in drawing up the reference: he had, in

---

1 All of these forms of action are examined in detail in Chapter 4.
2 [1994] 3 All ER 129.
3 Below at pp 103–104, 120–123.
4 [1964] AC 465.
5 [1993] 2 All ER 273, 1993 IRLR 122.
6 As it had been accepted in the New Zealand cases of *Bell-Booth Group Ltd v Attorney General* [1989] 3 NZLR 148 and *Balfour v Attorney-General* [1991] 1 NZLR 519.

other words, relied on the defendants stating facts accurately rather than on the facts themselves. Lord Keith dissented from the majority because he was unwilling to make this extension to the recognised categories of liability for economic loss. Most of the judges adopted a two-stage approach of finding that there was a sufficiently proximate relationship between the plaintiff and the defendant to impose a duty of care on the latter towards the former (which was relied upon by the former), and then holding that there was no reason in public policy to deny liability[1]. The fear of honest references being discouraged by allowing a plaintiff who could not establish malice to obtain damages was countered by the discouraging of careless or negligent references that the recognition of liability in negligence would effect.

Though this is an English case, it is one that falls into the sphere of negligence rather than defamation and the House of Lords is not likely to accept that the Scots law of negligence is any different from the English law of negligence. Though there are differences in the law of defamation, the defence of qualified privilege is to all intents and purposes identical in the two systems. And besides, there is old Scottish authority to suggest that in a case of verbal injury, if *animus injuriandi* cannot be proved, the pursuer can still obtain damages if he shows negligence on the part of the defender[2]. The result is that pursuers who can prove that a defender has made a defamatory statement negligently can choose whether to sue in negligence or in defamation. A claim in negligence has the advantage that it can be funded by legal aid[3], and in cases in which qualified privilege would be a defence in defamation a claim in negligence has the advantage that malice does not have to be proved. But the normal requirements for liability for economic loss caused by negligent misstatements will have to be established, that is duty, breach and causation, together with acceptance of responsibility by the defender and reliance thereon by the pursuer[4]: just how difficult it will be to establish these requirements when dealing with injurious words remains to be seen. It is likely that a claim in negligence will be available only to give damages for economic loss, for a claim based on insult alone would be met with the defence that emotional distress amounting to something less than a psychiatric illness does not found an action for damages in negligence[5]. Still to be resolved is the question of whether the other defences to defamation are as irrelevant to actions in negligence as the defence of qualified privilege. The policy considerations in absolute privilege, for example, are far stronger, and this defence would almost

1 Adopting the two-stage test laid down by Lord Wilberforce in *Anns v Merton London Borough Council* [1978] AC 728.
2 See *Craig v Hunter & Co* 29 June 1809, FC, in which the pursuer's name wrongly appeared in a commercial 'black-list' published by the defenders.
3 In the English case of *Joyce v Sengupta* [1993] 1 WLR 337 the Court of Appeal permitted legal aid in a case of malicious falsehood that could have been raised in negligence but for the fact that the plaintiff could not afford to do so. (That option is not open in Scotland since legal aid is denied to actions for both defamation and verbal injury – but not to negligence.)
4 See generally Thomson, *Delictual Liability* (1994) pp 67–75.
5 *Simpson v ICI* 1983 SLT 601. Insult founds an action for defamation because, technically speaking, defamation is an intentional delict which is limited by the extent of the intention: negligence, being unintentional, might be of unlimited extent if any form of emotional distress founded an action.

certainly prevent an action in negligence as it does in defamation. Truth is probably a defence in negligence, on the basis that telling the truth can cause no loss recognised by the law. Fair comment, or something similar, may also be a defence in negligence in the sense that there will seldom be the required proximity between defender and pursuer[1].

The future

While the law of defamation itself remains static, the law of negligence continues to expand its beneficent influence and now provides redress even for cases which previously were thought to come exclusively within the ambit of defamation. This is no bad thing. The action for defamation is, as we will see in the following chapters, full of anomalies. For one thing, it permits damages for affront as a means of clearing a person's name when all that is really required to do so is a declarator that the statement complained of is false. And for another thing, it permits economic loss to be recovered in circumstances in which the defender has neither intended loss nor been negligent in causing that loss. The presumption of malice or intent to injure (which is irrebuttable in cases in which qualified privilege does not apply) is the single most bizarre feature of the law of defamation. It is a leap of logic to say that because something is hurtful, therefore it was designed to hurt. The action for negligence on the other hand gives damages for economic loss when that loss has been caused carelessly and in breach of a duty not to cause it. The requirements for proximity, acceptance of responsibility, and reliance will keep that action within sensible bounds. This may be the future for attacks on character, honour and reputation – economic loss will be recoverable by actions for negligence when *culpa* is established, and the insult-only cases can be left to be dealt with under malice-based defamation. How neat it would be[2] if Scots law finally accepted that dichotomy which the Romans had recognised[3] and Smith[4] thought we previously had but had lost for ever.

---

1 These matters are explored in a little more depth in Norrie, 'Death-Knell for Defamation?' (1994) 39 JLSS 418.
2 Too neat, perhaps?
3 Above at pp 1–2.
4 *Short Commentary* pp 727–732.

CHAPTER TWO

Liability for defamation

Introduction

The action for defamation is by far the most common form of action arising from an attack on a person's character, honour and reputation, and in many respects it is the most peculiar. It is an intentional delict in which the intent to injure is usually irrebuttably presumed[1]. It is a delict only if the statement or communication upon which it is based is false, but with which falsity is rebuttably presumed leaving the defender with the onus of proving, as a defence, truth or *veritas*[2]. The pursuer does, however, always have the onus of proving that the statement or communication complained about is 'defamatory' and that it has been 'communicated' from the defender to either the pursuer alone or to some other person. Liability for defamation arises, therefore, only when the pursuer relevantly pleads and subsequently proves both elements.

The nature of a defamatory statement

Defamation is, literally, the taking away of one's fame[3] and to be actionable the pursuer must establish that the statement or communication is injurious in the sense of being capable of harming the pursuer's public character, honour or reputation. A defamatory statement or communication is one that is false, though not all false statements are defamatory; likewise it is one that is offensive, though not every statement that offends is defamatory. Rather, a statement that the law holds capable of harming character, honour or reputation is one that is derogatory or disparaging or demeaning or calumnious in the eyes of the reasonable person. At one time the law of Scotland seemed to take the view that a statement was defamatory only if it came within certain well defined categories. So for example Lord McLaren, whose judgments have been particularly influential in the Scots law of defamation, can be found saying that, 'by slander is meant the imputation of something which is criminal, dishonest, or immoral in the character or actions of the person

---

1 See further, below at pp 79–83.
2 See below at Chapter 9.
3 Green's *Encyclopaedia of Scots Law* vol 5, § 1102.

aggrieved'[1]. As an Outer House judge, he had previously described 'libellous' as meaning,

'the imputation of a crime or anything that would outrage the public conscience or sense of propriety . . . It is not necessary, in order that the statement should be calumnious, that it should impute a crime; a statement may amount to a libel if it accuses a person of what is universally considered to be an immoral act, or if it imputes conduct which is contrary to the generally accepted standard of honour or propriety amongst gentlemen – amongst the class of persons to which the individual aggrieved belongs'[2].

Coming out clearly from these dicta are two categories: criminality and immorality, the one as precise as the other is indeterminate. However, just as in the general law of delict the law has moved away from categorising wrongs and towards a general principle for delictual liability, so the law of defamation has moved away from a categorised to a more general definition. Cooper defines defamation as,

'the wrong or delict which is committed when a person makes an injurious and false imputation, conveyed by words or signs, against the character or reputation of another. Character or reputation must be here understood in the widest sense to include moral and social reputation and financial credit'[3].

In an earlier text, sadly neglected today, Sheriff Guthrie Smith[4] says that an injury to character may be caused in one or other of two ways:

'Directly, by the application to a particular individual of words or epithets tending to make him mean, disreputable, ridiculous, or contemptible; [or] indirectly, by the false imputation of such acts as may lower him in the estimation of the public, or make his society shunned by those with whom he is accustomed to associate'.

This second way by which defamation can be committed, authority for which Guthrie Smith finds in Grotius[5], is made the basis of the classic test for defamation in the English House of Lords decision in *Sim v Stretch*[6]. There Lord Atkin was at pains to free English law from the narrowness of the then accepted test for liability[7], which was 'exposing the plaintiff to hatred, ridicule and contempt'. Instead he proposed the following test: 'Would the words tend to lower the plaintiff in the estimation of right-thinking members of society generally?'[8]. The significance of this test cannot be overstated. Applied strictly, and the law can be kept within acceptable bounds and hurts will be compensated only when justly they should be; applied loosely, or ignored altogether, and the law ends up giving remedies for perceived hurts

1 *McLaughlan v Orr, Pollock & Co* (1894) 22 R 38 at 42.
2 *Macfarlane v Black & Co* (1887) 14 R 870 at 872–873.
3 Cooper, *Defamation and Verbal Injury* (2nd edn, 1906) p 1.
4 *The Law of Reparation* (1864) p 188. This text was substantially revised and expanded in 1889 and published as *The Law of Damages*: the neglect of this edition is a matter for less regret than the neglect of the 1864 book.
5 *Naturrecht*, ss 306.
6 [1936] 2 All ER 1237.
7 Now, doesn't that sound familiar?
8 [1936] 2 All ER 1237 at 1240. This test has been accepted as representing the law of Scotland in *Steele v Scottish Daily Record and Sunday Mail* 1970 SLT 53 and in *Thomson v News Group Newspapers* 1992 GWD 14–825.

and slights that all but the most sensitive or the most arrogant would shrug off with ease. Some of the claims that clutter the English courts indicate in a most unedifying manner that the law there pays less regard to this statement than it should and it is noticeable in that jurisdiction that defences to the effect that a statement which the plaintiff finds personally hurtful is not defamatory seldom meet with success. Yet Lord Atkin's 'right-thinking member of society' principle is as important in the law of defamation as his 'neighbourhood principle' is in the law of negligence, and strict attention should be paid to it.

Applying this test, a statement or communication is legally defamatory only when, if believed, reasonable or 'right-thinking' people would shun the pursuer or think significantly less of him or her. The important point is that the pursuer must be lowered in the estimation not of people generally, but of *right-thinking* people generally and it is the court that determines what right-thinking people think. In other words, the test is an objective one with the court determining whether members of society *ought to* regard a particular allegation as calumnious. This will invariably be influenced by whether members of society actually do regard it as demeaning, but it is not in every case determined by that fact. So for example an allegation that a person is insane may in fact result in that person being shunned by many – even most – people, but the allegation will be defamatory only if the court agrees that right-thinking members of society should shun the subject of the statement. A 'right-thinking' person we may take to be the law of defamation's equivalent to the 'man on the Clapham omnibus', or the reasonable person – that is the person without prejudice (for prejudice by definition is unreasonable) and who believes in proper standards of conduct. The question is,

'would a reasonable man, reading the publication complained of, discover in it matter defamatory of the pursuer? Or, put otherwise, the question is, What meaning would the ordinary reader of the newspaper put upon the paragraph which the pursuer complained of?'[1].

'The test, according to the authorities, is, whether under the circumstances in which the writing was published, reasonable men, to whom the publication was made, would be likely to understand it in a libellous [ie derogatory] sense'[2].

Whether the pursuer himself regarded the contentious statement as defamatory is nothing to the point, unless it reflects how the ordinary, decent person would regard it. Conversely,

'it is generally not relevant to construe the meaning of an alleged defamatory statement by the evidence of the defender as to what he intended to convey. No doubt this is on the principle that injury is done by the words actually used in their ordinary and natural sense rather than in any subjective sense intended by the defamer'[3].

---

1 *Duncan v Scottish Newspapers Ltd* 1929 SC 14 at 20 per Lord Anderson.
2 *Capital and Counties Bank Ltd v Henty* (1882) 7 App Cas 741 at 745 per Lord Chancellor Selborne, accepted as representing Scots law in *Russell v Stubbs Ltd* 1913 SC(HL) 14 and in *Muirhead v George Outram & Co* 1983 SLT 201.
3 *Fraser v Mirza* 1992 SLT 740 at 747 per Lord Murray. See also Lord Justice-Clerk Ross at 743D.

In applying this test words will, unless an innuendo is pleaded[1], be given their ordinary and natural meaning[2], with the result that,

'if the words of the writing complained of are unambiguous and harmless in themselves, and if no extrinsic facts are set forth tending to impress a defamatory meaning on the writing that is in question, then the defender is entitled to have the action dismissed, and is not bound to justify publication to a jury'[3].

On the other hand, if the primary meaning of the words used is clearly defamatory, the issue will simply put the question of whether the writing is of and concerning the pursuer, and is false and calumnious to his loss and damage and it will be for the defender to establish the existence of some defence[3]. The publication must, of course, be seen as a whole, and statements made in writing must be read in their context, and if the whole context bears a complimentary overtone, the court will not readily accept that one particular statement within the whole gives a cause of action. For example in *Thomson v News Group Newspapers Ltd*[4] a newspaper carried a report that a professional football player was hiding a knee injury and playing on while unfit in order to assist his team win a title. The pursuer alleged that this suggested that he was hiding his injury from his teammates, but other portions of the article suggested that his teammates were helping the pursuer hide his injury from the team's opponents. The article was false in various major respects, but read as a whole it was not an attack on the pursuer's character or reputation and it was not, therefore, defamatory.

Subjective elements in the test

The test is in its fundaments generally an objective one, referring to the views and opinions of society as a whole in determining whether the statement complained of is defamatory. However, the law does recognise that, just as the reasonable man must be set in his own context by being clothed with certain attributes of the defender, so too the right-thinking member of society is defined according to the section of society to which the pursuer belongs. Guthrie Smith[5] was quoted above as defining defamation as imputations which make the person's society shunned 'by those with whom he is accustomed to associate', and Lord McLaren talked of the standards of propriety accepted 'amongst the class of persons to which the individual aggrieved belongs'[6]. Lord Atkin added another consideration by recognising that his test 'is complicated by having to consider the person or class of persons whose reaction to the publication is the test of the wrongful character of the words

1 See below at pp 13–17.
2 *Fraser v Mirza* 1992 SLT 740 at 743D per Lord Justice-Clerk Ross.
3 *Sexton v Ritchie & Co* (1890) 17 R 680 at 696 per Lord McLaren.
4 1992 GWD 14–825.
5 *The Law of Reparation* p 188.
6 *Macfarlane v Black & Co* (1887) 14 R 870 at 873.

used'[1]. So in determining the views of the 'right-thinking member of society generally' the court has to take account of the type of person likely to hear or read the words complained about, the pursuer's own personal circumstances, and all the circumstances in which the statement is made. To allege that the pursuer broke the Sabbath will not be derogatory in the eyes of the generality of the readership of a local newspaper in, say, Edinburgh, but it might well be if the allegation is made in a local newspaper on one of the strongly Sabbatarian islands[2]; to allege that a person is full of sin may be meaningless to an atheist but utterly destructive of a zealot; to allege that a person knows nothing of medicine will not hurt the lawyer but may well hurt the doctor. In *Lloyd v Hickley*[3] one sportsman said of another that he was 'unsporting' and 'dishonourable'. These words may, in general, be fairly innocuous and would not hurt many people, but said of a sportsman, at a meeting of sportsmen, they were capable of disparaging the pursuer's character and reputation and were therefore actionable. However, it is always to be remembered that the pursuer's associates must be 'right-thinking' and if their views are unreasonable in the eyes of the court then they will be discounted in determining whether the statement is defamatory or not. In *Byrne v Dean*[4] the plaintiff averred that an allegation that he had reported his own club to the police for breach of regulations was a defamatory statement because the club members would regard this as an act of disloyalty. The Court of Appeal rejected that plea and held that to say of a man that he has put in motion the proper machinery for suppressing crime is a thing which cannot on the face of it be considered defamatory[5].

Matters of law and matters of fact

It is for the court to determine, as a matter of law, whether the words complained of are capable of the defamatory meaning which the pursuer seeks to ascribe to them[6], and in Scotland the court makes this determination before allowing an issue to be sent to the jury or before allowing a proof. It is therefore important that the pursuer's pleadings set forth clearly what

---

1 *Sim v Stretch* [1936] 2 All ER 1237 at 1240.
2 Cf Lord McLaren's comments in *Macfarlane v Black & Co*, above.
3 1967 SLT 225.
4 [1937] 1 KB 818.
5 Cf *Graham v Roy* (1851) 13 D 634, in which an allegation that the pursuer had given information to Excise officers against a distiller was held to innuendo him as a common informer acting from disreputable motives. *Kennedy v Allan* (1848) 10 D 1293 and *Winn v Quillan* (1899) 37 SLR 38 are to the same effect. In all three cases it was the innuendo of disreputable motives rather than the fact of being an informer that gave the ground of action. *Berry v Irish Times Ltd* [1973] IR 368 is an interesting example from the Republic of Ireland: in that case it was held not defamatory to accuse an Irish civil servant of helping to jail Republicans in England.
6 *Russell v Stubbs Ltd* 1913 SC(HL) 14 at 20 per Lord Kinnear, and at 24 per Lord Shaw of Dunfermline; *Sim v Stretch* [1936] 2 All ER 1237 at 1240 per Lord Atkin.

meaning he or she wishes to be ascribed to the statements complained of. If the words are on the face of them defamatory he or she need do no more but,

'if . . . the statement complained of is not defamatory in its own terms it is for the pursuer to aver on record what he says it really means and to set out in his pleadings any circumstances (leading up to or surrounding the utterance of the statement or affecting the minds of those to whom it was uttered) which may throw light on its true meaning'[1].

In such a case it is a question for the court, 'to determine whether the facts stated are such as to entitle the pursuer to have the case sent to a jury on an issue setting forth the innuendo or secondary meaning which he undertakes to prove'[2]. It is then for the jury or fact finder to determine whether as a matter of fact the statements have defamed the pursuer (that is, have injured his character, honour or reputation). Likewise, if the statement is ambiguous, that is if there are two meanings apparent to any intelligent person, one being inoffensive and the other being defamatory, the pursuer is entitled to have the case referred to a jury to determine which is the true meaning to be ascribed to the publication in the circumstances[3]. In other words, it is a question of law whether the statement complained of is capable of carrying a defamatory meaning, and a question of fact whether the statement does or does not defame.

Innuendo

In determining whether a statement or idea is defamatory, the court must examine the statement or idea in the light of the circumstances in which it was made or communicated. Statements made clearly in jest, or in the course of an argument, will not found an action, on the ground that those to whom the statements are directed will not hear them as being meant seriously[4]. However, to juxtapose an apparently innocent statement with surrounding circumstances which give it colour can amount to defamation, for 'the law looks to the substance of the words or acts, and if it is defamatory the utterer will not be protected because he has artfully disguised his libel'[5].

Thus to make a waxwork model of a person acquitted of a charge of murder at a famous trial might not be defamatory, but to place the model beside a room called 'The Chamber of Horrors', which contains models of convicted murderers, may well be[6]. Indeed, a false defamatory meaning can be communicated efficaciously with statements which are all true individually, but

---

1 *Gollan v Thompson Wyles Co* 1930 SC 599 at 602–603 per Lord President Clyde. See also *Lloyd v Hickley* 1967 SLT 225.
2 *Sexton v Ritchie & Co* (1890) 17 R 680 at 696 per Lord McLaren.
3 *Russell v Stubbs Ltd* 1913 SC(HL) 14 at 20 per Lord Kinnear.
4 See below at Chapter 11.
5 *Cooper* p 29.
6 *Monson v Tussauds* [1894] 1 QB 671.

where the omission of some important factor renders the impression conveyed false[1]. To accuse someone of taking your property may be factually accurate but if you have omitted to say that this was done with your permission then that omission might render the statement an allegation of theft. Words on the face of them nondescript, or even complimentary, may be defamatory if their context indicates an innuendo of a defamatory nature. Mark Antony praised Brutus as 'an honourable man' when he went to bury rather than to praise Caesar. But the mob knew that he meant exactly the opposite and that he was inciting them to revenge against Caesar's murderers[2].

It is therefore open to the pursuer to aver and prove that, due to the context or the circumstances of publication of the words or ideas, a meaning not apparent on the face of the words is nevertheless the appropriate meaning to be ascribed to them. This is innuendo, which is defined as 'an indirect or subtle reference, especially one made maliciously or indicating criticism or disapproval; insinuation'[3]. If innuendo is averred, the pursuer must state clearly in his pleadings the meaning that he attaches to the words, together with the extraneous factors or reasons why they should be held to bear a defamatory rather than their obvious meaning.

'In all actions for libel it is the duty of the pursuer to state on the record what he understands, and undertakes to shew, is the true meaning of the writing, taken as a whole. If he proposes to put upon words that are apparently harmless a defamatory meaning by reading them with some special application, then it is his duty to allege the extrinsic circumstances which he says prove that defamatory meaning; but if there is no occasion for alleging extrinsic facts at all, it is still . . . his duty, although he is not necessarily required to state extrinsic facts, to state distinctly the libellous meaning which he attaches to the writing'[4].

So when a woman claimed that a novelist was defaming her in a fictional story by making one character so similar to her that the reasonable reader would assume the character was meant to be her, she had to identify the parallels between the character's life and her own life[5].

An innuendo will nearly always be necessary when what is complained about is not words but actions. To make a signal with the hands, or to create an effigy of a person, requires explanation as to how it is defamatory. To be photographed and fingerprinted by the police without authority may be defamatory, but it can be proved to be so only if there are averments as to what these actions suggest[6]. This is also the case when the statement is made in a

1 *Duncan v Associated Scottish Newspapers Ltd* 1929 SC 14 – the action failed.
2 *Julius Caesar*, Act III, sc 2.
3 *Collins English Dictionary*.
4 *James v Baird* 1916 SC(HL) 158 at 165 per Lord Kinnear. See also *Sexton v Ritchie & Co* (1890) 17 R 680 at 685 per Lord President Inglis.
5 *Cuthbert v Linklater* 1935 SLT 94. The significant parallel, apart from a certain resonance of names, was that the character had shown her distaste for the Union by placing a Union Flag in a men's public toilet, while the pursuer had in real life shown her distaste for the Union by removing a Union Flag from its flagstaff at Stirling Castle. See further, below at pp 81–82.
6 *Adamson v Martin* 1916 SC 319.

foreign language: a jury is not to be expected to understand, without explanation, what a statement uttered in a foreign language, or in Gaelic, meant[1].

Matters of law and matters of fact

It is a matter of law to determine whether the words or ideas complained about carry a defamatory meaning, and the court may therefore refuse an issue on the ground that the action is irrelevant where in its opinion the innuendo is too strained or cannot be inferred from the circumstances. 'It is well settled that it is for the court to decide whether the innuendo is one which the words used may reasonably bear and for the jury in due course to decide as a matter of fact whether the words used should be construed in that sense'[2].

It is for the jury or fact finder to determine whether the statements complained of were in fact understood by those communicated to as bearing a defamatory sense; if they did not then the action will fail even although the words were capable of a defamatory meaning[3]. Just as in negligence a breach of duty is legally innocuous until it causes injury, so too in defamation a statement that is capable of causing hurt to reputation or justifiable affront creates no liability unless it actually does so. If the pursuer avers that the statement bears one defamatory meaning it is that meaning that has to be proved to have been understood by the listeners and damages will not be awarded if it is found that the statement carries another meaning, even if that other meaning is itself defamatory. The reason for this is that the other meaning is not the one the defender is being charged with.

Innuendo and the reasonable man

The test the court will adopt in determining whether an innuendo can be inferred is, again, that of the ordinary reasonable man being communicated to.

'Here again the court has . . . to apply the same standard of the presumed intelligence of the reasonable man, and has to determine whether the suggested innuendo is reasonable, whether, that is to say, it can reasonably be extracted from the language used'[4].

The court will not be too sensitive in finding a defamatory meaning from words merely because they are factually hurtful. The test is not whether the pursuer has been offended but whether the reasonable person in the circumstances of the pursuer would regard the words as offensive.

1 *Martin v McLean* (1844) 6 D 981; *Anderson v Hunter* (1891) 18 R 467; *Bernhardt v Abrahams* 1912 SC 748; *Macdonald v Morrison* (1912) 28 Sh Ct Rep 252; *McAskill v Silver* 1948 SLT (Notes) 63.
2 *Fairbairn v SNP* 1980 SLT 149 at 152 per Lord Ross. See also Lord President Dunedin in *Webster v Paterson & Sons* 1910 SC 459 at 469: 'It is trite law that it is for the bench to say whether a statement will possibly bear the innuendo which is placed upon it; but when the innuendo comes within the bounds of possibility, then it is not for the court, but for the jury, to say whether it actually does bear that innuendo'.
3 *Bernhardt v Abrahams* 1912 SC 748.
4 *Duncan v Associated Scottish Newspapers Ltd* 1929 SC 14 at 21 per Lord Anderson.

'Ordinary men and women have different temperaments and outlooks. Some are unusually suspicious and some are unusually naive. One must try to envisage people between these two extremes and see what is the most damaging meaning they could put on the words in question'[1].

As Lord Shaw of Dunfermline put it:

'I think the test in these cases is this: – Is the meaning sought to be attributed to the language alleged to be libellous one which is a reasonable, natural or necessary interpretation of its terms? . . . To permit . . . a strained and sinister interpretation, which is essentially unjust, to form a ground for reparation would be, in truth, to grant reparation for a wrong which had never been committed . . . The innuendo must represent what is a reasonable, natural, or necessary inference from the words used, regard being had to the occasion and the circumstances of their publication'[2].

Examples of innuendo

Innuendo has been held properly averred from a newspaper announcing the birth of twins to a couple who married the previous month (an imputation of premarital sexual intercourse)[3]; from a statement 'you have travelled twice with the same ticket', that the pursuer was attempting to defraud the defenders[4]; from a statement that the pursuer had been found liable in damages for slander, that he had acted out of animosity and was guilty of dishonourable conduct[5]; from an allegation that two clerks found together in an office toilet were 'worse than beasts', that the two had committed the criminal offence of sodomy or gross indecency[6]; from the police directing that a watch be kept on the pursuer's house, that she was a suspected criminal[7]; from the act of asking the pursuer to return to a shop to be questioned and searched, that she was a common thief[8]; from a reference to a pursuer as having played a leading part in a campaign against 'cheque-book journalism' coupled with an allegation that he had indulged in that practice himself, that he was a hypocrite[9]; from an allegation that an MP did not collect his mail, that he failed diligently to perform his duties as a member of Parliament[10]; from a newspaper article stating that a solicitor was being investigated by the Law Society of Scotland in regard to mortgage irregularities, that the solicitor had been negligent or

---

1 *Lewis v Daily Telegraph* [1964] AC 234 at 259 per Lord Reid.
2 *Russell v Stubbs Ltd* 1913 SC(HL) 14 at 23 and 24 per Lord Shaw of Dunfermline.
3 *Morrison v Ritchie & Co* (1902) 4 F 645. Cf *Cassidy v Daily Mirror Newspapers Ltd* [1929] 2 KB 331, in which the announcement of the engagement of a couple who were already married was held to innuendo that they had been living 'in sin', and *Bordeleau v Bonnyville Nouvelle Ltd* (1993) 97 DLR 4th 764, in which a newspaper congratulating a single 18–year-old girl on the birth of a child to her was held to innuendo aspersions against her moral character.
4 *Cumming v Great North of Scotland Railway Co* 1916 1 SLT 181.
5 *Lyal v Henderson* 1916 SC(HL) 167.
6 *AB v XY* 1917 SC 15.
7 *Robertson v Keith* 1936 SC 29.
8 *Neville v C & A Modes Ltd* 1945 SLT 51 (p 189).
9 *Stein v Beaverbrook Newspapers* 1968 SLT 401.
10 *Fairbairn v SNP* 1980 SLT 149.

fraudulent[1]; from an allegation that the mother of a deceased child had reacted to the sheriff's report after a fatal accident inquiry by saying 'I don't give a damn', that the pursuer was an uncaring and unfeeling mother[2]; and from an allegation that a policeman arresting the pursuer was after the pursuer's name, his job and his colour, that he had no reasonable grounds for charging him[3].

On the other hand, an innuendo was not relevantly averred when a newspaper published an article claiming that a hire purchase firm was being investigated by the Board of Trade: the court held that the reasonable, natural or necessary meaning of the article could not be held to be that the firm was untrustworthy, dishonest and oppressive[4]. Likewise the appearance of the pursuer's name in a list of debtors, with a note attached to the list that it implied nothing other than the fact that the name appeared in the court books, did not bear the innuendo that the pursuer was unable to pay his debts[5]. An innuendo could not be inferred that the pursuer was a liar when the Secretary of State for Scotland had refused to recommend the exercise of the prerogative of mercy towards the pursuer, who had been convicted of a crime, had had that conviction upheld on appeal, and had requested the Secretary of State to recommend mercy[6]. Nor were innuendos relevantly pleaded from a statement that a professional footballer had risked his career by concealing a serious knee injury (that he had deceived his employers)[7]; from a statement that the pursuer 'ostentatiously remained seated' during the national anthem (that he was disloyal to his country and was not prepared to honour it)[8]; from a statement that the pursuer's action for damages for slander had failed (that the original allegation was therefore true)[9]; from an allegation that the pursuer was neglecting his child (that he was guilty of criminal neglect)[10]; or from the placing of an advertisement 'wet nurse wanted immediately' at the pursuers' address (that the pursuers, only five months married, had been guilty of antenuptial fornication)[11].

Types of defamatory imputations

The sorts of statements that the right-thinking member of society generally would find derogatory or demeaning can be grouped together into a number of different categories, but such classification is useful only as illustration and

1 *Muirhead v George Outram & Co* 1983 SLT 201.
2 *McCabe v News Group Newspapers* 1992 SLT 707.
3 *Fraser v Mirza* 1993 SLT 527.
4 *NG Napier v Port of Glasgow Courier Ltd* 1959 SLT (Sh Ct) 54.
5 *Russell v Stubbs Ltd* 1913 SC(HL) 14. Cf *Mazure v Stubbs Ltd* 1919 SC(HL) 112.
6 *Leitch v Secretary of State for Scotland* 1983 SLT 394.
7 *Thomson v News Group Newspapers* 1992 GWD 14–825.
8 *Moffat v London Express Newspapers Ltd* 1950 SLT (Notes) 46.
9 *Duncan v Associated Scottish Newspapers Ltd* 1929 SC 14.
10 *Rae v Scottish Society for the Prevention of Cruelty to Children* 1924 SC 102.
11 *Wood v Edinburgh Evening News Ltd* 1910 SC 895.

has no legal consequence. Many defamatory imputations can fit into more than one category (for example, a statement that a person has been convicted of a crime of immorality), and some cannot readily fit into any (for example, an allegation that a person is heartless, or hard-hearted). However, the following classifications are offered to shed illustrative light on what the Scottish courts have regarded as defamatory imputations.

Imputations of criminality

To accuse a person of having committed a criminal offence is in many respects the archetypal defamatory statement. This is one of the categories long recognised by the law and, in numerical terms, is one of the most common types of allegation that comes before the courts[1]. This may well be because whether or not a person has committed a crime is a matter of fact that can be easily tested and because there is little room for argument that such an allegation would make 'right-thinking' people shun the subject of the allegation.

Many different allegations of crime have founded actions for defamation. So for example it is defamatory to accuse a person of having committed or been involved in murder[2] or in war crimes[3], or of having committed assault[4] or perjury[5] or fraud[6] or embezzlement[7] or theft[8], of being guilty of child neglect[9] or attempted abortion[10] or indecent exposure[11] or criminal sodomy[12] or breach of the peace[13] or spitting contrary to the byelaws[14], or of attempting to pervert the course of justice[15]. In cases in which a specific crime is alleged a plea of *veritas* can be taken even if the conviction is 'spent' in terms of the Rehabilitation of Offenders Act 1974[16]. Allegations, the substance of which are that the

1 It is possible to identify over 80 such cases in the Scottish law reports since 1900.
2 *Waddell v BBC* 1973 SLT 246; *Harkness v The Daily Record Ltd* 1924 SLT 759; *Wragg v DC Thomson & Co Ltd* 1909 2 SLT 315. See also *Young v Young* (1903) 10 SLT 367 (p 570) in which the action was dismissed as irrelevant, but only because it had been raised by a husband against his wife.
3 *Gecas v Scottish Television plc* 1992 GWD 30–1786.
4 *Smith v Graham* 1981 SLT (Notes) 19; *McTernan v Bennett* (1898) 1 F 333.
5 *McCluskie v Summers* 1988 SLT 55; *Dowgray v Gilmour* (1906) 4 SLT 51 (p 104).
6 *Turnbull v Frame* 1966 SLT 24; *Woods v Moir* (1938) 54 Sh Ct Rep 272; *Jardine v North British Railway Co* 1923 SLT 55; *Mitchell v Smith* 1919 2 SLT 115; *Mandelston v North British Railway Co* 1917 SC 442; *West v Mackenzie* 1917 SC 513; *McLeod v AR Ure & Young* 1915 1 SLT 151; *Smith v Walker* 1912 SC 224.
7 *Macdonald v Martin* 1935 SC 621; *Kufner v Berstecher* 1907 SC 797; *Dundas v Livingston & Co* (1900) 3 F 37.
8 *Sutherland v British Telecommunications plc* 1989 SLT 531; *Andrew v Penny* 1964 SLT (Notes) 24; *Borland v Denholm* (1942) 58 Sh Ct Rep 182; *Rogers v Orr* 1939 SC 121; *Harper v Provincial Newspapers Ltd* 1937 SLT 462; *Dunnet v Nelson* 1926 SC 764; *Smith v Paton* 1913 SC 1203; *Adams v James Templeton & Co* 1913 2 SLT 241; *Mills v Kelvin & James White Ltd* 1913 1 SLT 153.
9 *Rae v Scottish Society for the Prevention of Cruelty to Children* 1924 SC 102.
10 *Watson v McEwan* (1905) 7 F(HL) 109.
11 *Davidson v Anderson* (1905) 12 SLT 350 (p 679).
12 *AB v XY* 1917 SC 15.
13 *McGilvray v Bernfield* (1901) 8 SLT 300 (p 377).
14 *Buchanan v Corporation of Glasgow* (1905) 13 SLT 99 (p 203).
15 *Hines v Davidson* 1935 SC 30.
16 Section 8(3).

pursuer has breached the criminal law, though not in a specified way, are similarly defamatory. So for example to say to a person 'I will have you arrested'[1] imputes criminality[2], as do the actions of the police in fingerprinting a person and putting his photograph in their 'rogues' gallery'[3] or ordering a watch on the pursuer's house[4] or arresting the pursuer[5] (though it is to be noted that most actions of the police will be protected by qualified privilege[6]).

Not all allegations of criminal activity will be defamatory, for not all reflect upon the accused's personal probity[7]. So for example to allege that a person has been fined for illegal parking may not be considered to be defamatory, while to allege that a person has been convicted of drunk driving almost certainly is. The difference is that in the latter the person's character and reputation is being impuned: decent people think less of a person on discovering that he or she has committed this offence. There are of course grey areas here. For example an allegation that a person has been breaking the speed limit on the highway may not be defamatory in some circumstances, but it would probably be defamatory to infer that a person has speeded to such an extent as to be wickedly reckless as to the danger to life and limb thereby created.

Imputations of immorality

Attacks on the moral probity of the pursuer still today generate some cases of defamation, though not to the extent that they once did[8]. Today, when society has less self-confidence in its own judgments of right and wrong and is more tolerant of different views and different standards, these cases will be a good deal more difficult to establish than previously. Also, this aspect of defamation is subject to change more readily than others and so precedents must be read with especial care here. For society's morals shift, levels of tolerance increase in some circumstances and decrease in others, and what was considered derogatory yesterday may not be so considered today. The right-thinking person is a contemporary person who moves with the times and who does not maintain attitudes of 20 or even 10 years ago. It would, it is submitted, be difficult today for a female pursuer relevantly to plead defamation from an imputation that she lacked 'proper womanly delicacy'[9]

---

1 *Costa v Lumley* (1907) 15 SLT 101 (p 230).
2 On the other hand, many cases have involved such statements in which the action was dismissed as irrelevant because the court could not draw the defamatory imputation. See for example *Leon v Edinburgh Evening News Ltd* 1909 SC 1014; *Hunt v Paton* (1904) 12 SLT 295 (p 553); *Christie v Robertson* (1899) 7 SLT 163 (p 143); *Cockburn v Reekie* (1890) 27 SLR 454.
3 *Adamson v Martin* 1916 SC 319.
4 *Robertson v Keith* 1936 SC 29.
5 *Barclay v Chief Constable, Northern Constabulary* 1986 SLT 562.
6 See below, Chapter 8.
7 Clegg, *Reparation* (4th edn, 1955).
8 While it is possible to identify over 30 such cases this century, only a tiny handful based unequivocally on immorality can be identified since the end of the Second World War. There were many more in the nineteenth century.
9 Cf *Cuthbert v Linklater* 1935 SLT 94; *AB v Blackwood & Son* (1902) 5 F 25.

or for a male pursuer to complain of a statement that he 'lacked the manly virtues'. 'Womanly delicacy' and 'manly virtues' are phrases which have today lost the admiration they might once have generated[1]. To say that a person is 'ignorant of religion'[2] or is a 'scoffer at religion'[3] may once have been defamatory but is hardly a matter of regret today. To claim that a person was 'living in sin' was certainly defamatory in the middle years of the twentieth century and before[4], for such a statement was likely to lower the pursuer in the estimation of 'right thinking' members of society as then constituted; but this probably cannot be said today in most circumstances[5]. Parliament has given some recognition to cohabitation, for example in the Damages (Scotland) Act 1976, the Matrimonial Homes (Family Protection) (Scotland) Act 1981 and the Social Security Contributions Act 1991, and though this is a lesser degree of recognition than with marriage, it is still recognition that cohabitation is a valid relationship. The House of Lords too has recognised and accepted legal consequences for cohabitation. In *Tinsley v Milligan*[6] a lesbian couple's relationship was recognised as creating a constructive trust over their property and in *Barclay's Bank plc v O'Brien*[7] Lord Browne Wilkinson said, 'now that unmarried cohabitation, whether heterosexual or homosexual, is widespread in our society, the law should recognise this'. If Parliament and the courts accept the relationship of cohabitation then it will be accepted by the right-thinking member of society generally and it will not be defamatory to accuse a person of living with another in a union outwith marriage. Similarly, falsely to claim that a person is a homosexual was clearly defamatory in a previous age due to society's general intolerance of that state of being[8]. To describe someone as homosexual today could be regarded as defamatory only if the ordinary decent person shuns homosexuals and it is, of course, bigots only who do that[9]. It is submitted that an allegation of homosexuality is not, on its own, to be considered defamatory today[10]. If such an allegation causes a person to be exposed to public hatred, contempt and ridicule (as well it might since some members of the public are not always

---

1 It is still, of course, open to the pursuer to plead innuendo from such phrases.
2 *Dudgeon v Forbes* (1833) 11 S 1014.
3 *Macfarlane v Black* (1887) 14 R 870.
4 *Tamburinni v Ternahan* (1944) 20 Sh Ct Rep 62; *Bradbury v Outram* (1903) 11 SLT 71 (p 125).
5 Though there may still, of course, be circumstances which, added to the main charge, render a statement defamatory, such as (possibly) that both cohabitants are married to other people.
6 [1993] 3 All ER 65.
7 [1994] 1 AC 180 at 198.
8 *Richardson v Walker* (1804) Hume 623 (the allegation there was of sodomy rather than of homosexuality itself); *AB v XY* 1917 SC 15; *Kerr v Kennedy* [1942] 1 KB 409 (an allegation that the plaintiff was a lesbian). Cf *R v Queensbury* 3 April 1895, in which the defendant was charged with criminal libel having accused Oscar Wilde of 'posing as a somdomite (sic)'. The plea of *veritas* was successful, with tragic consequences for Wilde personally and for English literature.
9 In listing personal characteristics 'which are clearly consonant with the concept of the reasonable man' Lord Chief Justice Taylor included homosexuality in his list: *R v Morhall* [1993] 4 All ER 888 at 893.
10 For another (but slightly equivocating) view on this point, see Thomson, *Delictual Liability* (1994) p 208.

right-thinking) the appropriate remedy is in verbal injury rather than in defamation[1].

Conversely, society has become less tolerant of certain types of behaviour that were previously considered innocuous. Proverbs 13, 24 and Hebrews 12, 6 justify the beating of children and last century it was probably not defamatory to accuse a parent of visiting righteous wrath upon his child. Today a false accusation of beating a child, even to an extent that would not constitute a criminal offence, might well cause the right-thinking person to think less of the subject of the allegation, and it would, therefore, be defamatory.

Most examples of imputations against moral character have involved allegations of sexual impropriety, though they are not limited to that. To accuse a person of fathering a bastard has been held to be defamatory[2] and it might remain so today if the essence of the allegation is the neglect or denial of one's own child. An allegation of underage sex[3] clearly remains defamatory as does one of indecent exposure[4] for these are both criminal offences as well. Accusing someone of being a prostitute[5] is probably still defamatory today; but a mere allegation of sex outwith marriage, which was once sufficient to found an action[6] is almost certainly not now defamatory unless some other factor, such as gross sexual depravity, can be innuendoed. Adultery, containing as it does the innuendo of cheating on one's spouse, has founded cases[7] and may continue to do so. Other than direct allegations of sexual impropriety, it has been held defamatory to accuse a person of leading a disreputable life or being a bad character[8], or of being an evil influence[9], or of drunkenness[10], or of hypocrisy[11]. To call a person's honesty into question may, depending upon the facts, be defamatory[12]. In *McCabe v News Group Newspapers Ltd*[13] a newspaper published an article concerning a fatal accident inquiry into the death of a child, and commented upon the reaction of the pursuer, who was the mother of the child. The pursuer claimed that the article suggested that she was an uncaring and unfeeling mother. Such a suggestion would be defamatory, and the case was allowed to proceed to a jury to

---

1 See below at pp 55–56.
2 *C v M* 1923 SC 1; *McGrady v Urquart* (1912) 28 Sh Ct Rep 136; *M v H* 1908 SC 1130.
3 *AB v CD* 1919 2 SLT 46.
4 *Davidson v Anderson* (1905) 12 SLT 350 (p 679).
5 *Alberti v Bernardi* 1921 SC 468; *Finburgh v Moss' Empires Ltd* 1908 SC 928; *McKnight v Kelly* (1900) 16 Sh Ct Rep 30; *Reid v Scott* (1825) 4 S 5.
6 *Blair v Eastwood* (1935) 51 Sh Ct Rep 304; *R v S* 1914 SC 193; *Wood v The Edinburgh Evening News Ltd* 1910 SC 895; *Morrison v Ritchie & Co* (1902) 4 F 645; *Foote v Macdonald* (1900) 16 Sh Ct Rep 217.
7 *Fyvie v Waddell* 1923 SLT 518; *Pope v Outram & Co Ltd* 1909 SC 230.
8 *Boyd v BBC* 1969 SLT (Sh Ct) 17; *Donaldson v Connacher* (1915) 31 Sh Ct Rep 118; *McKnight v Kelly* (1900) 16 Sh Ct Rep 30.
9 *Rooney v McNairney* 1909 SC 90.
10 *Gillie v Labno* 1949 CLY 4792.
11 *Stein v Beaverbrook Newspapers Ltd* 1968 SLT 401; *Griffin v Divers* 1922 SC 605.
12 *Leitch v Secretary of State for Scotland* 1983 SLT 394; *Mackay v Grant* (1903) 41 SLR 18; *Watson v Duncan* (1890) 17 R 404. Cf *Agnew v British Legal Life Assurance Co* (1906) 8 F 422.
13 1992 SLT 707.

determine whether the mother had reacted to the verdict as the newspaper had suggested.

Imputations against the pursuer's professional competence

Most actions today are raised on the basis that the defender has impuned the pursuer's professional competence or conduct[1]. The frequency of these cases is probably explained by two reasons. First, people who are willing to ignore or to laugh off imputations of immorality may not be willing to do so with imputations concerning their professional competence or conduct. This is understandable, for such an allegation can readily diminish or destroy a person's career prospects and in that way affect both one's standing in the community and one's economic well-being. And secondly, many professional bodies which exist to protect the interests of their members (and thereby, of course, their own reputations) are willing to fund actions that would otherwise not be raised for financial reasons.

Actions on the basis of professional incompetence have been raised by a wide variety of people, for example by a doctor accused of gross negligence[2] or of not being properly qualified[3]; by a nurse accused of being untidy and not good at her job[4]; by a vet accused of unskilful treatment of a mare and foal[5]; by a solicitor accused of professional incompetence[6]; by an accountant accused of being fraudulent and inept and guilty of breach of trust[7]; by a teacher[8] and by a professor[9] alleged to have poor teaching abilities; by a hotelier alleged to be guilty of overcharging[10]; by the chief executive of a regional council accused of being childish and vindictive in the way he ran council meetings and business[11]; by a market gardener accused of inferior tillage and letting weeds gain ascendancy[12]; by a publican accused of being no good as a bar tender[13]; by a railway signalman accused of unsafe practices[14]; by a policeman accused by his chief constable of being a disgrace to the force and a danger[15]; by a shepherd accused of not looking after his flock properly[16]; by a seamstress accused of being unfit to hold her post[17]; and by an MP for an

---

1 Almost 90 cases in these two categories appear in the law reports since 1900.
2 *Simmers v Morton* (1900) 8 SLT 230 (p 285).
3 *Chisholm v Grant* 1914 SC 239.
4 *Wright v Thomas* (1931) 47 Sh Ct Rep 194. See also *Couper v Lord Balfour of Burleigh* 1914 SC 139.
5 *Mackenzie v Burgess* (1903) 19 Sh Ct Rep 44.
6 *Muirhead v George Outram & Co Ltd* 1983 SLT 201; *C v W* 1950 SLT (Notes) 8.
7 *Shanks v BBC* 1993 SLT 326.
8 *McKerchar v Cameron* (1892) 19 R 383. See also *Ross v Macleod* (1911) 27 Sh Ct Rep 30; *Leitch v Lyal* (1903) 11 SLT 222 (p 394).
9 *Auld v Shairp* (1875) 2 R 191.
10 *Macrae v Wicks* (1886) 13 R 732.
11 *Mutch v Robertson* 1981 SLT 217.
12 *Cadzow v The Distress Committee of Edinburgh* 1914 1 SLT 493.
13 *Macdonald v McColl* (1901) 9 SLT 127 (p 146).
14 *Dobson v Amalgamated Society of Railway Servants* (1901) 8 SLT 302 (p 378).
15 *Brown v Ross* 1907 SC 256.
16 *McDonald v McLachlan* 1907 SC 203.
17 *Vallance v Ford* (1903) 10 SLT 356 (p 555).

allegation that he did not perform his duties as a member of Parliament diligently and did not answer his mail[1].

Cooper suggests that a distinction should be drawn between cases of persons whose professions require qualifications (such as the doctor and the lawyer) and those whose trades do not (such as the seamstress and the MP)[2], on the ground that the law is entitled to presume competence in the former case but not in the latter. It is submitted that this distinction is not good: anyone who undertakes a task, whether professional or non-professional, is holding himself out as being competent to perform it properly[3] and the law can therefore presume competence in both cases.

Imputations of professional misconduct

Slightly different but no less actionable are allegations relating to a person's professional conduct that do not necessarily suggest incompetence. Persons holding certain offices are expected to behave in particular ways, often to a stricter standard than those who do not hold such offices, and allegations of certain conduct may be innocuous in relation to the latter but not to the former. It may not be defamatory to say of a man that he had sex with a woman who was not his wife, but it might become so if the man were a Roman Catholic priest, or the man were a teacher and the woman his student. So for example allegations that a policeman investigated or arrested a person not through reasonable suspicion but through malice or racism or some other bad motive are defamatory[4], as are statements that a prison warder had sexual intercourse with a prisoner[5], that a housing company was involved in a secret deal with senior civil servants[6], that a chartered accountant was guilty of conduct unbecoming of a chartered accountant[7], that a company director misrepresented the position of another director in the minutes of a board meeting[8], that a garage persuaded customers to have shock absorbers fitted to their cars when this was not necessary[9], that a journalist deliberately misquoted a source[10] or falsified facts to make his story more dramatic[11], that a policeman was drunk on duty[12], that a hire purchase firm was oppressive in the conduct of its business[13], that a soldier failed in his duty by ordering a surrender, which was a court-martial offence[14], that a veterinary surgeon was in breach of

1 *Fairbairn v SNP* 1980 SLT 149.
2 *Cooper* pp 60 and 61. (The examples are not his.)
3 *Wilsher v Essex Area Health Authority* [1986] 3 All ER 801; *Nettleship v Weston* [1971] 2 QB 691.
4 *Fraser v Mirza* 1993 SLT 527; *Anderson v Palombo* 1986 SLT 46; *Cassidy v Connochie* 1907 SC 1112.
5 *Winter v News Scotland Ltd* 1991 SLT 828.
6 *Waverley Housing Management Ltd v BBC* 1993 GWD 17–1117.
7 *Shanks v BBC* 1993 SLT 326.
8 *Chapman v Barber* 1989 SLT 830.
9 *Kwik-Fit-Euro Ltd v Scottish Daily Record and Sunday Mail* 1987 SLT 226.
10 *Cameron v Scottish Daily Record and Sunday Mail Ltd* 1987 GWD 29–1119.
11 *Stein v Beaverbrook Newspapers* 1968 SLT 401.
12 *Olsen v Keddie* 1976 SLT (Sh Ct) 64.
13 *NG Napier Ltd v Port Glasgow Courier Ltd* 1959 SLT (Sh Ct) 54.
14 *Gordon v John Leng & Co* 1919 SC 415.

professional propriety in giving a testimonial to a medicine in breach of regulations[1], that a bakery carried on business in an unfair and dishonourable manner and imposed oppressive conditions on its workers[2], that the pursuer deceived the public and traders by dishonest methods and practices in business[3], that a racehorse owner deliberately attempted to lose races in order to enrich himself[4], and that the chairman of a lunatic asylum had abused his position to have his father-in-law illegally confined in the asylum[5].

Imputations of financial unsoundness

To accuse a person of being in financial difficulties does not necessarily reflect upon honour or moral character, 'for men of the greatest honour and strictest honesty may become bankrupts by unavoidable misfortunes'[6]. There may be no element of insult, deliberate or otherwise[7], but because such an allegation is peculiarly potent in hurting a person's reputation as an economic asset, for a name that is good is as valuable as a good name, the law regards such an allegation as defamatory for which damages can be claimed. The element of insult being completely lacking, it may well be, as Smith suggests[8], that making the allegation to the pursuer alone would not be actionable, but it does not follow that solatium alone can never be sued for. If it is spread abroad that the pursuer is insolvent, he or she may well suffer personal distress and inconvenience, even when the allegation causes no economic loss, and solatium may be due for that[9]. Logically, the element of insult being missing, allegations of financial unsoundness ought properly to be dealt with as cases of verbal injury (or perhaps as negligence[10]) but the law does not adopt this approach, and the requisites for actionability stated in the cases are more nearly those for defamation than for verbal injury[11]. Given the lack of any personal aspersion this position is odd, but seems to be explained on the basis

1 *Bradley v Menley & James Ltd* 1913 SC 923.
2 *Walker v Miller* (1913) 29 Sh Ct Rep 177.
3 *Ogston & Tennant Ltd v The Daily Record (Glasgow) Ltd* 1909 SC 1000. See also *Crichton v Edwards* (1907) 23 Sh Ct Rep 70.
4 *Moffat v Coats* (1906) 14 SLT 183 (p 392).
5 *Mackenzie v Anderson and the Mail Newspapers* (1900) 7 SLT 449 (p 469).
6 Erskine, *Institute of the Laws of Scotland* IV, 4, 81.
7 Of course there might be insult if, say, fraud was innuendoed.
8 *Short Commentary* p 725.
9 *Murray v Bonn* (1913) 29 Sh Ct Rep 62.
10 The typical case, in which the pursuer's name is accidentally included in a 'blacklist', may most readily be dealt with as a case of negligence rather than verbal injury. The pursuer would have to establish the usual criteria for an action for negligence, but this is likely to be easier to establish than malice. For an early recognition that a claim in negligence would be relevant in these circumstances, see *Craig v Hunter & Co* 29 June 1809, FC.
11 See *Outram & Co v Reid* (1852) 14 D 577; *Russell v Stubbs Ltd* 1913 SC(HL) 14; *Mazure v Stubbs Ltd* 1919 SC(HL) 112; *Barr v Musselburgh Merchants' Association* 1912 SC 174; *Anderson v Drummond & Graham* (1887) 14 R 568. In none of these cases was malice required to be put in the issue (except in *Barr*, where privilege was pleaded in any case).

that the interest in character protected by the action for defamation is defined widely enough to include commercial character[1].

Defamatory allegations in this category include statements that the pursuer was not a suitable person to give credit to[2], that the pursuer's business was insolvent[3], that the pursuer's creditors were being forced to sell his goods[4], that the pursuer was unable to pay his debts[5], that the pursuer's business had been sold or transferred to the defenders[6], that the pursuer had been 'cleaned out and lost his all'[7], that the pursuer's company was about to be taken over by a rival[8], and that dealing with the pursuer represented more than an average risk[9].

Disease or disability

It has been said that to allege that a person is suffering from some loathsome disease[10] or is insane[11] is a defamatory remark, but such cases ought now to be read in the light of a greater public tolerance shown to disease or disability, and no such case has been traced this century. Insanity being a condition for which the sufferer cannot be held in any way to blame, it is submitted that falsely to claim another is insane is not an attack on character and cannot be defamatory since right-thinking members of society ought to show sympathy rather than distaste. The same can be said for physical diseases such as leprosy. An allegation that the pursuer is suffering from this disease may *actually* cause him or her to be shunned, but that is not the test: a statement is defamatory only if right-thinking people ought to shun the pursuer[12]. Other diseases, contracted by means which reflect harmfully upon the pursuer's character, may be dealt with otherwise: a false accusation that a person is suffering from a sexually-transmitted disease, such as gonorrhoea or syphilis, may still give a cause of action if it amounts to an innuendo of immoral conduct[13]. But a suggestion that a person is HIV positive ought to elicit sympathy rather than revulsion. As Professor Walker put it, 'An imputation of disease of

---

1 Just as a domestic servant's 'character' given by an ex-employer was an economic asset.
2 *Mazure v Stubbs Ltd* 1919 SC (HL) 112; *Barr v Musselburgh Merchants' Association* 1912 SC 174; *Hunter & Co v Stubbs Ltd* (1903) 11 SLT 81 (p 142).
3 *Carson v White* 1919 2 SLT 215; *Grand Theatre and Opera House (Glasgow) Ltd v George Outram & Co Ltd* 1909 2 SLT 75; *'Seaspray' Steamship Co Ltd v Tennant* (1908) 15 SLT 329 (p 874); *Aitchison & Sons Ltd v John McEwan* (1903) 10 SLT 316 (p 501).
4 *Murray v Bonn* (1913) 29 Sh Ct Rep 62.
5 *Russell v Stubbs Ltd* 1913 SC(HL) 14; *McLintock v Stubbs Ltd* (1902) 5 F 1.
6 *Wilson Advertising Co v Griffiths & Millington Ltd* (1906) 22 Sh Ct Rep 356.
7 *AB v CD* (1904) 7 F 22.
8 *General Accident Assurance Co Ltd v George A Miller* (1902) 9 SLT 426 (p 510).
9 *Bayne & Thomson v Stubbs Ltd* (1901) 3 F 408.
10 See Lord Deas in *Cunningham v Phillips* (1868) 6 M 926 at 928 (he was talking, though he did not like to mention its name, of impotency). He said the same thing in *Friend v Skelton* (1855) 17 D 548. See also Erskine IV, 4, 80 and Hume, 139, to similar effect.
11 *Mackintosh v Weir* (1875) 2 R 877.
12 Above at p 10.
13 Cf *A v B* 1907 SC 1154 (sub nom *Farrell v Boyd* (1907) 15 SLT 130 (p 327)).

mind or body which carries no implication of misconduct . . . is a misfortune, and no disgrace or dishonour attaches to one so afflicted'[1].

Aspersions against public character

Public figures are peculiarly susceptible to criticism, even ridicule, in the public domain. Attacks on a person's public character can be personally hurtful and professionally destructive. However, there are strong grounds of policy for granting a greater degree of freedom of expression to those criticising – and even abusing – public persons than to those referring to private persons, and the law of Scotland has long accepted that it should be more difficult to obtain damages for an attack on public character than it is for an attack on private character. Lord McLaren in *McLaughlan v Orr, Pollock & Co*[2] said:

'It is hardly necessary to point out that the constitution of this country tolerates the utmost freedom in the discussion of the conduct and motives of those who take part in its public business, whether in the higher plane of statemanship or in the conduct of local affairs. In such criticism ridicule is just as legitimate as any other rhetorical artifice. If, as the Lord Ordinary observes, this should take the form of rough language and unmannerly jests, the person aggrieved must put up with it . . . It is only when private character is attacked, or when the criticism of public conduct is combined with the suggestion of base or indirect motives that redress can be claimed on the ground of injury to reputation'.

It follows that a certain latitude is given to defenders accused of defaming pursuers' public character. This latitude has two quite distinct aspects. First, latitude is given in determining whether the words complained of carry a defamatory meaning at all.

'It . . . is well recognised in practice, that a different and stricter standard of construction is to be applied to calumnious expressions affecting a person in his business relations from that applied to expressions used of the same person in his public capacity'[3].

A person who takes part in public life must expect criticism and cannot react too sensitively when it is given. So in a case raised by the convener of a regional council[4] Lord Stott said,

'the appellant has chosen to be in the public limelight and having aspired to the position of chairman of a regional council cannot I think assume that his chairmanship will be immune from criticism. He must expect "such criticism as the law might not recognise as justified in the case of a merely private person, but readily admits when it is in the public interest that criticism should be brought to bear upon the conduct of public officials"'[5].

In this case, a verbal statement that the pursuer had conducted council meetings with a 'childish and vindictive attitude' was held to satisfy the test,

---

1 *Delict* (2nd edn, 1981) p 780.
2 (1894) 22 R 38 at 42 and 43.
3 *Waddell v Roxburgh* (1894) 21 R 883 at 885 per Lord McLaren.
4 *Mutch v Robertson* 1981 SLT 217.
5 1981 SLT 217 at 226 and 227, quoting from *Langlands v John Leng & Co* 1916 SC(HL) 102. Scots law consists, in this respect, with the jurisprudence of the European Court of Human Rights: see *Lingens v Austria* (1986) 8 EHRR 407.

but a letter requesting the Secretary of State for Scotland to instigate an inquiry did not. The test was stated to be whether,

'the ordinary man could reasonably infer from [the statements complained of] that the pursuer was dishonest or was guilty of dishonourable behaviour or if his public conduct was combined with the suggestion of base or indirect motives'[1].

The second aspect of the latitude given to the criticism of public character is that comments made about a public figure, if they relate to public affairs, will normally come within the protection of qualified privilege, for the public has an interest in the criticism of those who act on its behalf and in its name, as showing the person's incompetency or unfitness for office[2]. It would be unattractive to allow politicians and other public officials to rely on the presumption that those who criticise them are acting maliciously[3] and if the criticism concerns a matter of public interest then malice will normally have to be averred and proved[4]. Thus when members of a regional council wrote to the Secretary of State to the effect that the conduct of the convener of the council placed the proper conduct of council business in jeopardy, this would have been privileged had the statement in the letter been defamatory; publication of the letter to the council's constituents might also be an occasion of privilege since the matter was one of direct public interest and the public as such had an interest in receiving the information[5]. An allegation that the pursuer was not, as he claimed, a minister of the Free Church of Scotland, was likewise covered by qualified privilege[6], as was an allegation that the pursuer was not fit to be an elder[7]. And an attack on a baillie during a municipal election campaign was similarly privileged[8]. However, if the defender has gone outwith the scope of legitimate public criticism, that is if private character is attacked, or if the criticism of public conduct is combined with the suggestion of base or indirect motives, then the case is not properly one of privilege and redress can be claimed in the normal way on the ground of injury to reputation[9]. So to accuse burgh officials of corruption in the distribution of contracts[10] or to accuse an MP of failing to answer his mail[11] are not accusations that can be protected by qualified privilege[12].

1 *Mutch v Robertson* 1981 SLT 217 at 223 per Lord Kissen. See also *Caldwell v Bayne* (1936) 52 Sh Ct Rep 334 in which it was held that there was no defamation because the statements complained of made no reflection on the pursuer's private character or reputation.
2 *Coghill v Docherty* (1881) 19 SLR 96.
3 And indeed in the USA such a presumption was declared unconstitutional by the Supreme Court in 1964: *New York Times Co v Sullivan* (1964) 376 US 254. See further, below at p 69.
4 *Lyal v Henderson* 1916 SC(HL) 167.
5 See Lord Stott in *Mutch v Robertson* 1981 SLT 217 at 227.
6 *Wallace v Bremner* (1900) 16 Sh Ct Rep 308.
7 *Jack v Fleming* (1891) 19 R 1.
8 *Caldwell v Bayne* (1936) 52 Sh Ct Rep 334.
9 *McLaughlan v Orr, Pollock & Co* (1894) 22 R 38 at 43 per Lord McLaren.
10 Cf *Waddell v Roxburgh* (1894) 21 R 883.
11 *Fairbairn v SNP* 1980 SLT 149.
12 Section 10 of the Defamation Act 1952 provides that statements made by or on behalf of election candidates are not privileged even although the statement is material to a question in issue in the election.

Communication of a defamatory idea

Once the pursuer has established the defamatory nature of the statement or idea complained about, there is liability only if he or she then goes on to prove that it has been communicated by the defender to another person. Communication is necessary for liability because without it no lowering of the pursuer's reputation can occur, and the pursuer can feel no affront and suffer no loss[1]. It is no wrong for a person to think defamatory thoughts, or even to commit them to paper, but if these thoughts are expressed to any other person, including the pursuer, verbally, in writing, or in any other way, then communication has occurred and the wrong becomes actionable. The communication may be made deliberately, recklessly, negligently or inadvertently: the sole question is whether the idea has passed from one person to another. In English law, where defamation is more purely concerned with public reputation, the communication (there called 'publication') must be to someone other than the plaintiff in a civil claim[2] and there are various technical rules for determining whether communications between two individuals concerning a third are or are not 'publications' for the law of defamation[3]. These issues have not troubled Scots law where, as we will see, communication to the pursuer alone gives a good ground of action and, while the circumstances of the publication may affect the level of damages[4], the element of communication is normally treated as a simple one of fact[5]. If the pursuer comes to hear of the defamatory statement, there has been communication at least to him and he can claim damages by way of solatium for the affront; if economic loss, or damage to reputation as an economic asset, is to be claimed a causal link between the defamation and that loss, in the form of communication to a third party, must be shown.

Communication to pursuer alone

The action for defamation in Scotland is designed to give reparation for loss caused and also to provide a solace for the affront or insult felt by the pursuer.

---

1 As Lord McLaren put it in *Evans & Sons v Stein & Co* (1904) 7 F 65 at 68, 'It appears to me that it is of the essence of an injury of the nature of defamation that the defamatory charge should reach its destination, or should at least become known to someone'. In that case (discussed more fully below at p 185) the First Division held that the wrong of defamation was not committed when a letter was sent but when it was received.
2 *Pullman v Hill* [1891] 1 QB 524 at 527 per Lord Esher MR. (A charge of criminal libel may be made in England when the communication is made only to the person defamed.)
3 Problems arise for example when a businessman dictates defamatory words concerning another person to his secretary, or when a husband speaks to a wife concerning someone else: see Carter-Ruck, *Libel and Slander* (4th edn, 1992) pp 62–69.
4 See below at p 169.
5 In *Evans & Sons v Stein & Co* (1904) 7 F 65 the question arose whether there had been publication to a third party because the wrong was committed in England. Lord Kinnear said at 72, 'Whether there has been such communication or not is a question of fact; and if a pursuer complains of publication as a wrong, he is bound to state specifically to whom the language complained of was made known'. The pursuer had argued that there had been communication by the defenders at least to their clerks who had been dictated to and had typed the defamatory letter but the action was dismissed because, inter alia, the clerks were not identified.

While economic losses can only be caused if publication of the defamation is to third parties, affront or insult can be suffered even when the defamatory remarks are addressed to and heard by the pursuer alone. It follows that a calumnious attack upon the pursuer will, even when no-one but the pursuer hears it, justify an award of at least nominal damages and often much more than that[1]. If a pursuer himself gives publicity to a private attack he cannot claim damages for anything other than the private attack, for he will be the author of his own further loss[2]: a person attacked privately does not need litigation to clear his name which, in the circumstances, has not been sullied[3].

Methods of communication

Communication sufficient to found an action can be by any means that are efficacious in passing from one person to another an idea of and concerning the pursuer, whether by speech, direct or by telephone, telegraph, radio or television[4], by writing[5], on paper, in print, by telex, telegramme[6], FAX or electronic mail[7], by physical act[8] or signal[9], or by representation in drawings[10], cartoons, photographs[11], effigies[12], puppets or film[13].

Repetition of defamation

Any repetition of a defamatory communication by the original defamer may compound the wrong and increase the level of damages that may appropriately be awarded, as will repetition by someone else which is authorised by the original defamer[14] or which is a natural and probable consequence of the

---

1 *Mackay v McCankie* (1883) 10 R 537; *Ramsay v MacLay & Co* (1890) 18 R 130.
2 *Wallace v Bremner* (1900) 16 Sh Ct Rep 308.
3 *Will v Sneddon, Campbell & Munro* 1931 SC 164.
4 See eg *Shanks v BBC* 1993 SLT 326; *Waverley Housing Management Ltd v BBC* 1993 GWD 17–1117; *Gecas v Scottish Television plc* 1992 GWD 30–1786.
5 In *Gulf Oil (GB) Ltd v Page* [1987] 3 All ER 14 the defamatory statement was made in a banner towed by a light aircraft over the crowd at a race meeting.
6 *Thomson v Kindell* 1910 2 SLT 442; *Robertson v Taylor* (1903) 10 SLT 371 (p 575).
7 It was reported in *The Lawyer* 25 January 1994 that a writ had been served (in England) against Dr Phillip Hallam-Baker for placing an allegedly defamatory notice on a public access computer system known as USENET concerning Dr Laurence Godfrey.
8 See for example *Barclay v Chief Constable, Northern Constabulary* 1986 SLT 562; *Neville v C & A Modes Ltd* 1945 SLT 51 (p 189).
9 'Suppose a man only so much as holds up his finger to you, if you offer to prove that he meant by that to make an imputation on your character, that is relevant': *Kennedy v Allan* (1848) 10 D 1293 at 1296 per Lord Cockburn.
10 *Whyte v Smith* 3 March, 1798 (Borthwick, 186) (unchaste pictures insinuating a woman's want of chastity).
11 *Hood v WH Smith & Son Ltd* (1937) Times, 5 November.
12 *Monson v Tussauds* [1894] 1 QB 671 (waxwork model).
13 *Youssoupoff v MGM Pictures* (1934) 50 TLR 581 (portraying a real person on the silver screen).
14 *Parkes v Prescott* (1869) LR 4 Exch 169.

original defamation[1]. Not only that, but any repetition of the defamation is actionable against the person, other than the original defamer, responsible for repeating the defamation, publishing it, or otherwise putting it in circulation[2]. This rule causes some difficulties in relation to newspapers which carry reports of statements made by those for whom they are not responsible, and for television and radio companies which broadcast (perhaps live) words that are defamatory[3]. A pursuer would in these circumstances have the choice of suing the original defamer or the publisher or broadcaster, and in many cases would choose the latter on the ground that more damages might be obtained because of the wider circulation given by the publication or broadcast, and might well have more chance of recovering any damages awarded. Yet the publisher or broadcaster will usually be less culpable than the original framer of the defamatory idea and might indeed be entirely innocent[4]. The defence of innocent dissemination[5] is normally regarded as limited to situations in which the distributor cannot be aware of the defamatory content of the material being distributed but an argument can be made for its extension to broadcasters and original publishers[6].

Repetition of rumour

It is no defence for a newspaper or broadcaster to say that a story it publishes is merely a rumour or that someone else alleged it, for 'the existence of a slanderous report, or its prevalent currency, is no justification for repeating it. Each repetition is a new injury to the party slandered'[7]. 'The injury to the pursuer is exactly the same, whether the writer himself affirms the truth of the story, or whether he says that some lawyer or other person has affirmed it'[8]. For a newspaper or magazine to report that a certain rumour is current while stating that it is untrue is usually considered not to protect the defender if the rumour is defamatory. However, if, as was shown above, a statement is defamatory only if the ordinary reasonable listener or reader would accept it as

---

1 *Weld-Blundell v Stephens* [1920] AC 956. On the question of remoteness of damage, see further below at pp 171–173.
2 See for example *Hayford v Forrester-Paton* 1927 SC 740, in which a friend of the defender had written to him in terms which were defamatory of the pursuer. The pursuer sued the defender who had then circulated the letter rather than the person who had written it.
3 See Heerey, 'Publishing the Defamatory Statements of Others' (1985) 59 Aust LJ 371.
4 As eg in *Morrison v Ritchie & Co* (1902) 4 F 645, in which a newspaper published a birth notice handed in by a member of the public, or in the case of a live television or radio broadcast in which a speaker over whom the broadcaster has no control defames on air.
5 See below at pp 87–90.
6 See below at pp 89–90.
7 *Marshall v Renwick* (1835) 13 S 1127 at 1129 per Lord President Hope.
8 *Pope v Outram* 1909 SC 230 at 235 per Lord McLaren. See also *Fairbairn v Scottish National Party* 1980 SLT 149 at 153 per Lord Ross.

a seriously meant allegation, then such a report would not be defamatory when the ordinary reasonable reader would accept the statement of untruth as accurate: a statement that no-one believes cannot harm reputation[1]. If such a disclaimer is not sufficient to take away the defamatory quality of the communication, it may nonetheless be relevant to mitigate any damages awarded[2].

1 Mr John Major, when Prime Minister, raised an action against the *New Statesman* magazine for publishing, on 29 January 1993, an article which detailed a rumour of sexual impropriety and went on to state that there were no grounds for believing it to be true. The case was settled, but it is not clear whether a statement of that nature would be sufficient in the eyes of the ordinary reasonable reader to render the whole article non-defamatory. It is interesting to note that his claim was based on one of the rumours to which it was possible to give credence (an affair with a woman who provided catering services to Downing Street) and not on the other rumours to which it was not possible to give credence (such as that he was having an affair with a black left-wing councillor, or that he was having an affair with a gay football player).
2 *MacCullochs v Litt* (1851) 13 D 960; *Morrison v Ritchie & Co* (1902) 4 F 645 at 652 per Lord Moncreiff. And see further, below at pp 168–170.

CHAPTER THREE

Liability for verbal injury

Introduction

The action for defamation is not the only form of redress available to a person who feels that his or her character, honour or reputation has been attacked, but to base the action on defamation itself does have certain significant advantages for the pursuer. For once it has been established by the pursuer that the statement or communication complained about is defamatory in the sense described above[1], the law will presume that the statement is false, that it had been made with intent to injure (or, as it might be put, maliciously), and that at least some loss, injury or damage has been caused thereby. These advantages do not accrue if the statement cannot be proved to be defamatory, but it does not follow that the statement is not actionable at all. Rather, for redress to be available for non-defamatory statements, the elements of falsity, intent to injure, and actual injury must be averred and proved by the pursuer. There is no doubt that the law of Scotland recognises the actionability of non-defamatory statements and communications which injure a person's character, honour or reputation; the basis upon which that actionability is founded, and its requisites, is less clear. It is the purpose of this chapter to examine the proper terminology to be used in relation to non-defamatory attacks on a person's character, honour and reputation, to delineate the available classes of action, and to identify the different requisites appropriate to each class. The chapter immediately following will examine the different factual types of non-defamatory statements which have been held to be actionable.

The taxonomy of verbal injury

The correct classification of actions arising from attacks to character, honour and reputation has been the source of some dispute amongst academic writers, but while the judges have certainly contributed to the confusion by loose terminological usages, the actual law they apply, as gleaned from the decided cases, is (as we will see) fairly clear. Professor Walker[2] points out that

---

1 See above at pp 8–12.
2 *Delict* (2nd edn, 1981) pp 730–736.

the term 'verbal injury' was used by the Institutional Writers in the generic sense of *injuria verbis* covering all attacks on character, honour and reputation and being distinguished from real injuries such as assault and other physical attacks[1]. There is old statutory authority for using the phrase 'verbal injury' in this way[2] and, rather more surprisingly, modern (though oblique) authority for doing so[3]. Notwithstanding the institutional authority for this usage, the phrase 'verbal injury' has taken on in the modern era a different meaning and normally it is used to refer not to the genus itself, but to one of the classes within the genus. The phrase 'verbal injury' in this sense is an actionable wrong *other than* defamation which is an attack on character, honour and reputation and it has been used thus by many judges[4] and at least two statutes[5]. The title of Cooper's work *Defamation and Verbal Injury*, as well as the treatment contained therein, indicates a similar understanding on the part of that author, and it is this approach that this book will adopt. The term 'verbal injury' is much less useful today in delineating all injuries that are not real or physical. The law in modern times has developed other forms of action which could just as easily be described as verbal injuries, but which are clearly not within the ambit of *injuria verbis*. Most particularly actions based on negligent

1 See most clearly Erskine, *Institute of the Law of Scotland* IV, 4, 80; Hume, *Lectures on the Law of Scotland* III, 133; and in Roman law D 47, 1. Other authors adopt this approach. Glegg, 'The Law of Slander' (1894) 1 SLT (News) 585 talks of 'forms of verbal injury, either defamation or *convicium*'; Stewart, *Delict* (1993) entitles his chapter on defamation, *convicium* and malicious falsehood 'Verbal Injuries'. Professor Thomson, *Delictual Liability* (1994), on the other hand adopts the approach to be expounded in the text above.

2 Section 28 of the Court of Session Act 1825 talks of 'all actions on account of injury to the person, whether real or verbal, as assault and battery, libel or defamation'.

3 The schedule to the Damages (Scotland) Act 1993 amends s 13 of the Administration of Justice Act 1982 to talk of 'defamation and *any other* verbal injury' – suggesting that defamation is a form of verbal injury and that Scots law recognises other forms of verbal injury. Lord Fraser in *Trapp v Mackie* 1979 SLT 126 (HL) at 132 uses a similar formula, describing the claim in that case as being based 'not on defamation but on *some other form* of verbal injury, either *convicium* or malicious falsehood' (emphasis added).

4 See for example Lord Justice-Clerk in *Sheriff v Wilson* (1855) 17 D 528 at 530; Lord Ordinary Kincairney in *Waddell v Roxburgh* (1894) 21 R 883 at 884; Lord Justice-Clerk in *Andrew v Macara* 1917 SC 247 at 250; Lord Blackburn in *Lamond v Daily Record (Glasgow) Ltd* 1923 SLT 512 at 514 and Lord Hunter in *Argyllshire Weavers Ltd v A Macaulay (Tweeds) Ltd* 1965 SLT 21 at 35; Lord Wheatley in *Steele v Scottish Daily Record* 1970 SLT 53 at 60, Lord Milligan at 63 and Lord Fraser at 65; Lord Kirkwood in *Thomson v News Group Newspapers Ltd* 1992 GWD 14–825.

5 The Defamation Act 1952, s 3 (as applied to Scotland) provides a special rule for actions of 'verbal injury'; the English version of s 3 provides the same special rule (ie one not applied to actions for defamation) for actions of 'slander of title, slander of goods or other malicious falsehood'. The Legal Aid (Scotland) Act 1986 provides that legal aid is not to be available in actions for defamation or for verbal injury: the latter is clearly meant to be distinguished from the former, and not the genus within which the former is a class. Curiously, the English Legal Aid Act 1988, Sch 2, Part 2, para 1, excludes from legal aid only actions for defamation and does not exclude malicious falsehood, slander of title and slander of goods. In *Joyce v Sengupta* [1993] 1 WLR 337 a plaintiff who could not afford to raise an action for defamation applied for and obtained legal aid to seek redress for malicious falsehood. Though the Court of Appeal was careful to point out that the appropriateness of the award was for the Legal Aid Board rather than for the court it did spend some time emphasising the differences between defamation and malicious falsehood and concluded that since the statute denied legal aid only for the former it was still available for the latter. It is also to be noted that various statutes grant absolute privilege to certain reports 'for the purposes of the law relating to defamation'. Whether this includes malicious falsehood is examined elsewhere.

misstatements, of the *Hedley Byrne* sort[1], are actions arising from injury caused verbally but are properly classified, of course, as a species of claim within the genus of negligence. So too actions like *Spring v Guardian Assurance plc*[2], in which the House of Lords held that a negligently drawn-up reference was actionable in negligence even though it would not be actionable in defamation or malicious falsehood, was clearly an injury caused verbally, but was not a 'verbal injury' in the generic sense used by the Institutional Writers[3].

In an important sense it really does not matter what a particular action is called, so long as the defender is made aware of the charge he or she is being asked to answer and so long as the law is clear as to the requisites to be established by the pursuer[4] and it is proposed to adopt the following terminology in this book. The genus of actions which, quite apart from negligence, provide redress for attacks on character, honour and reputation will be referred to as *injuria verbis*; within that genus the only classifications that it is legally pertinent to make are those that have legal consequence and therefore, as will be seen, there are two classes – defamation (whose requisites for liability have already been discussed) and verbal injury (sometimes known as malicious falsehood). A taxonomy based on one genus and two classes is rejected by Professor Walker, partly on the basis of the misuse of the phrase 'verbal injury' to mean a class within the genus rather than the genus itself, and partly on the ground that within the genus there are in fact three rather than two classes of action[5]. The three classes he identifies are defamation, malicious falsehood, and *convicium*. In order to determine whether Walker is correct, we have to examine the cases involving non-defamatory actionable statements to see whether the law makes a two-fold or a three-fold classification – and in doing so we must look to what the courts do rather than to what the courts (and the reporters and the writers) call the various actions.

Verbal injury, or malicious falsehood

Within the class which Walker calls 'malicious falsehood' can be included cases of slander of title, slander of property, slander of business and other false statements made maliciously that are not covered by these descriptions. These cases tend to be referred to by the judges as cases of verbal injury (in the sense of a class different from, rather than including, defamation), though the phrase malicious falsehood, summing up as it does the essentials of the claim,

---

1 See *Hedley Byrne v Heller & Partners* [1964] AC 465.
2 [1994] 3 All ER 129.
3 One of the important consequences of the action being raised in negligence rather than defamation is that qualified privilege imposes a duty on the plaintiff to prove malice in the latter but not the former action.
4 See further, Norrie, 'Hurts to Character, Honour and Reputation: A Reappraisal' 1984 JR 163.
5 *Walker* pp 732–736. See also his comment on *Steele v Scottish Daily Record* 1970 SLT 53 at 1970 JR 157.

may well be a more apt title[1]. There is no doubt that the law distinguishes between cases of defamation and cases of malicious falsehood (and recognises both). When the pursuer shows the statement complained of to be defamatory, both falsity and intent to injure will be presumed in his or her favour and the burden of proving truth will fall on the defender. If the statement complained of cannot be shown to be defamatory then falsity will not be presumed since the presumption of freedom from derogatory characteristics does not apply, and malice cannot be presumed since the words, not being derogatory, will contain nothing in themselves to suggest intent to injure[2]. It follows that malice and falsity will both have to be proved by the pursuer: hence the appropriateness of the title malicious falsehood[3].

At common law there was a further difference between defamation and malicious falsehood. Defamation is actionable even in the absence of averments of special damage, since the law presumes that insult at least has been suffered and Scots law recognises that damages are available for that alone. However, at common law in cases of malicious falsehood or other verbal injuries some damage had always to be averred and proved. This is no longer so and it has been statutorily provided[4] that in actions for verbal injury it is not necessary to aver and prove special damage if the words founded on are calculated to cause pecuniary damage to the pursuer. This rule is applicable in English law to what is called there slander of title, slander of goods and malicious falsehood[5].

Convicium

Thus far there is no difference between the Walker taxonomy and the one suggested above, save the terminological one that Walker calls malicious falsehood that which is usually today referred to as verbal injury. Walker's real innovation comes in his suggestion that there is a third class within the genus *injuria verbis*, different from both defamation and malicious falsehood, and with different requisites for liability from either. This third class he calls *convicium*, and the distinguishing feature of this class is, according to Walker,

---

1 *Trapp v Mackie* 1977 SLT 194 (OH), 1979 SLT 126 (IH and HL) is one of the few reported Scottish decisions referring to the claim as one of malicious falsehood. The phrase is much more commonly used in England.

2 *Steele v Scottish Daily Record* 1970 SLT 53 at 63 per Lord Milligan. Though he distinguishes between 'slander' and 'verbal injury' in this way rather than 'defamation' and 'malicious falsehood', the term 'slander' can be taken, in Scotland, as synonymous with defamation. See also Lord Hunter in *Argyllshire Weavers Ltd v A Macaulay (Tweeds) Ltd* 1965 SLT 21 at 35, distinguishing between what he calls 'defamation proper' and 'verbal injury'; and Lord Deas in *North of Scotland Banking Co v Duncan* (1857) 19 D 881 at 887.

3 It has to be admitted that in *Bruce v JM Smith & Co* (1898) 1 F 327, a case of slander of property (a form of malicious falsehood), an issue was permitted which deliberately omitted any mention of malice. This might be explained by the fact that the case was at least as close to defamation as to malicious falsehood (see particularly Lord Moncrieff at 332), in which, as was stated, malice is only relevant in cases of privilege.

4 Defamation Act 1952, s 3, as applied to Scotland by s 14. Discussed further, below at pp 47–48, 55.

5 See the English version of s 3 of the 1952 Act.

that truth is not an absolute defence. There is no authority whatsoever for this proposition, and there is no case in the law reports that unequivocally describes itself as one of *convicium* as an action different from defamation[1]. It exists only in the writings of the commentators.

The word itself does appear in the law reports and even in statute, but never in such a context as indicates a form of action separate from defamation or verbal injury. The word '*convicium*' was used by many nineteenth-century judges to mean, quite simply, 'defamation'. This is seen most clearly in the cases discussing whether *veritas* is or is not an absolute defence to the action for defamation[2], or, as it was put, whether *veritas convicii excusat* or *veritas convicii non excusat*[3]. No judge uses the word *convicium* to mean something different from defamation until after the first edition of Walker's *Delict* was published. In *Steele v Scottish Daily Record*[4] the sheriff-substitute, using Walker as authority, describes the case as one of *convicium* though he does not accept Walker's assertion that truth is no defence to such an action, thereby rejecting the only feature of Walkeresque *convicium* distinguishing it from other forms of verbal injury: the Inner House describes the case as one of verbal injury and lays down that falsity must be averred and proved by the pursuer. The only other case in which the word appears is *Trapp v Mackie*[5], where Lord Fraser of Tullybelton says[6] that the claim there is 'not based on defamation but on some other form of verbal injury, either convicium or malicious falsehood'. Walker does not cite this case as an example of *convicium*. The word also appears in one statute. The Prescription and Limitation (Scotland) Act 1973 was amended in 1985[7] to provide a three-year limitation period for actions for 'defamation'; and the new provision[8] defines 'defamation' to include '*convicium* and malicious falsehood'. The aim of the provision is clearly to ensure the same limitation period for all claims based on attacks on character, honour and reputation and the word *convicium* was added, it is submitted, merely for the avoidance of doubt.

Gleggian convicium

Cooper describes *convicium*, almost as an aside, as follows: 'the wanton and malicious publication of some old scandal or of some physical deformity'[9]. He

---

1 Indeed there are only two cases in which the word is apparently used to mean something other than the Latin term for defamation: *Steele v Scottish Daily Record* 1970 SLT 53 and *Trapp v Mackie* 1979 SLT 126.
2 Eventually resolved, of course, in favour of being an absolute defence: see below at pp 125–127.
3 *Macdonald v Macdonald* 2 June 1813, FC; *Scott v McGavin* (1821) 2 Mur 484; *Mackellar v Duke of Sutherland* (1859) 21 D 222; *Paul v Jackson* (1884) 11 R 460. See also *Brodie's Commentaries on Stair's Institutions* (1826) I, 4, 4.
4 1970 SLT 53.
5 1979 SLT 126.
6 1979 SLT 126 at 132.
7 Law Reform (Miscellaneous Provisions) (Scotland) Act 1985, s 12(5).
8 Prescription and Limitation (Scotland) Act 1973, s 18A.
9 Cooper, *Defamation and Verbal Injury* (2nd edn, 1906) p 210.

took this definition from Glegg[1] who, after giving the definition, goes on to state that truth is no defence to such actions[2]. If this were so then this would be a significant difference from both defamation and malicious falsehood, and *convicium* would indeed constitute a third category of action. However, Cooper and the later editor of Glegg are not convinced that the authorities cited by Glegg support his proposition. *Macdonald v Macdonald*[3] and *Dyce v Kerr*[4] both date from a time when it was very uncertain whether *veritas* was a complete defence in an action for defamation[5], and in the former indeed a majority of the court allowed the defender to lead evidence to prove the truth of the statement complained of – that is to prove the *veritas convicii*. The other authority used by Glegg is a statement by Lord Deas as Lord Ordinary in *Friend v Skelton*[6] in which he states 'truth is not always a justification of libel' and gives as his example the allusion to a bodily defect or to a family misfortune or some old generally forgotten immoral act or act of impropriety[7]: in such cases Lord Deas suggests that truth might be an aggravation. It is unlikely today that in the absence of liability for breach of privacy (perhaps through an extension of the delict of breach of confidentiality[8]) the publication of one's physical defects or diseases would be regarded as actionable[9]. The raking-up of an old forgotten allegation of immorality would be regarded as defamatory[10] and there is no doubt that truth is today an absolute defence in cases of defamation[11].

Walkeresque convicium

When Walker talks about *convicium* as the third category of verbal injuries, he is not primarily meaning cases of the raking-up of old scandals or the publication of secret bodily defects, though he does include such actions within his heading of *convicium*[12]. Rather, Walker defines the question in a case of *convicium* as follows: 'whether the defender falsely, or probably even truly, and

---

1 *Reparation* (2nd edn) pp 145–148: the third and fourth editions of *Glegg*, written by Sheriff James Lindsay Duncan, take a quite different line, which is closer to the one to be propounded in the text above.
2 The first edition of *Glegg* was published in 1892. He repeated this view in 'The Law of Slander' (1894) 1 SLT 585.
3 2 June 1813, FC.
4 9 July 1816, FC.
5 This matter is examined more fully in Chapter 9.
6 (1855) 17 D 548 at 551.
7 In the Inner House Lord Deas says much the same in *Cunningham v Phillips* (1868) 6 M 926 at 928 in which he suggests that a true publication of impotency might be actionable.
8 See cases involving breaches of medical confidentiality: *AB v CD* (1851) 14 D 177; *AB v CD* (1904) 7 F 72. Cf *Stephens v Avery* [1988] 2 All ER 477 in which a personal relationship gave rise to a duty of confidentiality, whose breach was held actionable. The tort of breach of confidentiality is discussed in relation to English law in (1994) 14 LS 313.
9 Nineteenth-century comments on diseases and disabilities, mental or physical, must be read bearing in mind nineteenth-century attitudes, ignorances and prejudices. It is unlikely to be held defamatory today to suggest that a person is insane, or suffering from some 'noxious' disease: see above at pp 25–26.
10 See Lord Shaw of Dunfermline to this effect in *Sutherland v Stopes* [1925] AC 47 at 74.
11 See below, at Chapter 9.
12 *Walker* pp 736–737.

maliciously communicated of and concerning the pursuer an idea calculated to bring him into public hatred, ridicule and contempt and caused him loss, injury or damage thereby'[1]. He is, in other words, primarily referring to the 'public hatred and contempt' cases[2]: 'where the ground of action is convicium rather than defamation the issue is one of "holding up to public hatred, contempt and ridicule" as well as or instead of wounding the pursuer's feelings and degrading him in the estimation of society'[3].

Now, there is a small number of cases in which issues have been allowed to go to the jury asking them whether the defender's communications have deliberately held the pursuer up to public hatred, contempt and ridicule or the case has been argued before a judge on that basis[4], and a similar number of cases in which the case has been held irrelevant or issues of this sort have, for various reasons, been refused[5]. However, it must be noted that in not one of these cases is the word 'convicium' ever used, except in the most recent case, Steele v Scottish Daily Record[6], in which the sheriff-substitute describes the case as one of convicium. That case, however, is not available for Walker to use as authority for describing this sort of case as one of convicium, since the authority used by the sheriff-substitute was Walker himself. The Inner House described the case as one of 'verbal injury'. The only part of Walker's reasoning not accepted by the sheriff-substitute is his assertion that truth is no defence in such an action: the Inner House expressly holds that falsity has to be established by the pursuer. Steele can be regarded as authority for nothing more than the proposition that the public hatred cases might be called convicium, and it lays down no different criteria to be applied to these cases from those applied to other actions for verbal injury. There is no legally separate class, and it is suggested that the terminology of convicium should be avoided lest one is led into the error of thinking that there is.

Exposing to public hatred, contempt and ridicule as a verbal injury

Though the cases which involve issues of holding up to public hatred, contempt and ridicule have been regarded for well over a century now as

---

1 *Walker* p 736. See also Smith, *Short Commentary on the Law of Scotland* p 731, note 62; *Stewart* p 173; Butterworths, *Glossary of Scottish Legal Terms* p 20 who also define *convicium* in this way. The earliest such usage of the word that has been found is in Guthrie Smith, *The Law of Damages* (2nd edn, 1889), where it is accepted that truth is no defence, on the basis that public derision might lead to public disturbance. No such proposition was made in the first edition (1864).
2 Discussed fully, below at pp 50–57.
3 *Walker* p 738.
4 *Sheriff v Wilson* (1855) 17 D 528; *McLaren v Ritchie* (1856) (unreported: issue set out in 14 R at 873 and 874); *Cunningham v Phillips* (1868) 6 M 926; *Paterson v Welch* (1893) 20 R 744; *Andrew v Macara* 1917 SC 247; *Lamond v Daily Record (Glasgow) Ltd* 1923 SLT 512; *Steele v Scottish Daily Record* 1970 SLT 53.
5 *Macfarlane v Black & Co* (1887) 14 R 870; *Waugh v Ayrshire Post* (1893) 21 R 326; *Waddell v Roxburgh* (1894) 21 R 883; *McLaughlan v Orr, Pollock & Co* (1894) 22 R 38; *Burns v Diamond* (1896) 3 SLT 397 (p 256); *Lever Bros v Daily Record* 1909 SC 1004; *Caldwell v Bayne* (1936) 52 Sh Ct Rep 334; *Moffat v London Express Newspapers* 1950 SLT (Notes) 46.
6 1970 SLT 53.

actions not of defamation but of non-defamatory actionable communications, it is clear that this was not always so. The phrase, or similar, appears in the Scottish law reports from very early times as a general definition for defamation. In for example *Society of Solicitors v Robertson*[1] the claim was on the basis that a newspaper article concerning the pursuers was malicious and tended 'to expose to ridicule and contempt, and to vilify, [the pursuers] . . . and that the said paragraphs [were] calculated, by lessening their estimation, to injure the pursuers'. This is clearly an action for defamation[2]. Such issues are regarded as issues in defamation in later cases also, even after it is recognised that there can be actions based on something other than defamation. Lord Kinnear for example in both the Court of Session[3] and in the House of Lords[4] equates 'exposure to public hatred or contempt' with 'slanderous'[5]. In England similar claims are still today treated as cases of defamation, for the formula was the classic definition of a defamatory statement in that jurisdiction until *Sim v Stretch*[6] in which Lord Atkin, specifically in order to escape the narrow trammels of that test, laid down the modern test of 'tending to lower the plaintiff in the estimation of right thinking members of society', while at the same time retaining, for appropriate cases, the older test.

However, there is no doubt that the modern practice in Scotland is to regard such a cause of action as something different in kind from defamation[7]. The change may well have been accidental, with the precise formulation of the issues doing no more than reflecting the facts of the cases in question, but the alteration was important since the move away from defamation denied to pursuers the presumptions of malice and falsity in their favour, which characterise the action for defamation. It seems likely that the movement from defamation to verbal injury came about in the following manner.

1 (1781) Mor 13935.
2 See also *Taylors v Swinton* (1824) 2 Shaw 245, and, most clearly, *Drew v Mackenzie & Co* (1862) 24 D 649 at 660, where Lord Deas defined defamation as a statement that 'held up the pursuer to scorn, ridicule, and contempt in the eyes of the public'.
3 *Waddell v Roxburgh* (1894) 21 R 883 at 886 and *Lever Bros v Daily Record* 1909 SC 1004 at 1008 and 1009.
4 *Russell v Stubbs Ltd* 1913 SC(HL) 14 at 19.
5 See also the defamation cases of *Wheatley v Anderson & Miller* 1927 SC 133 at 134 and *Cuthbert v Linklater* 1935 SLT 94 in which issues of holding up to public hatred, contempt and ridicule were presented as issues of defamation (and disallowed).
6 [1936] 2 All ER 1237.
7 In *Sheriff v Wilson* (1855) 17 D 528 the Lord Justice-Clerk stated that there was a claim for damages for articles holding the pursuer up to public ridicule 'whether they contain defamatory statements or not'. In *Cunningham v Phillips* (1868) 6 M 926 at 927 Lord Deas pointed out that the form of issue proposed by the court (from which he dissented) 'is avowedly applicable to a class of cases in which there is no slander'. In *Macfarlane v Black & Co* (1887) 14 R 870 at 874 Lord Young pointed out that the issue permitted was one of defamation but that there had been an argument 'that possibly the case was one of another category, that is in which a party complains of being injuriously held up in a series of attacks to public hatred, contempt and ridicule'. In *Paterson v Welch* (1893) 20 R 744 at 749 Lord President Robertson said 'But assuming, as I now do, that the words sued on do not found a claim for damages on the head of slander, it by no means follows that they are not actionable'. The matter has not been doubted since *Paterson*. In *Caldwell v Bayne* (1936) 52 Sh Ct Rep 334 at 345 Sheriff Malcolm said, 'while slander on the one hand and holding up to public hatred, odium and contempt on the other, are each actionable wrongs giving ground for a good claim for damages, they are quite distinct from one another, and the latter is not slander. It is known as verbal injury'.

The early public hatred cases all involved public figures like magistrates, or ministers, or teachers, or candidates for election, municipal or parliamentary. It has long been a feature of Scots law that public figures are expected to be rather more thick-skinned than the purely private individual, because criticism is to be expected of a person holding or seeking public office[1]. To be actionable therefore the criticism must be more than mere ridicule. To be defamatory, the criticism must impute criminality or refer to the person's private life; attacks on a person's public persona that do not impute criminality are actionable only if they go much further than ridicule and amount to the holding up of the person to public odium, or hatred, contempt and ridicule. The reason for this is that it is to the good of democracy that persons in public positions have their actions and opinions open to criticism or even to ridicule. Any member of the public has an interest and possibly even a duty to criticise public figures, for public debate on matters of public importance is of the essence of democratic life and an essential bulwark against abuse of position[2]. This of course is coming very close to the notion of qualified privilege, and it had the same effect: in order for a public figure to raise an action based on criticism he would have to show that the defender had acted with intent to injure him, that is had acted maliciously[3]. The fact that malice was required to be proved by the pursuer took the action right away from defamation (where it is, of course, presumed) and put it into a separate category. It is emphasised in most of the relevant cases that the fundamental part of the claim is the averment that the defender had acted with intent to injure[4]. Once recognised as something different from defamation this form of action could not be limited to public figures (a concept that cannot be defined with precision in any case)[5].

Truth and the public hatred cases

While the need to prove malice or intent to injure clearly distinguishes the public hatred cases from defamation, that does not in itself distinguish them from other cases of verbal injury where intent to injure is also a requirement. As we have seen, Walker claims that the feature distinguishing the public

1 See above at pp 26–27.
2 The significance of the fact that the pursuers in the developing cases were in public positions is recognised in *Steele v Scottish Daily Record* 1970 SLT 53 at 64 by Lord Milligan and at 65 by Lord Fraser.
3 Non-defamatory statements on public or political questions have to be treated with great care: *Cunningham v Phillips* (1868) 6 M 926 at 928 per Lord Deas, and in *McLaughlan v Orr Pollock & Co* (1894) 22 R 38 at 42 per Lord McLaren.
4 See for example the comments of Lord Deas in *Cunningham v Phillips* (1868) 6 M 926 at 928; of Lord Kinnear in *Waddell v Roxburgh* (1894) 21 R 883 at 886; of Lord Ordinary Kyllachy in *Waugh v Ayrshire Post* (1893) 21 R 326 at 328 and Lord Adam at 329; of Lord Ordinary Kincairney in *McLaughlan v Orr Pollock & Co* (1894) 22 R 38 at 41; and of Lord Fraser in *Steele v Scottish Daily Record* 1970 SLT 53 at 65.
5 In *Lamond v Daily Record (Glasgow) Ltd* 1923 SLT 512 the pursuer was a variety artiste – a person in the public eye possibly, but scarcely a public figure. In *Steele v Scottish Daily Record* 1970 SLT 53 the pursuer was a garage proprietor.

hatred cases from both defamation and malicious falsehood is the position of truth, for he argues that in such cases truth is no defence, or, as it might be put, *veritas convicii non excusat*. This suggestion is surprising, for in most of the cases that Walker himself cites as being examples of *convicium*[1] it is stated quite clearly that one of the fundamental requisites for actionability is that the statements complained of be proved by the pursuer to be false[2], and only in relation to *Steele v Scottish Daily Record* does Walker contend that the court 'mistakenly' included falsity as one of the requisites for actionability[3]. Indeed in the first case in which the issue was clearly not one of defamation, the Lord Justice-Clerk held that, at the pleading stage, the court had to assume the remarks complained of to be false and calumnious (and that at trial falsity and calumny would have to be proved to the jury)[4]. However, Walker's view does have a certain logic to it: if the essence of the case is intention to injure by holding up to public hatred and this can be achieved by publishing true facts, then it can be argued that it ought not to destroy the case that the defender has achieved his or her malicious aim by spreading the truth. Walker might be able to find some support in the public hatred cases prior to *Paterson v Welch*[5], that is *Sheriff v Wilson*[6], *McLaren v Ritchie*[7] and *Cunningham v Phillips*[8], for falsity appeared in none of the issues allowed in these cases. However, though not expressly overruled, these cases must be regarded as, at the very least, superseded by later developments and, whatever the state of the earlier law, falsity has been specified as one of the conditions for actionability in every public hatred case since 1893. The policy considerations in balancing freedom of speech with the right to individual privacy suggest that the overruling of the modern law and the restoration (if restoration it is) of the actionability of truthful statements should be a matter for legislative rather than judicial development. It is submitted that such a development ought to be resisted.

Solatium for verbal injury

In the English case of *Joyce v Sengupta*[9] the plaintiff raised an action for malicious falsehood and claimed damages both for economic loss and for the

---

1 *Walker* p 740, notes 76–84.
2 See eg *Paterson v Welch* (1893) 20 R 744 at 749; *Waugh v Ayrshire Post* (1893) 21 R 326 at 328 per Lord Ordinary Kyllachy (the Inner House held that the proper issue in that case was the normal one of defamation); *Lever Bros v Daily Record* 1909 SC 1004 at 1008 per Lord President Dunedin; *Moffat v London Express Newspapers* 1950 SLT (Notes) 46; *Steele v Scottish Daily Record* 1970 SLT 53 at 61 per Lord Wheatley and at 65 per Lord Fraser. In *Andrew v Macara* 1917 SC 247 a counter-issue of *veritas* was permitted (and found established by the jury: the Second Division, for that reason alone, refused the bill of exceptions). See also *Parlane v Templeton* (1896) 4 SLT 234 (p 153).
3 *Walker* p 738, note 63.
4 *Sheriff v Wilson* (1855) 17 D 528 at 530.
5 (1893) 20 R 744.
6 (1855) 17 D 528.
7 Issue set out in 14 R at 873 and 874.
8 (1868) 6 M 926.
9 [1993] 1 WLR 337.

distress and injury to feelings that she suffered as a consequence of certain newspaper articles. The Court of Appeal held that she was entitled to rely on section 3 of the Defamation Act 1952 to seek more than nominal damages, but the judges expressed doubt (though refused to decide the issue) on the question of whether it was competent to seek damages for injury to feelings as a separate head in an action for malicious falsehood, rather than using such injury to aggravate the economic loss. (All previous English cases of malicious falsehood had, rather surprisingly, concerned economic loss.) The English law of damages is very different from the Scots law, particularly in this field of law[1]. However, in Scots law too it has sometimes been suggested that solatium cannot be claimed for verbal injury[2]. Certainly particular forms of verbal injury will be inept to cause the insult for which solatium is claimable. So with slander of property or slander of business the essence of the wrong is the economic loss the slander causes and it is unlikely that the court will accept that any emotional hurt can be caused. But that is simply a factual conclusion (which may well be invariable with slander of property or slander of business) and it cannot be taken to lay down any rule that solatium is never available for any form of verbal injury. Damages (even solatium) in Scots law is reparation for injury caused and if the facts show no injury no damages will be awarded; but if injury, whether in the form of insult or otherwise, is caused by a legal wrong the law will provide redress. Insult and emotional damage can most readily be seen to be caused in the public hatred cases, where the pursuer's peace of mind as well as his or her reputation may be attacked. Solatium was expressly claimed in *Sheriff v Wilson*[3], and though it is seldom clear in later cases what types of damages are being claimed, the matter was put beyond doubt by the Second Division in *Steele v Scottish Daily Record*[4]. That case is important not only for its affirmation of the requisites for actionability laid down in *Paterson v Welch* but also for the application of these requisites, without differentiation, to both the claims made in that case, ie for patrimonial loss and for solatium. There was no suggestion that solatium cannot be claimed in an action for verbal injury, or that it can only be claimed when patrimonial loss is claimed also. Lord Fraser indeed[5] in discussing whether actual injury had been properly averred, stated that such averment was required to make it clear whether the injury complained of consisted of holding the pursuer up to public hatred or of damaging him in his business. The former would attract solatium, the latter damages for patrimonial loss. He then dealt with the two claims separately (and applied the same requisites to each). The primary harm in the public hatred cases is the loss of public standing and esteem, and the personal hurt that causes is appropriately compensated by solatium. The loss

---

1 See further, Chapter 12.
2 This was a matter of (surprising) concession by counsel for the pursuer in *Waddell v Roxburgh* (1894) 21 R 883. See also the Lord Ordinary and the Lord Justice-Clerk in *Broom v Ritchie & Co* (1904) 6 F 942: though that case was argued in defamation it might more relevantly (as explained below at pp 59–60) have been argued in verbal injury. Cf *Thomson v Fifeshire Advertiser* 1936 FN 56.
3 (1855) 17 D 528.
4 1970 SLT 53.
5 1970 SLT 53 at 65.

of public esteem may also, consequentially, cause patrimonial loss in the shape, for example, of lost business, and if that can be proved then that too can be claimed for. There is no room in modern Scots law for the suggestion that verbal injury founds a claim only for patrimonial loss. Indeed Lord Wheatley pointed out that 'in *Paterson v Welch* the injury was said to be one of holding the pursuer up to public hatred, and the action was restricted accordingly to a claim for solatium'[1].

Conclusion

The true position in the modern law is, it is submitted, as follows. Attacks on a person's character, honour and reputation, that is *injuria verbis*, are actionable under one of two heads, and the pursuer can choose, on the basis of what he or she can prove, which head is more appropriate[2]. If the attack can be shown to be defamatory then defamation is the appropriate ground of action, and on proof that the statement complained of is defamatory both intent to injure and falsity will be presumed. If the attack cannot be shown to be defamatory then what is normally today called verbal injury is the appropriate ground of action, though here the pursuer will have to prove both falsity and intent to injure. All the public hatred cases are subsumed into the category of verbal injury, which includes, as will be seen in the next chapter, slander of title, of business and of property, third party slander, and other malicious falsehoods. Solatium can be claimed when insult as well as or instead of patrimonial loss has been caused by the verbal injury. *Convicium* does not exist as a separate ground of action in Scotland, though the word is sometimes, misleadingly, used to refer to that form of verbal injury involving the holding up of the pursuer to public hatred, contempt and ridicule. The conditions for the cases described by Walker as cases of *convicium* are the same as for all other verbal injuries and there is, therefore, no need in law to separate them out.

---

1 1970 SLT 53 at 60. The report of *Paterson* gives no indication that solatium was included in the claim, far less that the claim was restricted to solatium alone. Professor Blackie, having analysed both the decision and the comments on it at around the time it was decided, has concluded that the claim in that case was in fact for patrimonial loss only.

2 Alternative claims in the same case are not permitted: *Cunningham v Phillips* (1868) 6 M 926 at 928 per Lord Deas; *Lever Bros v Daily Record* 1909 SC 1004 at 1008 per Lord President Dunedin and at 1007 per Lord Ordinary Guthrie; *Steele v Scottish Daily Record* 1970 SLT 53 at 61 per Lord Wheatley.

CHAPTER FOUR

Verbal injury: specific claims

Introduction

It was seen in the previous chapter that attacks on a person's character, honour and reputation can lead to the remedy of damages under one of two quite distinct heads: on the one hand there is the more common action for defamation, and on the other hand there is the very much less common action for what is called verbal injury or malicious falsehood[1]. Within the second category there are a number of different fact situations that can lead to liability, but for each the basic requirements are the same and the legal consequences of liability are also the same. This chapter will examine a number of fact situations in which non-defamatory statements can be or have been held to be actionable, though it must be emphasised that the classification presented is a factual one only, and any differences in the way the claims are dealt with are consequences of the facts rather than of different legal principle.

Slander of title, property or business

The Scottish section 3 of the Defamation Act 1952 lays down a rule[2] applicable to 'any action for verbal injury'. The English section 3 lays down the same rule for any action 'for slander of title, slander of goods or other malicious falsehood'. It can be seen therefore that one of the major forms of verbal injury or malicious falsehood is what is called in England (and sometimes in Scotland too) slander of title or slander of goods. This form of verbal injury is the wrong committed when a person maliciously communicates to a third party some falsehood about the pursuer's property or title to property or his business in a manner intended to cause and with the result of causing loss (invariably economic) to the pursuer. Though there are very few cases in the Scottish law reports to illustrate this wrong, there is no reason in principle why, so long as the normal conditions for actionability of verbal injury are satisfied, these fact situations should not give rise to liability. It will be a

---

1 The House of Lords in England accepts that in appropriate cases such an attack might also be sued for as negligence: see *Spring v Guardian Assurance plc* [1994] 3 All ER 129 discussed above at pp 5–7.
2 Discussed below at pp 47–48, 55.

defence for the defender to show the lack of one of the requisites for liability; and absolute privilege will also act as a defence[1].

Slander of property

It is unlikely that an allegation concerning a person's property will be defamatory of that person, for it will seldom amount to an attack on a person's character, honour and reputation to state that the property he or she owns is defective in some way. Yet it is easy to imagine how such an allegation might be the direct cause of economic loss to the owner. If, for example, an item of property is being advertised for sale, attacks on its quality may easily reduce its marketability and value. This is particularly so in certain volatile commercial sectors such as the art market, where an allegation that, say, a particular painting is not by some renowned artist could greatly diminish its value. If it can be innuendoed that the owner is trying to commit a fraud by passing the item off as something that it is not, an action for defamation will be available, but if that innuendo cannot be established an action based on verbal injury can be used to compensate the owner for his or her loss caused by the malicious falsehood.

The earliest Scottish case usually cited as an example of slander of property is that of *Hamilton v Arbuthnot*[2], the short report of which can be given in full: 'A person having spread a calumnious report against a merchant advertising a sale, that the goods were an imposition, and rotten and mill-dewed trash, the Lords condemned him in £40 Sterling of damages to the party injured'. Given the brevity of this report it cannot be stated with certainty whether the case is truly one of slander of property or one of defamation in which an innuendo of fraud by the merchant was drawn; and in any case the report dates from a time in which the distinction between defamation and other actionable statements was not made. Most of the later cases contain clear elements of defamation, which serves to confuse the picture[3]. So in *Broomfield v Greig*[4], in which a doctor alleged that a baker's bread was unfit for human consumption, the court refused an issue on that allegation but allowed one on the innuendo that the pursuer adulterated bread and flour on his premises, in violation of the law. There is little to suggest that this case is anything other

1 *Trapp v Mackie* 1979 SLT 126. Walker, *Delict* (2nd edn, 1981) p 903, citing *McLean v Adam* (1885) 16 R 175 indicates that qualified privilege is a defence also. This cannot be right since the only effect of qualified privilege is to impose upon the pursuer the burden of proving malice, or intent to injure; in cases of verbal injury the pursuer already has this burden. As we will see *McLean* was as much a case of defamation as of verbal injury.
2 (1750) Mor 13923.
3 *Walker* p 905, suggests that slander of property and of title are necessary in England due to the narrowness of the principles of libel and slander, but are not necessary in Scotland, where all the decided cases could have been dealt with under the general head of defamation. This may well be so, but it is easy to imagine situations in which aspersions of property are clearly not defamatory of the owner, such as a statement that his oil painting of a bowl of sunflowers is not, after all, by van Gogh.
4 (1868) 6 M 563.

than one of defamation. In *McLean v Adam*[1] a doctor stated that an outbreak of typhoid fever could be traced to the pursuer's dairy, and though Lord Young was of the opinion that the statement complained of 'contains no imputation on the character of the pursuer'[2], Lord Lee expressly described the case as one of defamation[3]. *Bruce v JM Smith*[4] involved a newspaper report that a building owned by the pursuer was likely to fall down, as a result of which its sale value was greatly reduced. The Lord Ordinary, Lord Kincairney, treated the case as one of 'slander of property', which he accepts as part of the law of Scotland, though in the Inner House Lord Moncrieff states 'I should like to add that I think that we have here not merely slander of property, but slander of the pursuer himself in connection with his trade'[5].

Though the case of *Bruce* contained defamatory elements, it is a clear acceptance that Scots law recognises as actionable statements which disparage a person's property. The Defamation Act 1952 provides support as we have seen, with the Scottish section 3 describing as 'verbal injury' what the English section 3 describes as 'slander of title, slander of goods or other malicious falsehood'. Further support is provided by the case of *Argyllshire Weavers Ltd v A Macauley (Tweeds) Ltd*[6]. In this case the pursuers sought an interdict against the defenders to prevent them alleging that the cloth produced by the pursuers was not genuine 'Harris tweed'[7]. Though the case failed, this was on the ground of lack of proof rather than relevancy, for the pursuers failed to prove the falsity of the defenders' statements (ie had failed to prove that their own cloth could properly be described as Harris tweed). Lord Hunter's judgment is interesting for a number of reasons[8]. There is, first, an unequivocal recognition that the case is an example of what can be called verbal injury[9]. Then there follows a clear enumeration of the requisites for actionability, which are threefold.

First and foremost the disparaging remarks must be shown to be false. 'Whatever view' Lord Hunter said, 'may be taken of the ingredients of verbal injury, the fundamental requirement must in my opinion be that the statement should be false'[10]. If a person states that a building is falling down

---

1 (1888) 16 R 175.

2 (1888) 16 R 175 at 181.

3 (1888) 16 R 175 at 182. The discussion of qualified privilege also suggests that the case is truly one of defamation rather than verbal injury. See above, p 45, note 1.

4 (1898) 1 F 327.

5 (1898) 1 F 327 at 332.

6 1965 SLT 21 (OH).

7 Cf *Webster v Paterson & Sons* 1910 SC 459, which involved an action for interdict against one coffee manufacturer claiming that its coffee was the same as that of another's with the implication that the other's was, therefore, inferior.

8 Quite apart from the detailed history of Scottish tweed-making it contains.

9 'The nature of the wrong which the pursuers contend they have suffered . . . falls in my opinion into the category which has been referred to in Scotland as verbal injury, and in England by a variety of terms, including the general description injurious falsehood, of which slander of goods, and slander of title or property are examples': 1965 SLT 21 at 35.

10 1965 SLT 21 at 35. That this is one of the main distinctions from defamation proper was recognised by Lord Ordinary Kincairney in *Bruce v JM Smith* (1898) 1 F 327 at 331: 'The statement complained of must be alleged to be false, and I rather think must be proved to be false; for I see no reason for adopting that presumption for falsehood which is, by rooted practice, with or without reason, recognised in actions of slander of character'.

and it is falling down then the owner cannot claim damages for the diminution in its value, because the diminished value is its real value. To put it another way, if a person's property is diminished in value due to its true worth being published, then the owner has suffered no loss that the law can take cognisance of.

Secondly, the disparaging remarks must be made with intent to cause loss to the pursuer[1]. Though in *Bruce v JM Smith*[2] an issue was permitted which, expressly, did not contain any reference to malice, this can be explained – at least partly – by the fact that there were defamatory elements to the claim. There is too much authority with the other types of verbal injury to suggest that this type alone has the specialty that malice does not need to be averred and proved. So, if a defender points out to a potential purchaser of an oil painting owned by the pursuer that it is not the work of the artist whom the purchaser believed it to be there is no liability even if this comment is false and causes loss, unless the pursuer can show that the comment was made with malicious intent to harm the pursuer. If it is made in a genuine attempt to protect the interests of the potential purchaser or in the course of a genuine dispute about attribution then there is no malice and the remark will not be actionable[3]. The law will not presume malicious intent (as it does with defamation) and the onus is therefore on the pursuer to aver and prove it. It may well be that the relative rarity of cases based on this form of verbal injury – and indeed of the other forms – stems from the difficulties in proving intent to injure.

Thirdly, the remarks must have caused the pursuer loss, and it is not sufficient merely that they are capable of causing loss[4]. It follows that, unlike with defamation, this form of verbal injury can be committed only when the contentious statements are communicated to a third party, for there will be no diminution of value if the 'slander' is communicated only to the owner of property. At common law it was a rule that in actions based on verbal injury (of whatever form) rather than defamation, special damage, in the sense of particular economic harm, had to be averred and proved by the pursuer, but this was a heavy and often impossible burden for the pursuer to discharge, and so today section 3 of the Defamation Act 1952 provides that 'in any action for verbal injury it shall not be necessary for the pursuer to aver and prove special damage if the words on which the action is founded are calculated to cause pecuniary damage to the pursuer'. The effect of this section would seem to be that it is presumed that words calculated to cause pecuniary loss do indeed cause pecuniary loss, even when they cannot be precisely identified. The pursuer will still have to make averments as to the quantification of his loss and the section does not restrict those who rely on it to nominal damages only.[5]

---

1 'The pursuer must prove that the false assertion was made maliciously. Malice is not presumed': *Argyllshire Weavers* 1965 SLT 21 at 35 per Lord Hunter.
2 (1898) 1 F 327.
3 Cf the English case of *Re Lewis's Declaration of Trust* [1953] 1 All ER 1005.
4 *Argyllshire Weavers* 1965 SLT 21 at 35 per Lord Hunter.
5 *Joyce v Sengupta* [1993] 1 WLR 337 (CA).

Section 3 is limited in its terms to pecuniary loss and it is likely that this is all that can be claimed in this type of verbal injury. The solatium element in defamation is designed to provide compensation for the insult contained within the defamatory remarks and for the personal affront that the insult is assumed to cause, and while section 3 of the 1952 Act may allow the courts to assume that patrimonial damage has arisen from words intended to have that effect, the courts are unlikely to accept that sufficient hurt feelings or insult can arise from aspersions on the quality of one's property. So the action was dismissed as irrelevant in *Thomson v Fifeshire Advertiser*[1] when the alleged slander was directed only against the pursuer's goods and business and there were no averments of damage of a patrimonial kind. It does not follow from this that solatium cannot be claimed for other types of verbal injury: all that is suggested here is that no recognisable personal hurt flows from slander of property or of title[2].

Slander of title

An aspersion on a person's title to property might more readily than slander of property be innuendoed as an aspersion on a person's character, as containing a possible allegation of theft or fraud. As always, if a defamatory innuendo can be established then the case can be treated as one of defamation[3]. If no such innuendo can be drawn then an action might be based on 'slander of title', as an example of verbal injury. So, an allegation that a seller of property does not have a good title thereto could easily occasion loss by disrupting the sale. The allegation will not, however, be actionable unless it is false, was made maliciously, and caused actual harm. Statements made during a genuine dispute as to ownership of an item of property will not normally be actionable, notwithstanding any harm caused, because of the lack of intent to injure.

In *Philp v Morton*[4] an auction sale was in process when the defender's law agent declared, in the hearing of those attending the sale, that the seller was not entitled to sell the items. Damages for the loss occasioned thereby were recovered. In *Yeo v Wallace*[5] agents of a landlord intervened during the sale of a tenant's furniture and declared that anyone purchasing items did so at their own risk and would be responsible for anything they removed. The action failed because there was no allegation of malice and because the statement alleged to have caused the loss was not false. In *Harpers v Greenwood & Batley*[6] the defenders had raised an action for interdict against the pursuer seeking to prevent him from infringing certain patents to which they laid claim. The pursuer alleged that the action had been raised maliciously and without

---

1 1936 SN 56.
2 See further, above at pp 41–43.
3 And of course the pursuer has strong incentive in raising the action on the basis of defamation rather than anything else (ie the presumptions of falsity and malice).
4 (1816) Hume 865.
5 (1867) 5 SLR 253.
6 (1896) 4 SLT 177 (p 116).

probable cause and was designed to cast aspersions on his right to the patents. The case failed on two grounds: first that no averments of special damage had been made (a ground that has since been superseded[1]), and secondly that there were no relevant averments of malice. Malice was not to be inferred simply from the fact that the defenders had raised an action which they knew had little chance of success, for every person is entitled to test their potential rights in a court of law.

From these cases it is clear that the action for 'slander of title' is accepted by Scots law as an example of verbal injury, and that the three requirements appropriate to a case of slander of property must be averred and proved by the pursuer here also; that is to say, falsity, intent to injure and actual injury. The comments relating to patrimonial loss and the availability of solatium for slander of property[2] apply with equal force in cases of slander of title.

Slander of business

Slander of business is the form of verbal injury most closely linked to defamation, for most statements made about a person's professional or business competence will be within the accepted definition of defamation, which includes aspersions on a person's business practices or competence[3]. In the few cases in which the statement complained of is not defamatory, the action may be raised on the basis of verbal injury, but in that case the onus will be on the pursuer to prove falsity, intent to injure and actual injury. So in *Buchan v Walch*[4] a claim was held irrelevant when the defender, a landlord, had allegedly stated that the pursuers, his tenants, had not paid their rent and did not understand the business they carried on, because it had not been averred that the statement was made with the intention of injuring the pursuers. And in *Parlane v Templeton*[5] the pursuer alleged that the defenders had published his name in a list which suggested that he had been a member of the defenders' association and had been expelled therefrom for unfair and dishonourable conduct in connection with his trade[6]. An issue in defamation was permitted and one for verbal injury refused. On the other hand, a claim based on verbal injury was successfully pursued in *Lamond v Daily Record (Glasgow) Ltd*[7], in which a variety artiste sued a newspaper which had published a fictitious interview with her in which it attributed to her certain unpopular opinions about prohibition in the United States of America. She alleged that this had been done with intent to injure her standing in the public eye and so to diminish her chances of being employed on the stage. Lord Blackburn held the claim relevant: 'In my opinion the article inflicts on her a verbal injury, resulting

1 Defamation Act 1952, s 3.
2 Above at p 48.
3 See above at pp 22–24.
4 (1857) 20 D 222.
5 (1896) 4 SLT 234 (p 153).
6 A printers' trade union published what they termed 'The Register of Rats'.
7 1923 SLT 512. This case might also be considered with the 'public hatred' cases discussed below.

in general damage to her trade or business, and amounts to an actionable wrong which she is entitled to have submitted to a jury'[1]. When the case was sent to a jury, Lord Constable said in his charge that the case belonged to the category called verbal injury, which was different from defamation, and for which an award of damages was due if the statements were proved to be false and to have been made with intent to injure and did in fact injure[2]. The jury found that the pursuer had proved all these things, and awarded her £500. It is worthy of note that Lord Constable charged the jury to the effect that if they found the article to be false and injurious this was enough to show that the publication was 'wrongful', but this is not to be taken to mean that malicious intent is to be presumed from the falsity of the statement complained of. The finding that the article was false in this particular case was necessarily a finding that the defenders knew it was false, since it was alleged that they had made the whole interview up: making a statement knowing it to be false is good and sufficient evidence of malice[3].

A case of this sort which would have been successful, but for the fact that the pursuer sued the wrong defenders[4], is that of *Craig v Inveresk Paper Merchant Ltd*[5]. Here, sales representatives of the defenders had informed customers of the pursuer that he was on the point of going out of business. Lord Leechman held, after proof, that the pursuer had established that the statements were false, that they had been made with intent to injure him in his business, and that they had caused some loss of orders and therefore injury to the pursuer's business. This once again illustrates the three requisites that have to be averred for the claim to be relevant and that have to be proved by the pursuer for the claim to be successful.

The public hatred, contempt and ridicule cases

It has already been shown how the law came to accept as actionable on grounds other than defamation injuries allegedly caused by the defender holding the pursuer up to public hatred, contempt and ridicule[6]. It is clear that such actions are today to be regarded as examples of verbal injury and that the same requirements have to be fulfilled in this type of case as for all other forms of verbal injury. The requirements are that the pursuer prove that the statements complained of are false, that they were made with intent to injure, and that they did in fact cause the injury intended. There are a number of reported decisions in which the claim has been based solely on this type of

1 1923 SLT 512 at 514. And see *Thomson v Fifeshire Advertiser* 1936 SN 56.
2 1923 SLT 512 at 515.
3 See below at p 122.
4 The defenders were the employers of the wrongdoers and the pursuer could not establish that the latter were acting in the course of their employment, and therefore could not establish vicarious liability.
5 1970 SLT (Notes) 50.
6 Above at pp 38–40.

verbal injury, though like slander of title, property or business, successful claims are exceedingly rare. A number of them have certain (factually) common elements.

Series of statements designed to ridicule

The first set of cases concerns pursuers who complain about newspapers or magazines publishing series of articles about them, which individually might not be defamatory but the cumulative effect of which is to destroy the pursuer's peace of mind and public esteem. The earliest case in which such a claim was made in circumstances in which it is clearly not one of defamation is that of *Sheriff v Wilson*[1], in which a teacher complained about a series of newspaper articles lampooning his personal habits and accusing him of being a glutton. An issue was sent to the jury asking whether the series of articles 'was written in pursuance of an intention to expose the pursuer to ridicule and contempt, to wound his feelings as a private individual and to degrade him in the estimation of the society in which he resides, to the loss, injury and damage of the pursuer?'. Similar issues were allowed on similar facts in *McLaren v Ritchie*[2] and in *Cunningham v Phillips*[3], the latter of which involved a minister who had been vociferous in the great and important public debate about whether organs should be used in Church of Scotland worship. It is to be noted that while intent to injure was regarded as being of the essence in the issues allowed in *Sheriff* and in *Cunningham*[4], falsity did not appear in either of the public hatred issues in these two cases (though it appeared in an additional issue of defamation in *Sheriff*). However, in *Sheriff*[5] the Lord Justice-Clerk did state in his opinion that falsity would require to be proved by the jury for the action to be successful. Falsity has been stated as a requisite in every case since 1893[6].

In *Macfarlane v Black & Co*[7] an issue of verbal injury was not proceeded with, notwithstanding promptings from the bench that this would be more appropriate in the particular case than defamation, an issue of which was proceeded with. Because defamation is less burdensome for the pursuer than verbal injury, the judicial suggestion to counsel that verbal injury would be appropriate in this case indicates that the bench did not consider that the pursuer could prove that he had in fact been defamed. (The case involved a parliamentary candidate who was described in a newspaper article as a 'scoffer' at religion and as a person who permitted the boat crew from his yacht to go

---

1 (1855) 17 D 528.
2 1856, unreported, issue set out in 14 R at 873 and 874.
3 (1868) 6 M 926.
4 See particularly Lord Deas at 927 and 928. Also, in *McLaughlan v Orr, Pollock & Co* (1894) 22 R 38, though the Inner House disallowed the issue, the Lord Ordinary, Lord Kincairney, was prepared to approve it, so long as it put the question whether the series of articles was intended to cause the injury complained of.
5 (1855) 17 D 528 at 530.
6 See further, above at pp 40–41.
7 (1887) 14 R 870.

fishing on a Sunday.) An issue of verbal injury was also refused in *McLaughlan v Orr, Pollock & Co*[1] when a series of articles ridiculed a burgh magistrate, because the articles were not so disparaging that they could achieve the effect of holding the pursuer up to public hatred, contempt and ridicule[2]. And in *Burns v Diamond*[3] an issue was refused to a candidate at a municipal election when a series of articles in *The Glasgow Observer and Catholic Herald* accused him of being irreligious, the reason being that a charge of change of religion does not expose a person to public hatred and contempt[4].

Attributions of unpopular sentiments

The next series of cases starts with *Paterson v Welch*[5] in which the pursuer complained that the defender had attributed to him certain unpopular opinions and sentiments. The defender was alleged to have stated publicly on two occasions that the pursuer, a candidate for municipal election, had expressed the view that to allow children from a public school to attend Madras College in St Andrews would 'contaminate the genteel children' currently attending that institution. An issue was allowed and Lord President Robertson laid down three conditions for actionability: the pursuer must show that '(1) the statement . . . is false; (2) the statement was made with a design to injure; and (3) injury has resulted'[6]. This case is significant for two reasons. First, it was the first case in which an issue of holding up to public hatred, contempt and ridicule was permitted when only one statement and a repetition was being complained about rather than, as before, a series of articles[7]. Secondly, while the previous cases had emphasised that design to injure was the element which made the communication wrongful, Lord President Robertson expressly laid down that falsity was a matter to be proved by the pursuer, and for the first time required that that be put in the issue. In *Waddell v Roxburgh*[8], which was decided shortly after *Paterson*, a newspaper stated that a printing contract had been secured 'in a mean and contemptible manner' and the First Division held that an issue in defamation was appropriate rather than an issue of verbal injury. *Paterson* was commented upon in the Inner House by Lord Kinnear, who clearly wished to limit the effect of the earlier case. He said: 'It was not intended by the Court in that case to lay down that whenever

---

1 (1894) 22 R 39.
2 On that point, see below at pp 56–57.
3 (1896) 3 SLT 397 (p 256).
4 See also *Lever Bros v Daily Record* 1909 SC 1004 in which an issue of defamation was permitted and one of verbal injury disallowed since once the defamatory elements were removed from the contentious articles there was nothing injurious left.
5 (1893) 20 R 744.
6 (1893) 20 R 744 at 749.
7 Lord Ardmillan, who as Lord Ordinary in *Sheriff v Wilson* allowed the issue because of a series of attacks, said in *Cunningham v Phillips* (1868) 6 M 926 at 929 that he was not prepared to say that a single attack, though holding a person up to public contempt, could afford a ground of action. A single statement was thought by the judges to be sufficient in *Macfarlane v Black & Co* (1887) 14 R 870, but the pursuer proceeded only in defamation rather than verbal injury.
8 (1894) 21 R 883.

the words of which a pursuer complains are not in themselves slanderous, he may have an issue whether they exposed him to public hatred and contempt'[1]. Rather, Lord Kinnear emphasised that intent to injure is the fundamental point of such an issue. It is doubtful whether this really does limit the effect of *Paterson*, since intent to injure was clearly specified there as one of the fundamental requisites to be proved. The effect of *Paterson* was, indeed, explicitly to recognise the onus on the pursuer of proving not only malicious intent but also falsity.

A similar case to *Paterson* is *Waugh v Ayrshire Post Ltd*[2], in which a newspaper had published a fictitious letter ascribing to the pursuer the opinion that Roman Catholic blood ought to be spilt. An issue along the *Paterson* lines, requiring the pursuer to prove falsity, intent to injure, and actual injury was permitted by the Lord Ordinary (Kyllachy), though the First Division held that the publication was defamatory and that an issue of defamation rather than verbal injury was therefore the appropriate one. The case of *Andrew v Macara*[3] is more significant. Here the defender had ascribed to the pursuer (the secretary of a local YMCA) the statement that the troops at that time fighting in France during the First World War were in the trenches to have an easy time. Lord Salvesen emphasised that falsity was necessary to make the defender's comments actionable. Lord Hunter stated:

'the essence of such an issue, as I understand it, is that the defender has falsely ascribed to the pursuer odious or unpopular sentiments, and that he has done that, and is proved to have done it, with the design and with the result of holding the pursuer up to public contempt'[4].

A counter-issue of *veritas* was allowed in order to permit the defender to lead evidence that the pursuer had made the statement alleged, and indeed the defender was successful in proving just that. The fact that a counter-issue was permitted should not, however, be taken to mean that the defender has the onus of proving truth in actions for verbal injury. The counter-issue, as Lord Hunter makes clear[4], was designed to have the jury's attention very strictly directed to the essentials of the case. The onus remains on the pursuer to prove that the defender's assertions are false, and nothing in *Andrew v Macara* is designed to alter that principle.

Another case in this class is *Lamond v Daily Record (Glasgow) Ltd*[5], which is also an example of slander of business. Here a newspaper printed a fictitious interview with a variety artiste in which she had allegedly stated that American audiences were less responsive to her due to the deleterious effects on the American citizenry of alcohol prohibition. The issue proposed by the Lord Ordinary (Blackburn) contained all the three elements specified in *Paterson v Welch*, ie falsity, intent to injure, and actual injury. In charging the jury, Lord

---

1 (1894) 21 R 883 at 885 and 886.
2 (1893) 21 R 326.
3 1917 SC 247.
4 1917 SC 247 at 253.
5 1923 SLT 512.

Constable emphasised[1] that it was necessary for the pursuer to prove that the statement was false, and that she had suffered damage as a result of the statement. In this particular case malice was inferred from the facts that the statement was false and that the publisher, having invented the interview, knew the statement to be false.

Finally, there is *Caldwell v Bayne*[2] in which the pursuer, during a municipal election, had been accused of voting against the provision of free milk to necessitous school children and was therefore a 'baby-starver'. The claim based on verbal injury failed because it had not been pleaded with sufficient clarity on record to give the opponent fair notice of the case that was being set up against him. The case indicates the importance of pleading clearly that the claim is laid in verbal injury rather than in defamation and the importance of setting out all the requisites.

Other cases

After 1936 there was no reported case of verbal injury in which the pursuer complained of being held up to public hatred, contempt and ridicule until 1969, when *Steele v Scottish Daily Record*[3] was decided. In this case a newspaper had published an article in its legal advice and consumer rights page in which a car-dealer was shown in what he considered an unfair light. The article was headed: 'Have a heart, that's my message to Motor Dealer Mr Steele' and it suggested that the pursuer, the car dealer, had refused to accommodate a customer who was in financial difficulties by refusing to cancel a hire-purchase agreement. The case failed on the ground that the article, fairly read, was not calculated to, and indeed could not, bring the pursuer into public hatred and contempt, but its importance lies in the affirmation by the Second Division, for all types of verbal injury, of the three requirements to be proved by the pursuer which had been laid down in *Paterson v Welch*[4]. Lord Wheatley pointed out that the pursuer was claiming both solatium and damages for injury to his business. He said:

'Each of these has to be examined separately. Under the first head the pursuer has to aver and prove (1) that the article, though not slanderous, was false at least in some material respect; (2) that the falsity was intended to bring him into public hatred and contempt; and (3) that it did so. Under the second head the pursuer has to aver and prove (1) the falsity of the article as above; (2) that the falsity was intended to injure him in his business; and (3) that it did so.'

Lord Fraser[5] agreed that the three requisites laid down by Lord President Robertson in *Paterson* had to be established, and he stated, 'I note in passing that the second of these elements [intent to injure] constitutes one of the main

1 1923 SLT 512 at 515.
2 (1936) 52 Sh Ct Rep 334.
3 1970 SLT 53.
4 (1893) 20 R 744.
5 1970 SLT 53 at 65.

distinctions between an action for verbal injury and one for defamation'. Under neither head did the pursuer prove his case.

The third requirement, under both heads, has not been rendered otiose by section 3 of the Defamation Act 1952, which provides that in an action for verbal injury, it is not necessary to aver and prove special damage, for it is still necessary to show that some injury has been suffered.

'The pursuer has to aver that the false statement was designed to injure him in a particular way and in fact did injure him in that way. Merely to refer to injury *in vacuo* does not seem to me to be enough'[1].

'In my opinion the submission of the defenders to the effect that in a case of verbal injury a pursuer must aver and prove in what particular way the words or article complained of were designed to injure him is well founded . . . A bare averment that the words or article were designed "to injure the pursuer" is not sufficient'[2].

Section 3 is designed to ensure that the law grants a remedy despite the difficulty in proving actual loss. It will seldom be possible for the pursuer to lead direct evidence that the public hate him and consequently have stopped doing business with him, still less that consequently he has been hurt in his feelings[3], and section 3 does no more than provide that the case is still actionable despite the absence of such direct evidence.

Public hatred since Steele

There has been no reported case in the Scottish courts since *Steele* in which the pursuer's complaint is that he has been held up to public hatred, contempt and ridicule and in that way has suffered a verbal injury. This is not, however, to say that such a complaint is no longer possible. Certainly it will be a difficult claim to pursue, due to the heavy burden (to be discussed shortly[4]) of proving public hatred, contempt and ridicule: the last successful case seems to be that of *Lamond v Daily Record (Glasgow) Ltd* in 1923; or, if that is really a case of slander of business, the last successful case which involved only the holding up to public hatred, contempt and ridicule was in 1893 with *Paterson v Welch* itself. However, the action, though clearly difficult to prove, may well have some continuing use in providing redress for false statements which, though hurtful and harmful are nevertheless not defamatory.

A statement is defamatory only if it lowers the pursuer in the estimation not of society as it actually is but of 'right-thinking members of society'[5]. This objective test involves a determination by the court of how people *ought* to regard certain allegations, and it does not necessarily reflect how people *actually do* regard these allegations. It is easy to imagine a statement being made

---

1 1970 SLT 53 at 60 per Lord Wheatley.
2 1970 SLT 53 at 63 per Lord Milligan.
3 *Paterson v Welch* (1893) 20 R 744 was an exception since there was evidence to show quite clearly public hatred: the pursuer had been burned in effigy after the defender's remarks.
4 Below at pp 56–57.
5 See above at pp 8–12.

which right-thinking people ought not to regard as being derogatory but which large sections of society do in fact regard as being derogatory, and if such a statement is made by a defender deliberately in order to hurt the pursuer, and it does hurt the pursuer, then liability may be affirmed under this ground. So for example a false allegation of homosexuality would not today, it is submitted, be regarded by 'right-thinking members of society' as one that makes them less willing to associate with the subject of the allegation[1]. Yet homosexuals are legally barred from the armed forces and are effectively socially barred from other employments such as the police. If a defender puts it about that a particular person is a homosexual and this is done to prevent the person from being employed, say in the army, or as an actor in a 'macho' role, and it has this effect, the subject of the allegation may be able to claim damages if he can establish all the requisites for the action: that is that it is false, that it is made with intent to injure him and that it does so injure. An action of this nature based on public hatred would be rare, because there are few allegations that can be made which will hold a person up to public hatred but which 'right-thinking' members of society do not regard as derogatory, but perhaps a false allegation of homosexuality is an example, homophobia being one of the few remaining respectable bigotries. Attribution of highly unpopular opinions might be another example: it may not be defamatory to accuse a person of holding certain beliefs[2] because in a democracy everyone is entitled to their own opinions, but false attribution for malicious motive may well be actionable if it holds the pursuer up to public hatred. Most other claims would simply be based on malicious falsehood.

What is public hatred, contempt and ridicule?

A malicious falsehood that leads to no harm is not actionable, notwithstanding section 3 of the Defamation Act 1952. Some harm must therefore be caused before verbal injury is actionable, and the harm in the public hatred cases is that the pursuer has been exposed to public hatred, contempt and ridicule and has thereby been lowered in public standing and esteem, causing affront and patrimonial loss. Successfully to show that a person has been held up to public hatred, contempt and ridicule will be difficult. Mere contempt or ridicule is not sufficient to cause that harm. In *McLaughlan v Orr, Pollock & Co*[3] an issue was refused in which the pursuer claimed that he had been held up to contempt and ridicule. Lord McLaren pointed out[4] that in earlier cases,

'the question was whether, by the words libelled, the pursuer was "held up to public hatred, contempt and ridicule" and I cannot help thinking that the expression "public hatred", which the pursuer of this issue rejects, is the most important and significant part of an issue of the form proposed'.

1 To hold such an allegation defamatory a court would have to affirm that it is right and proper to be prejudiced towards homosexuals. See above at p 20.
2 Though it may be, eg a belief in racism.
3 (1894) 22 R 39.
4 (1894) 22 R 39 at 42.

Later he stated, 'I am certainly not prepared to send to a jury a claim of damages founded on the fact that the public conduct of the pursuer has been held up to ridicule'[1].

The matter was again discussed in the most recent case, *Steele v Scottish Daily Record*[2]. In that case the sheriff-substitute said that the words 'hatred and contempt' are

'strong words which, in my view, import more than simple disapprobation or dislike of an individual . . . The pursuer must show that the statement complained of reasonably read is likely to do more than make him the object of disapproval, adverse comment or criticism'[3].

Lord Wheatley in the Inner House considered that the sheriff-substitute applied too strict a meaning to the words 'hatred and contempt'. He said:

'I agree that the words complained of must produce something more than public disapproval, adverse comment or criticism. I do not consider, however, that people would have to "hate" the complainer in the full sense of that word. In my opinion, something in the order of condemn or despise is the proper test. This I would regard as something stronger than the test laid down in England by Lord Atkin in *Sim v Stretch*[4], namely, "tending to lower the plaintiff in the estimation of right-thinking members of society"'.

Lord Fraser is to similar effect, holding[5] that the expression 'public hatred and contempt' must mean something more than merely lowering the pursuer in the public esteem. Lord Milligan was of the view that the article complained about in this case could not reasonably be said to have possibly had that effect: at most it showed the pursuer to be a hard-hearted businessman[6].

As with defamation, it is for the court to determine whether the words complained of are capable of achieving the hurt recognised by the law. It is therefore a matter of relevancy, and the court can hold irrelevant a claim based on words that are incapable of holding the pursuer up to public hatred. So for example in *Burns v Diamond*[7] an accusation that a politician was irreligious was held not capable of holding him up to public hatred. And in *Steele* the words complained of showed, at most, the pursuer to be 'hard-hearted': this was not sufficient and the case failed on the point of relevancy.

Third party slander

Defamation, because it has a strong element of personal insult, requires that the pursuer's own character, honour or reputation be attacked. Communications which attack the reputation of someone may be actionable as defamation by

---

1 (1894) 22 R 38 at 42. The case did, of course, involve a public figure, with which a certain leeway in criticism and even ridicule is permitted by the law.
2 1970 SLT 53.
3 1970 SLT 53 at 58.
4 [1936] 2 All ER 1237.
5 1970 SLT 53 at 65.
6 1970 SLT 53 at 64.
7 (1896) 3 SLT 397 (p 256).

that person, but will not be actionable as defamation by anyone else. However, if the attack is not defamatory of the pursuer it may nevertheless still be actionable by the pursuer if it causes him or her loss. This has already been seen in relation to slander of property. The pursuer's character, honour and reputation is not attacked, but the slander causes him loss which is reparable. The same must be true when the attack is not on property but of another person. The pursuer can sue in defamation if he is personally attacked, or if, by innuendo, an attack on another can reasonably be read as an attack on him[1], and he can sue in verbal injury if he can show that by attacking another person the defender is intending to cause loss to the pursuer and actually did so[2]. So to say of a woman, with the intent of injuring her, that her father was a footman and her mother kept a brothel will be actionable at her instance, not on the ground of defamation, for she has not been defamed (unless it can be shown that right-thinking members of society are not willing to associate with the daughters of footmen and brothel-keepers) but on the basis of verbal injury[3]. (The mother could, of course, sue for defamation.)

This was early recognised by Lord Deas in *North of Scotland Banking Co v Duncan*[4], in which he said:

'It is quite easy to conceive that one party may be injured by a slander directed against another. For instance, if it were spread abroad that my factor or agent had defrauded me and absconded with all my funds, this might seriously injure my credit, but I could have no action of damages for the slander, without alleging that it had been uttered with intent to injure me. A slander against one member of a family may deeply injure the other members – for instance, to attack the character of one daughter may deeply injure another daughter, but unless the latter alleges that the slander was intended to injure her she cannot claim damages'[5].

Though this principle must be sound, there is no case in the Scottish law reports in which such an action has been successfully pursued, and indeed some dicta seem to preclude actionability on this basis. However, it is submitted that if all the requisites for actionability on the basis of verbal injury can be established by a pursuer then the law of Scotland will grant redress. The dicta suggesting otherwise are all probably explained by a misunderstanding of the distinction between defamation and verbal injury[6]. Lord Deas

1 See *Bradbury v Outram & Co* (1903) 11 SLT 71 (p 125) in which a newspaper reported an accident in which a certain person was killed. It referred to the deceased as 'unmarried' and his widow sued on the ground that this innuendoed that she had been 'living in fornication'. An issue was disallowed on the ground that the innuendo could not reasonably be drawn.

2 Cooper, *Defamation and Verbal Injury* (2nd edn, 1906) p 1. In Roman law it was recognised that the *pater familias* could sue for an *injuria* directed against his family since this would be regarded as an insult to his own honour: see D 47, 10, 1.

3 *Symmond v Williamson* (1752) Mor 3435.

4 (1857) 19 D 881. Though a dissenting judgment, the dissent was only in relation to who had been defamed: the majority held that the bank had been directly defamed through allegations concerning its officers, while Lord Deas thought that only the officers had been directly defamed and that the bank could therefore sue only on the basis of third party slander.

5 (1857) 19 D 881 at 887.

6 In *Shearlock v Beardsworth* (1816) 1 Mur 196 a colonel successfully sued for damages for defamation of his regiment. There was disapproval by both the Lord Ordinary and the Lord Justice-Clerk in *Broom v Ritchie & Co* (1904) 6 F 942, but both cases were distinctly cases of defamation and the point being made here, that the case could be relevantly pleaded as verbal injury, was not mentioned.

seems to suggest that the difference between the cases lies only in the fact that with third party slander intent to injure cannot be presumed, and he does not indicate whether the pursuer must also prove falsity or whether that too can be presumed. The reason why, in defamation, falsity is presumed is that the pursuer is to be presumed to come to court with clean hands and to be free of derogatory characteristics; but it is a different thing to suggest that persons other than the pursuer are also to be presumed free from these characteristics. It is submitted that there is no reason why falsity should be presumed in such cases and that, as in all other forms of verbal injury, actions for third party slander should be successful only if the pursuer can prove falsity, intent to injure, and actual injury.

In *Finburgh v Moss' Empires Ltd*[1] a man and his wife were asked to leave a theatre, the theatre manager (mistakenly) calling the wife a 'notorious prostitute'. The wife successfully raised an action for defamation, and the husband also sued, on the ground that he too had been slandered. His action was dismissed, on the ground (Lord Stormonth-Darling) that it was not slanderous to suggest that a man kept company with a prostitute[2], or (Lord Ardwall) that the injury to the husband was too remote and consequential[3]. The case was not dealt with as one of verbal injury of the husband by slander of the wife, but if it had been then the husband would have had a relevant claim had he been able to aver the three necessary requisites, that is falsity, intent to injure, and actual injury. If the husband had shown that the allegation was false (which had been established by the wife's successful action of defamation), that it had been made with the deliberate and malicious intent to injure him, and that it had in fact lowered his standing in the esteem of others, then it is difficult to see how relevancy could have been denied. This is not inconsistent with Lord Ardwall's reasoning, for intended consequences are never too remote[4].

In *Broom v Ritchie & Co*[5] the pursuer raised an action for solatium on the ground of her hurt feelings due to an article which appeared in the defender's newspaper suggesting that her deceased husband had committed suicide. The Lord Ordinary, Lord Kincairney, dismissed the action on the ground that it was incompetent to claim solatium alone in such circumstances, even although solatium can be claimed by the person defamed. The decision was upheld on appeal, Lord Justice-Clerk Macdonald following the reasoning of the Lord Ordinary. However, the Lord Justice-Clerk did point out that if the defamation of the third party could be innuendoed as a direct defamation of the pursuer, or if the defamation of the third party affected the pursuer's patrimonial interest, the action would be competent. The latter ground of action could only be on the basis of verbal injury, but if that is so it is difficult to see why only patrimonial loss and not also solatium could be claimed[6]. Lord

---

1 (1908) 16 SLT 61 (p 116).
2 (1908) 16 SLT 61 at 120.
3 (1908) 16 SLT 61 at 121.
4 See below at p 171.
5 (1904) 6 F 942.
6 See above at pp 41–43.

Trayner agreed with the Lord Justice-Clerk, holding that an action for damages for defamation is a purely personal action to which the maxim applies *actio personalis moritur cum persona*[1]. That is certainly so, but it does not address the verbal injury point. Lord Young's opinion is far the most interesting. He accepted that the present action failed[2], but disagreed strongly on the point of principle. He pointed out that certain relatives can sue for solatium for the death of a person through a defender's negligence, and that 'on the same ground' the widow and children of a dead man whose character has been defamed have a right – indeed a duty – to seek to clear his character and to seek solatium.

At the end of the day, all that *Broom v Ritchie & Co* decides is that a person cannot sue for defamation of a deceased relative[3]. It does not decide that a person cannot sue for verbal injury they themselves suffer through the defamation of another, and it is submitted that if the three requisites for verbal injury are properly averred then the claim is not made incompetent either because the statement complained of refers to someone other than the pursuer (alive or dead) or because the only injury complained of is emotional and solatium alone is claimed. If the defender uses false words about the pursuer's agent or banker or business partner intending thereby to cause patrimonial loss to the pursuer, then the loss he does cause is clearly reparable. Similarly, if the defender had deliberately set out to injure the feelings of the pursuer, by casting aspersions on the pursuer's deceased father or mother, or even more distant relatives, and the defender achieved his malicious intent, the pursuer ought in principle to be able to sue, so long as he avers falsity, malicious intent and actual injury. It is to be noted that Lord Deas, quoted at the beginning of this section[4], did not limit his remarks to the causing of patrimonial loss and expressly envisaged the case of one family member being upset as a result of aspersions about another member. Such upset would, of course, be relevant only for solatium. An analogy might be drawn with cases in which relatives have been upset by the unauthorised carrying out of post-mortems on deceased relatives' bodies: in such cases a claim for solatium alone has been regarded as competent[5]. In verbal injury cases it will of course be difficult to establish that insult or upset has been caused deliberately, but the right to attempt such proof should not be denied, and the heavy onus on the pursuer will be sufficient disincentive to the raising of frivolous claims based on hurts and upsets too slight to be justiciable.

---

1 This decision appears not to take account of Bankton I, 10, 29: 'It is always the interest and concern of the heir that the character of the deceased be vindicated'. This could not be achieved if the restoration of reputation were possible only when its destruction had caused patrimonial loss.

2 On the ground, apparently, that it was not defamatory to suggest that someone had committed suicide.

3 See Woolman, 'Defaming the Dead' 1981 SLT (News) 29.

4 Above at p 58.

5 See *Pollok v Workman* (1900) 2 F 354; *Conway v Dalziel* (1901) 3 F 918; *Hughes v Robertson* 1913 SC 394.

Other cases of verbal injury

There are a few cases in the Scottish law reports which do not fall into any of the above factual classifications. This, of course, will not deny actionability, because the basis of liability is not the fitting of the case into one of the recognised categories but the establishment of the three requisites specified (repeatedly) above: falsity, intent to injure, and actual injury.

In *Moffat v London Express Newspapers*[1] officials of a trade union sued for both defamation and verbal injury when a newspaper published an article headed 'What Makes a Man Spit at his Country?' and which reported that the officials had 'ostentatiously remained seated' during the playing of the British National Anthem. In relation to the issue of defamation Lord Strachan allowed the defence of fair comment to go to the jury; and he held the issue of verbal injury irrelevant, citing the three requisites, but failing to indicate upon which of the three the case foundered. However it may be conjectured that if fair comment was a successful plea in defence to the action for defamation then intent to injure could not have been found.

In *Trapp v Mackie*[2] the pursuer, a former rector of a school, had been dismissed by his employers, and during a statutory inquiry into the dismissal the chairman of the local authority education committee made certain statements which were not defamatory but which, the pursuer alleged, were false and made with a design to injure him. Though the main importance of the case lies in the discussion of the application of absolute privilege to statutory inquiries[3], the case is an example of verbal injury based on malicious falsehood. Lord Ross in the Outer House said:

'Counsel pointed out that there was no precedent for an action based on malicious falsehood, but accepted that in principle such an action might be put forward being in essence an instance of verbal injury. From Walker on *Delict* and *Steele v Scottish Daily Record Ltd*, which was a case of verbal injury, it appears that there are three requisites of actionability: (1) the statement must be proved to be false; (2) there must have been *animus injuriandi;* and (3) actual damage must have resulted'[4].

This is an acceptance that the same three requisites apply to all forms of verbal injury or, as it might be called, malicious falsehood. The matter was not commented upon in the Inner House, but in the House of Lords Lord Diplock may be found laying down as a matter of public policy: 'that the law should provide a remedy to the citizen whose good name and reputation is traduced by malicious falsehoods uttered by another'[5]. Lord Fraser of Tullybelton explained that it was unnecessary to form a view on the precise nature of the present action, since the judges were all agreed that the case was one to which absolute privilege attaches[6]. Nevertheless, it is clear from this case that

---

1 1950 SLT (Notes) 46.
2 1977 SLT 194, 1979 SLT 126.
3 See below at pp 99–100 for fuller discussion of the case on this point.
4 1977 SLT 194 at 197.
5 1979 SLT 126 at 129.
6 1979 SLT 126 at 132.

the notion of malicious falsehood can be accepted by Scots law as an example of verbal injury and will apply in any circumstance in which the requisites can be averred and proved by the pursuer and which does not fall within any of the above factual categories.

CHAPTER FIVE

Parties to the action

Introduction

Any person, natural or legal, who is capable of suffering the loss complained of has title to sue for defamation or verbal injury, and will have interest to do so if the loss is actually suffered. The qualification for title in all cases is the capacity to suffer hurts that are legally recognised and protected. However, the law does not accept that all persons can suffer all the types of losses for which compensation may, in other circumstances, be due. For example, solatium for hurt feelings may not be claimed by a corporate body, for such an entity has no feelings that the law recognises as capable of being hurt. Conversely, any person, whether natural or otherwise, who is capable of being sued for an intentional delict can be found liable for defamation or verbal injury, and this is not altered by the fact that for non-natural persons, the intention necessary to found liability is as artificial as their very existence[1]. No distinction is to be drawn in this context between defamation and verbal injury[2], but the rules concerning title to sue and to be sued therefor are rather different for *injuria verbis* than for negligence and this chapter will concern only the former. For negligence, the specialist texts on that subject should be consulted.

Individuals as pursuers

The typical pursuer in an action for defamation or verbal injury is an individual person, complaining of some false and harmful statement that has been made about him or her. To be actionable the statement must be shown to refer to the pursuer, whether directly, for example by name, or indirectly, for example by reference to an office which he or she holds[3] or by description which only he or she fits. It is a matter for the jury or fact-finder to determine whether the statement actually does refer to the individual pursuer[4] and the action will be dismissed as irrelevant if it is not established that the pursuer is

---

1 See further, below at p 79.
2 *Highland Dancing Board v Alloa Printing Co Ltd* 1971 SLT (Sh Ct) 50 at 52 per Sheriff AB Wilkinson.
3 *Beattie v Mather* (1860) 22 D 952.
4 *Hulton & Co v Jones* [1910] AC 20; *Browne v DC Thomson & Co* 1912 SC 359.

referred to in the statement complained of[1]. Sometimes the statement or communication complained of refers to more than one individual, in which case each person defamed can raise an action in his or her own name without reference to the others, so long as the pursuer can prove that he or she as an individual was included in the statement[2]. It is different if the defamation is of a class of person: in that situation no individual member of the class may sue[3], unless the context is such that the statement could reasonably be taken to refer to an individual[4]. So for example to say 'the Campbells are all liars and thieves' is not defamatory of each individual person with that surname[5], but it might be actionable by one Campbell if an innuendo towards him as an individual can be made out, for example if the remark had been made in the context of a criticism directed towards that person. Similarly, a reference to a small determinate body may well be defamatory of each member of the body[6], though the larger the body the less likely it is that the statement will be held to refer to particular individuals[7].

Corporate bodies as pursuers

One of the attributes of legal personality, such as that which attaches to corporate bodies, is the capacity to sue and to be sued in the body's own name. The law of Scotland has for long recognised that actions for damages for defamation can be raised by legal as well as by natural persons[8], though confusion frequently arises since the same statement can often refer both to the corporate body itself and to individual members of the body. If the defamation is truly of the individual members then the corporation cannot sue[9] for no-one can sue for the defamation of another person[10]. If both a corporation and its members are defamed, each has a right of action independent of the others[11]: if the corporate body has been defamed and injured thereby, the right of

---

1 *Caldwell v Munro* (1872) 10 M 717; *McFadyen v Spencer & Co* (1892) 19 R 350.
2 *Browne v DC Thomson & Co* 1912 SC 359; *Campbell v Wilson* 1934 SLT 249.
3 *Wardlaw v Drysdale* (1898) 25 R 879; *Braddock v Bevins* [1948] 1 KB 580.
4 *Campbell v Ritchie & Co* 1907 SC 1097; *Campbell v Wilson* 1934 SLT 249; *Campbell v Toronto Star Newspapers Ltd* (1990) 73 DLR 4th 190.
5 Cf *Wardlaw v Drysdale*, above, which involved a violent attack on the alcoholic liquor trade.
6 *McFadyen v Spencer & Co* (1892) 19 R 350; *Macphail v Macleod* (1895) 3 SLT 137 (p 91); *Browne v DC Thomson & Co* 1912 SC 359.
7 Walker, *Delict* (2nd edn, 1981) p 747.
8 *Society of Solicitors v Robertson* (1781) Mor 13935; *Incorporation of Fleshers of Dumfries v Rankine* 10 Dec 1816, FC; *North of Scotland Banking Co v Duncan* (1857) 19 D 881; *Argyllshire Weavers Ltd v Macauley (Tweeds) Ltd* 1965 SLT 21; *Kwik-Fit-Euro Ltd v Scottish Daily Record and Sunday Mail Ltd* 1987 SLT 226.
9 *Incorporation of Fleshers of Dumfries v Rankine* 10 Dec 1816, FC. See *North of Scotland Banking Co v Duncan* (1857) 19 D 881, in which Lord Deas dissented from his brethren on the ground that the statements complained of in that case were properly of and concerning individual members of the bank's board and not the bank itself.
10 Though as is argued above (at pp 57–60) the defamation of one person may amount to verbal injury of another if done with intent to injure that other.
11 *Hustler v Allan & Watson* (1841) 3 D 366.

action is not destroyed by the fact that certain individual board members of the corporate body have also been defamed and have also raised actions for the individual injury they suffered[1].

It has been held in England that corporate bodies can be defamed only by statements accusing them of actions which they are capable of performing[2]. In a limited sense this is true: to accuse a corporation of, say, adultery or incest cannot be defamatory. However, this is not simply because the pursuer is incapable of the act it is accused of. It would be as defamatory of an impotent man as of a potent man wrongly to accuse him of rape. Rather the nature of the statement is such that it cannot be taken seriously[3]. If this is so then allegations of legally impossible acts, which might be taken seriously by the general public, could well be held to be defamatory. For example in *Dean v John Menzies Holdings Ltd*[4] it was held that a company could not be guilty of the common law crime of shameless indecency, because of the particularly human characteristic of 'shame'[5]. But to accuse a trading company of shameful acts might well be defamatory if those who hear the accusations take them seriously and are less willing to associate with the company as a consequence, notwithstanding that, legally, the act is impossible. Accusations of impossibility can easily innuendo the possible.

Typical defamatory statements against a trading company would be allegations of fraud or corruption, or comments on the quality of goods or services it supplies[6], but actionable statements are not limited to this type of allegation and could include aspersions upon the company's policies, employment practices[7], business methods[8], or indeed anything else that would make reasonable persons less willing to associate or deal with it. To accuse a respectable bookshop or magazine store of selling pornographic or semi-pornographic material may be defamatory if such an allegation would make the reasonable person less likely to patronise the store, and if such an allegation were not defamatory in that sense it could nevertheless amount to a verbal injury if made with the intent, and having the effect, of reducing or destroying the store's business[9]. In *South Hetton Coal Co v Northeastern News*[10] an allegation that the housing provided to employees by a coal mining company was insanitary and in a poor condition was held by the Court of Appeal to be defamatory and actionable by the company. And in *Waverley Housing Management Ltd v BBC*[11] an allegation

1 *North of Scotland Banking Co v Duncan* (1857) 19 D 881 at 885 per Lord Ardmillan (Ordinary).
2 *Manchester Corporation v Williams* [1891] 1 QB 94; *D & L Caterers Ltd and Jackson v D'Ajou* [1945] KB 364 at 366 per Goddard LJ.
3 *D & L Caterers Ltd and Jackson v D'Ajou* [1945] KB 364 at 366 per Goddard LJ.
4 1981 JC 23.
5 See Gordon, *Criminal Law*, 2nd Supp (1992) pp 31 and 32.
6 Comments on the quality of the business products may also amount to a verbal injury, for which there are different requirements for actionability: see pp 45–48.
7 *Derbyshire County Council v Times Newspapers* [1993] 1 All ER 1011 at 1017 per Lord Keith.
8 *Gulf Oil (GB) Ltd v Page* [1987] 3 All ER 14.
9 See pp 49–50.
10 [1894] 1 QB 133.
11 1993 GWD 17–1117.

that a housing company won contracts through secretive and collusive deals with civil servants was held by the Lord Ordinary to be actionable[1].

Damages claimable by corporations

Though a corporate body can sue for defamation, it has long been accepted by the law that it cannot claim solatium for hurt feelings, for the simple reason that a corporate body has no feelings to hurt[2]. Only patrimonial loss can be claimed and an action in which a corporate pursuer does not specify patrimonial loss in its statement of claim will be dismissed as irrelevant. However, while specific losses must, in general, be averred, the courts will accept averments of patrimonial losses of a more speculative nature than it normally would, such as loss of goodwill which, though difficult to quantify, is a valuable asset. As Lord Reid put it, 'A company cannot be injured in its feelings, it can only be injured in its pocket. Its reputation can be injured by a libel but that injury must sound in money. The injury need not necessarily be confined to loss of income. Its goodwill may be injured'[3]. This was reiterated by Lord Cullen in *Waverley Housing Management Ltd v BBC*[4], when he said:

'I am satisfied that as a matter of principle it is open to the second pursuers to claim general damages, as opposed to specific damages based on the loss of particular contracts or the diminution of turnover. However, it has to be recognised that the fundamental basis of any award of damages to a company pursuer is patrimonial loss'.

It can be argued[5] that corporations are sufficiently protected by their right to sue for malicious falsehood or verbal injury (slander of business), which would require proof of intent to injure and that they ought not to be able, in addition, to sue for defamation. It is not, however, the current law that corporate pursuers are barred from raising actions for defamation and are limited to raising actions for verbal injury, though there is no doubt that it should be, for the element of insult, inherent in defamation but not verbal injury, is entirely missing.

Partnerships and voluntary associations as pursuers

Partnerships in Scotland are able to raise actions in their own names. This is a consequence of section 4(2) of the Partnership Act 1890, which provides that,

---

1 There may be problems in principle in permitting corporations a like right to sue for defamation as private individuals, for freedom to criticise potentially hugely important organisations might thereby be compromised: for a discussion, see Patfield, 'Defamation, Freedom of Speech, and Corporations' 1993 JR 294.
2 *North of Scotland Banking Co v Duncan* (1857) 19 D 881 at 885 per Lord Ardmillan (Ordinary); *Derbyshire County Council v Times Newspapers* [1993] 1 All ER 1011 at 1017 per Lord Keith.
3 *Lewis v Daily Telegraph Ltd* [1964] AC 234 at 262.
4 1993 GWD 17–1117.
5 Patfield, 'Defamation, Freedom of Speech, and Corporations', above.

'In Scotland a firm is a legal person distinct from the partners of whom it is composed'. One of the necessary attributes of legal personality is the ability to sue, and this has been recognised to be so in actions for defamation[1]. Partnerships are voluntary associations in which business is carried on with a view to making a profit[2], though title to sue for defamation in Scotland flows not from the purposes of the particular association but the economic value of its reputation. It follows that other voluntary associations with economically valuable reputations are also entitled to defend these reputations by raising actions for defamation. A plea of no title to sue was repelled in *Scottish Co-operative Society v Bishop*[3]. In *Highland Dancing Board v Alloa Printing Co Ltd*[4] a Highland dance association sued a newspaper which had published an article suggesting that the association had little knowledge of Highland dancing and were imposters and that official judges appointed by the association for competitions would adjudicate unfairly. The sheriff-substitute[5] could see no good ground for distinguishing between partnerships and voluntary associations formed for non-trading purposes and he held that a voluntary association such as the pursuer in the present case had title to sue for defamation. However, he went on to point out that, while in the normal action for defamation the pursuer is prima facie entitled to solatium, because it is presumed that damage has been done at least to the pursuer's feelings, that reasoning did not apply in cases in which the pursuer has no feelings to hurt. It followed in the present case that the pursuer had to set out in its pleadings the loss that it alleged had been caused, and its failure to do so rendered its claim in this case irrelevant as lacking in specification.

As with claims by corporate bodies[6], specific elements of patrimonial loss will make up the bulk of any claim by a voluntary association though general damages for harm to reputation as an economic asset, which is necessarily more speculative, might also, in appropriate cases, be awarded.

Trade unions as pursuers

Trade unions are in a peculiar position in relation to capacity to sue for defamation. Before 1974 trade unions were regarded as having a 'quasi-corporate' status, which was sufficient to allow them to sue and to be sued in their own name[7], and this permitted them even to sue for defamation if the statements

---

1 *McVean & Co v Blair* (1801) Hume 609 (Cooper, *Defamation and Verbal Injury* (2nd edn, 1906) p 15); *Le Fanu v Malcomson* (1848) 1 HL Cas 637. In *Adams & Sons v Scottish Agricultural Publishing Co* 1926 SLT 255 a sole partner brought an action in the partnership name on the basis that the firm had been defamed.
2 Partnership Act 1890, s 1(1). And see Brough, *Miller on Partnership* (2nd edn, 1994) pp 1–6.
3 (1897) 5 SLT 121 (p 88).
4 1971 SLT (Sh Ct) 50.
5 AB Wilkinson.
6 Above, at p 66.
7 *Taff Vale Railway Co v Amalgamated Society of Railway Servants* [1901] AC 426.

touched their own reputation rather than that of their members[1]. However the Trade Union and Labour Relations Act 1974 provided that 'a trade union . . . shall not be, or be treated as if it were, a body corporate'[2], though the section went on to provide that trade unions shall be capable of suing and being sued in their own names[3]. The precise status this created is open to much doubt, though the effect was to put trade unions in a position that was not dissimilar to Scottish partnerships.

Actions for defamation may well be different from all other actions, due to the peculiar character of the interest that is being protected. In *EETPU v Times Newspapers Ltd*[4] the English court held that notwithstanding a union's ability to sue and be sued in its own name, a union could not sue for defamation, because defamation is an attack on personality and the 1974 Act specifically provided that a trade union shall not be a body corporate (ie shall have no legal personality capable of being attacked). The current statute is even blunter. Section 10(1) of the Trade Union and Labour Relations (Consolidation) Act 1992 provides that 'a trade union is not a body corporate'. The decision in *EETPU* suggests that capacity to be defamed depends not on capacity to sue but on possession of a personality capable of being defamed. Yet defamation in Scotland today involves more than an attack on personality, and includes (as English law does) attacks on reputation as an economic asset. The Scottish cases (none of which involves a trade union) suggest that voluntary associations that lack legal personality can sue for defamation if they have a reputation attacks upon which can cause patrimonial loss[5], and a trade union clearly has such a reputation. For example, an unjustified and slanderous statement about a union may cause members to leave or inhibit potential new members from joining, causing the union to lose subscription fees. If it is reputation as an economic asset rather than legal personality that gives title to sue for defamation in Scotland, then *EETPU*, which even in its own (English) terms is anomalous, does not represent the law of Scotland. However, the fact that the status of trade unions is governed by a UK statute suggests that, as a matter of statutory interpretation, the same result will probably be reached in both jurisdictions. It may be that trade unions are unique institutions and that analogies with other forms of organisation cannot validly be drawn. On the other hand, it may be that *EETPU*, a first instance decision, is quite simply wrong. It is interesting to note that, on the question of whether a local authority could sue for defamation, the House of Lords[6] expressly adopted policy reasoning to provide the answer. Trade unions ought to be held unable to sue for defamation only if there are policy reasons to justify that approach.

---

1 *Carter & Pratt v Glasgow Typographical Society* (1894) 10 Sh Ct Rep 248; *National Union of Bank Employees v Murray* 1949 SLT (Notes) 25.
2 Section 2(1).
3 Section 2(1)(c).
4 [1980] QB 585.
5 See above, at pp 66–67.
6 *Derbyshire County Council v Times Newspapers* [1993] 1 All ER 1011. See below at pp 69–72.

Government as pursuer

There is little authority in Scots law on the question of whether a government body, such as a local authority or a department of state, can sue for defamation, though the matter has been authoritatively determined by the House of Lords in England[1]. In *Banchory Local Authority v Duncan*[2] the sheriff-substitute had dismissed an action as incompetent when a local authority sued on the basis of the 'indignity of the burgh'. The sheriff recalled the interlocutor and allowed a proof[3]. The sheriff-substitute had envisaged that the case might have been competent had the local authority been attempting to recover its financial loss, but he assumed that a local authority had no feelings to hurt. Though English law does not give damages for hurt feelings, it is likely that Scots law today will take its rule from the English House of Lords case shortly to be discussed.

There had been a conflict of authority in England on the question of whether local councils could sue for defamation. In *Manchester Corporation v Williams*[4] it was held that a town corporation could sue for a libel affecting property (that is for slander of property or, in Scottish terms, verbal injury[5]) but not for a wrong merely affecting personal reputation (that is, for defamation)[6]. On the other hand, in *Bognor Regis UDC v Campion*[7] it was held that, just as a trading company has a trading reputation which it is entitled to protect by bringing an action for defamation, so a local government corporation has a 'governing reputation' which it is equally entitled to protect in the same way. This conflict was resolved by the House of Lords in *Derbyshire County Council v Times Newspapers*[8], in which *Bognor Regis* was overruled. In this case, articles in a Sunday newspaper had suggested that a county council's superannuation fund had been subject to 'improper behaviour and legally doubtful transactions'. The judge at first instance, founding on *Bognor Regis*, held that a municipal corporation could sue for defamation in order to protect its governing or administrative reputation. The Court of Appeal overruled this[9], taking account, significantly, of Article 10 of the European Convention on Human Rights, which protects freedom of expression. The House of Lords affirmed the decision of the Court of Appeal that local authorities cannot sue for defamation, though it came to its decision not on the basis of

---

1 *Derbyshire County Council v Times Newspapers* [1993] 1 All ER 1011.
2 (1892) 8 Sh Ct Rep 142.
3 The defender marked an appeal to the Court of Session, but the case was settled before the appeal was heard.
4 [1891] 1 QB 94.
5 See pp 45–48.
6 This has for long been the case in the USA, where the constitutionally protected right to freedom of speech is considered to outweigh the right of governmental bodies to sue for defamation: see *City of Chicago v Tribune Co* (1923) 139 NE 86; *New York Times v Sullivan* (1964) 376 US 254. In the latter case a public official was held entitled to sue only on the basis of alleging and proving malice.
7 [1972] 2 All ER 61.
8 [1993] 1 All ER 1011.
9 [1992] 1 QB 770.

the ECHR but on the state of the English common law as it declared it. Lord Keith gave the leading judgment, with which the other four members of the Judicial Committee concurred.

Lord Keith started by pointing out that there are certain rights which are available to private citizens which are withheld from the institutions of government, unless these institutions can show that it is in the public interest that these rights should be available. The right to raise actions for breach of confidence is one such right[1]; the right to sue for defamation is another. Lord Keith went on to hold that it was contrary to the public interest to allow the organs of government, whether central or local, the right to sue for libel, since this would place an undesirable fetter on freedom of speech[2]. He held that there are features of a local authority which distinguish it from other types of corporation, whether trading or non-trading:

'The most important of these features is that it is a governmental body. Further, it is a democratically elected body, the electoral process nowadays being conducted almost exclusively on party political lines. It is of the highest public importance that a democratically elected governmental body, or indeed any governmental body, should be open to uninhibited public criticism. The threat of a civil action for defamation must inevitably have an inhibiting effect on freedom of speech'[3].

For this reason of policy, local authorities are, he concluded, entirely barred from seeking damages for defamation. There is little doubt that this case reflects the law of Scotland, for which the policy considerations are equally persuasive.

Lord Keith did not deny the right of individuals who have been defamed by attacks on a council (such as council members) to seek redress themselves, and he pointed out that it is open to the controlling body to defend itself by public utterances and in debate in the council chamber[4]. Interestingly, he also held that the council would be able to sue for malicious falsehood[5], which may well have been all that *Manchester Corporation* decided in any case. It is, of course, perfectly proper that local authorities be able to sue for slander of property[6], because they must protect the value of their assets for the good of the electors on whose behalf they hold these assets. But it is to be remembered that to be successful in an action for malicious falsehood or verbal injury the pursuer would have to plead and prove intent to injure or malice[7], making the action more difficult to sustain than defamation. Alternatively, following *Spring v Guardian Assurance plc*[8], a local authority could sue in negligence for its economic loss caused by defamatory statements. That action would be

---

1 And in *Attorney General v Guardian Newspapers (No 2)* [1990] 1 AC 109 it was held that the government had demonstrated its public interest.
2 [1993] 1 All ER 1011 at 1019.
3 [1993] 1 All ER 1011 at 1017. The logic of this approach is questioned by Loveland in 'Defamation of "Government": Taking Lessons from America' (1994) 14 LS 206.
4 [1993] 1 All ER 1011 at 1020.
5 [1993] 1 All ER 1011 at 1021.
6 On which, see above at pp 45–48.
7 Above at p 47.
8 [1994] 3 All ER 129.

based not on loss of reputation but a loss of economic standing and the normal requisites for an action for negligently caused economic loss would have to be established by the pursuers.

Other governmental institutions

It is to be noted that the decision in *Derbyshire County Council* was not limited to local authorities as plaintiffs, and that Lord Keith put central government departments, and central government itself, in exactly the same position as municipal corporations[1]. However, beyond these categories, it is not clear how 'organs of government' is to be defined for this purpose. The question of the Sovereign's right to sue is likely to remain entirely hypothetical, but even in her private capacity (if she has one) similar considerations to those referred to by Lord Keith apply. The constabulary and the armed forces are almost certainly to be considered 'organs of government', though neither in themselves has legal personality. On the other hand, the management of nationalised industries are likely to be considered to be in the same position as the management of ordinary corporate pursuers. The position of quasi-autonomous non-governmental organisations such as health boards, NHS trusts, school boards, water boards, the Scottish Development Agency, and the Church of Scotland is open to more doubt. The test is not whether they have an economic reputation to protect, for a local authority undoubtedly has that. The test postulated by the House of Lords in *Derbyshire County Council* was one of public policy, being the necessary democratic freedom of being able to criticise government. The question seems to be this: are the interests of democracy compromised by allowing the body to sue in defamation? Democracy is compromised when the ability to sue inhibits the free speech to which the body ought to be answerable. The boards of management of NHS trusts are not elected and their accountability lies not to the democratic process but to the Scottish Office. It is too simplistic to say that directly elected bodies cannot sue while those answerable to government can: indeed, Lord Keith said, 'It is of the highest public importance that a democratically elected governmental body, *or indeed any governmental body*, should be open to uninhibited public criticism'[2]. Governing bodies appointed by and answerable only to government departments are already protected from the rigours of debate and electoral challenge and it may be that democracy would be further compromised by allowing them to inhibit press criticism by threatening actions for defamation in which they can rely on an irrebuttable presumption of malice. For this reason it is suggested that, following the philosophy evident in *Derbyshire County Council*, quasi-autonomous non-governmental organisations answerable only to government itself, such as the boards of management of NHS trusts and the state church, should be able to sue only in

1 [1993] 1 All ER 1011 at 1019.
2 [1993] 1 All ER 1011 at 1017, emphasis added.

circumstances in which government itself can sue, that is to say, only for verbal injury[1].

Government members and officials

Another important issue concerning the extent of the decision in *Derbyshire County Council* is whether its *ratio* can be applied to individual members of government and government officials as well as the organs of government themselves. We have already seen that the law permits a certain leeway in the criticism of public figures, which it would not allow with private individuals[2], but it could be argued that the law should go further and, in the interests of freedom of expression, disallow actions for defamation for criticism of government members' or officials' performance of their public roles. Lord Keith clearly does not go this far, and it may be considered that individual members of government, being answerable to the electoral process, ought to be able to protect their own governmental reputations. Yet there is something deeply unattractive in allowing politicians to take the benefit of a presumption that those who criticise them are acting maliciously, and the approach of the American courts[3] whereby public officials can sue only when they can aver and prove malice (effectively conferring qualified privilege on criticism of public officials) has much, it is submitted, to commend it. It may be that this, in fact, is the position in this country already[4]. The same might be said in relation to political parties[5].

Executors as pursuers

Communications made before death

Until 1993 the law of Scotland treated defamation and verbal injury as it treated the other delicts on the question of the title of executors to pursue claims[6]. In all actions for damages a distinction was made between those raised by the injured person during his life and those raised by his executor after his death. If an action had been raised by an injured person during his life, but he then died, the executor could continue the action in place of the deceased, and would be able to recover damages both for patrimonial loss and

---

1 On the blurring of the distinction between governmental and corporate activities, see Patfield, 'Defamation, Freedom of Speech, and Corporations' 1993 JR 294.
2 See above, at pp 26–27.
3 See in particular the seminal case of *New York Times v Sullivan* (1964) 376 US 254.
4 See above at p 27.
5 See Loveland, 'Defamation of "Government": Taking Lessons from America' (1994) 14 LS 206 at 213–214.
6 Unlike English law, where the right of action in defamation dies with the plaintiff (and indeed with the defendant): Law Reform (Miscellaneous Provisions) Act 1934, s 1(1).

for solatium (referrable to the period before death)[1]. If, on the other hand, no action had been raised before the deceased's death upon an injury suffered during his life the executor could raise an action but could recover only such pecuniary loss as had been caused to the estate before the death[2]; he could not recover solatium. These rules had been subject to some criticism and the law was changed in 1993. Section 2(1) of the Damages (Scotland) Act 1976[3] now provides as a general rule that there shall be transmitted to executors of deceased persons the like right to damages in respect of personal injuries, including solatium, as was vested in the deceased immediately before his death. In other words, an executor who raises an action afresh after a deceased's death can now claim solatium as well as patrimonial loss. However, as an exception to this new statutory rule, the common law position is preserved in relation to actions for defamation and for verbal injury. It is provided:

'In so far as a right to damages vested in the deceased comprised a right to damages (other than for patrimonial loss) in respect of injury resulting from defamation or any other verbal injury or other injury to reputation sustained by the deceased, that right shall be transmitted to the deceased's executor only if an action to enforce that right had been brought by the deceased before his death and had not been concluded by then'[4].

Communications after death

The above rule applies when the defamatory or injurious communication has been made during the life of the person defamed or injured. There is no authority allowing executors or successors to sue upon a communication made after the death of the subject of the communication, and indeed some authority against the proposition[5]. These authorities might however be to no more effect than that a successor cannot sue in a personal capacity for defamation directed against someone else. Successors or other relatives might be able to sue for verbal injury if they can prove the communication was designed to injure them, and did so[6]. Indeed there is, it is submitted, nothing in principle to prevent an executor seeking to recover patrimonial loss to an estate under his charge caused by communications made after the death of the deceased: it is likely, however, that the correct basis of the claim would be one for verbal injury rather than defamation, since the insult element is entirely

1 *Haggart's Trustees v Hope* (1824) 2 Shaw App 125; *Tullis v Crichton* (1850) 12 D 867; *Neilson v Rodger* (1853) 16 D 325.
2 *Auld v Shairp* (1875) 2 R 191 (as explained in *Bern's Ex v Montrose Asylum* (1893) 20 R 859); *Smith v Stewart & Co* 1961 SC 91.
3 As substituted by s 3 of the Damages (Scotland) Act 1993.
4 Damages (Scotland) Act 1976, s 2(4). An action is not concluded while any appeal is competent or before any appeal taken has been disposed of: s 2A(2), as inserted by the Damages (Scotland) Act 1993.
5 *Broom v Ritchie & Co* (1904) 6 F 942; *Agnew v Laughlan* 1948 SLT 512. See *Walker v Robertson* (1821) 2 Mur 508 and 516 (disapproved in *Broom v Ritchie & Co*). See also Woolman, 'Defaming the Dead' 1981 SLT (News) 29.
6 This might – though one cannot really tell from the report – underlie *Walker v Robertson*, above.

missing and the analogy would be with slander of property (the estate) rather than with defamation itself. This would not, of course, be a representative action for any wrong done to the deceased, but would rather be an action on a wrong done directly to the successors[1].

Individuals as defenders

An individual is liable for his or her own delicts, committed either personally or through the medium of another. To instruct one's employee to defame another is to commit the wrong oneself[2] (though the employee will be personally liable too[3]). If more than one person joins in the defamation each is personally liable for the whole loss to the pursuer, for, notwithstanding that the defamation is committed by more than one person, liability is individual and not joint and several[4]. (It might be different if there is a conspiracy or common purpose between several defenders[5].) So one person may make a defamatory allegation while another person repeats it, or a statement may be made on behalf of two individuals: in either case both will be personally liable for the whole loss and the pursuer can choose whom to sue. Indeed, the action may be raised against both[6], subject to what was said above. That a defence is available to one does not in itself provide a defence to the other, and if the case is one of privilege malice must be found against both if both are to be held liable[7].

Corporate bodies as defenders

Legal persons such as corporate bodies can only act through agents and employees, and their liability in delict is, basically, vicarious liability[8]. A corporate body will therefore be liable for defamation or verbal injury committed by employees while acting within the scope of their employment[9], and for defamation or verbal injury committed by agents acting within their authority[10], just as they are liable thus in negligence. The employer will not be responsible for a defamatory or otherwise injurious statement of an employee

---

1 See *Smith v Stewart & Co* 1961 SC 91.
2 *Rogers v Dick* (1863) 1 M 411.
3 (1863) 1 M 411 at 415 per Lord Deas.
4 *Turnbull v Frame* 1966 SLT 24 per Lord Fraser.
5 See Thomson, *Delictual Liability* (1994) pp 41–46.
6 *Keay v Wilsons* (1843) 5 D 407.
7 *Keay v Wilsons*, above, in which malice could be proved in relation to one defender but not the other.
8 *Walker* p 78.
9 *Citizens' Life Assurance Co Ltd v Brown* [1904] AC 423; *Ellis v National Free Labour Association* (1905) 7 F 629; *Finburgh v Moss' Empires Ltd* 1908 SC 928; *Jardine v North British Railway Co* 1923 SLT 55.
10 *Ramsay v Nairne* (1833) 11 S 1033; *Goodall v Forbes* 1909 SC 1300.

or agent if it is no part of the latter's job to make statements[1], or if in doing so he goes beyond his authority[2] or beyond the scope of his employment[3]. In *Eprile v Caledonian Railway Co*[4] the view was expressed by Lord Kincairney that written words are more likely to be within the scope of a person's employment than spoken words, but this lays down neither rule nor presumption. Many types of employees, such as actors, ministers, solicitors, lecturers, teachers, and television and radio presenters, are employed to speak and to comment: slander within the course of their work and scope of their employment will render their employer vicariously liable. The employer's liability does not, of course, detract from the employee's or agent's personal liability.

It is no longer the law – if it ever was – that a non-natural person cannot be guilty of malice, and therefore cannot be guilty of defamation or at least defamation in cases of qualified privilege where the pursuer must show malice[5], for to accept that would be to hold that qualified privilege turns into absolute privilege whenever a non-natural person is the defender[6]. The existence of malice is proved by facts that can relate to a company as well as to an individual, and 'it is a mere metaphysical subtlety to say that a company cannot be guilty of malice where the very nature of the proceeding in which the plea is taken necessarily implies that the *persona* has a power of action and a power of judgment'[7]. It is worth noting that the criminal law has long accepted that companies can have some degree of criminal intent[8].

Partnerships as defenders

Partnerships may be liable either vicariously for the wrongs of their employees, or under the terms of the Partnership Act 1890 for the wrongs of the partners. Vicarious liability for employees follows the normal rules and there is no specialty arising from the fact that the employer is a firm. Section 10 of the Partnership Act 1890 provides as follows:

'Where, by any wrongful act or omission of any partner acting in the ordinary course of the business of the firm, or with the authority of his copartners, loss or injury is caused to any person not being a partner in the firm, or any penalty is incurred, the firm is liable therefor to the same extent as the partner so acting or omitting to act'.

---

1 *Eprile v Caledonian Railway Co* (1898) 6 SLT 87 (p 65); *Riddell v Glasgow Corporation* 1911 SC(HL) 35; *Adamson v Martin* 1916 SC 319; *Mandelston v North British Railway Co* 1917 SC 442.
2 *Wilson v Purvis* (1890) 18 R 72.
3 *Beaton v Corporation of Glasgow* 1908 SC 1010; *Craig v Inveresk Paper Merchant Ltd* 1970 SLT (Notes) 50.
4 (1898) 6 SLT 87 (p 65).
5 *Gordon v British and Foreign Metaline Co* (1886) 14 R 75; *Citizens' Life Assurance Co Ltd v Brown* [1904] AC 423.
6 *Gordon v British and Foreign Metaline Co* (1886) 14 R 75 at 86–87 per Lord Rutherfurd Clark.
7 (1886) 14 R 75 at 84 per Lord Justice-Clerk Moncreiff.
8 *DPP v Kent & Sussex Contractors* [1944] KB 146; *Dean v John Menzies Holdings Ltd* 1981 JC 23.

The liability imposed by this provision arises either if the partner is acting in the ordinary course of the business of the firm or if the partner acts with the authority of his co-partners[1]. There are numerous situations in which a partner can be acting in the ordinary course of the business of the firm and at the same time uttering defamatory remarks, such as during the course of business negotiations, or in dealing with an employee of the firm, or in publishing advertisements, or in correspondence with clients[2]. In addition, if the making of a statement is not within the normal course of the partnership business but it has been authorised by the co-partners, then the firm itself will be liable for defamation. This is so even although the partner making the statement is not expressly authorised to defame: the general position in partnership law is that firms are liable for authorised acts carried out wrongfully as well as authorised wrongful acts[3]. It has been held in England that in a case of privilege if only one of a number of the partners can be found guilty of malice it is only that one who can be held liable[4]. It is doubtful whether this would be followed in Scotland. In England firms have no personality and the primary liability attaches to individual partners. In Scotland on the other hand the liability of the partnership is vicarious. It has been held that this makes a firm responsible for a partner's fraud[5] and there is no reason to prevent the firm (ie the whole partnership) from being vicariously liable for a single partner's malice[6]. If partners are sued as individuals, however, one partner's malice will not taint the others. Liability under section 10, though vicarious, involves that every partner is liable jointly with his co-partners and also severally for every such thing for which the firm while he is a partner therein becomes liable[7]. Claims should be made first against the partnership, and then against the individual partners, who may be charged on a decree directed against the firm[8].

Voluntary associations as defenders

As with corporate bodies, voluntary associations may be guilty of malice, but they can be sued for defamation only in so far as they are capable of being sued at all. Trade unions cannot now be sued. In *Murdison v Scottish Football Union*[9] Lord Kinnear was not prepared to say that if a body such as the Scottish Football Union published defamatory material to the world it could not be sued for defamation[10]. In *Gray v Scottish Society for the Prevention of Cruelty*

---

1 See 14 *Stair Memorial Encyclopaedia* para 1041.
2 See for example *Will v Sneddon, Campbell & Munro* 1931 SC 164; *Evans & Sons v Stein & Co* (1904) 7 F 65.
3 *Kirkintilloch Equitable Co-Operative Society v Livingstone* 1972 SC 111.
4 *Meekins v Henson* [1962] 1 All ER 899.
5 *Thomson & Co v Pattison Elder & Co* (1895) 22 R 432.
6 For a different view, see Brough, *Miller on Partnership* (2nd edn, 1994) pp 319–321, 348–349.
7 Partnership Act 1890, s 12.
8 Ibid, s 4(2).
9 (1896) 23 R 449.
10 See also *Blasquez v Lothian Racing Club* (1889) 16 R 893.

to Animals[1] an unincorporated association was sued for defamation in the name of its office-bearers, and in *Smith v Presbytery of Auchterarder*[2] a church court of the state church was sued in its own name[3]. In *Fairbairn v SNP*[4] the constituency association of a political party was sued. In *Argyllshire Weavers Ltd v Macauley (Tweeds) Ltd*[5] the Harris Tweed Association was sued through the individual corporations of which it was comprised[6], while in *Barr v Musselburgh Merchants' Association*[7] a trade association was sued in its own name.

Children as defenders

The age of capacity to commit delictual acts has never been authoritatively laid down in Scots law. There is authority to suggest that even very young children can be guilty of contributory negligence[8], and these cases seem to be based on the view that the test is one of determining the individual capacity of the child to recognise and understand the danger he or she is placing him or herself in. However, though this may provide the rule for negligence itself, the consideration is far less significant in relation to intentional delicts and it has been held in an old case that pupil[9] children cannot be guilty of spuilzie[10]. It is suggested that the analogy between intentional delicts, like defamation, and crime is sufficiently close in determining liability therefor that the same age for both is appropriate[11]. In the words of Guthrie Smith[12], 'If criminally responsible, they must be so civilly'. If this is so then the rule today would be that no child below the age of eight can be found liable for defamation or verbal injury. This seems sensible. On like reasoning the mentally incapax probably cannot be found liable for defamation or verbal injury, as being incapable of the *animus injuriandi* which, though presumed in defamation, is the foundation of liability in both actions.

Actions against a child should be raised against the guardian as representative of the child, though the child's name will appear as first defender[13].

---

1 (1890) 17 R 1185.
2 (1850) 12 D 296.
3 Cf *Edwards v Begbie* (1850) 12 D 1134 in which the members of a non-state church were sued in their own names.
4 1980 SLT 149.
5 1965 SLT 21.
6 See also *Parlane v Templeton* (1896) 4 SLT 234 (p 153).
7 1912 SC 174.
8 *Frasers v Edinburgh Street Tramways Co* (1882) 10 R 264; *Banner's Tutor v Kennedy's Trs* 1978 SLT (Notes) 83; *Harvey v Cairns* 1989 SLT 107.
9 The concept of pupillarity remains relevant for determining criminal and civil responsibility: Age of Legal Capacity (Scotland) Act 1991, s 1(3)(c).
10 *Bryson v Sommervill* (1565) Mor 8906. In *Somerville v Hamilton* (1541) Mor 8905 a six-year-old child was apparently found liable in spuilzie, but it has been suggested that this case should more properly be regarded as one of unjust enrichment: see Stewart, 'Liability for Pupils in Delict' 1989 SLT (News) 404.
11 See *Cooper* p 26; Wilkinson & Norrie, *Parent and Child* (1993) p 376.
12 *A Treatise on the Law of Reparation* (1864) p 22.
13 *Wilkinson & Norrie* p 368.

Executors as defenders

The estate of a person who defames and then dies is liable in damages, including solatium for wounded feelings, to the person injured thereby[1], and the executor can be sued as the deceased's representative.

1 *Evans v Stoole* (1885) 12 R 1295 (an action for seduction).

CHAPTER SIX

Unintentional defamation

Introduction

The law of defamation can be hard on defenders, and nowhere is this more apparent than in relation to unintentional defamation, which can found liability just as much as intentional defamation. The theoretical requirement for malice, or intent to injure, to exist may give the impression that defamation is an intentional delict, in which the motive of the defender is always highly relevant; but the fact that wrongful intent is (apart from cases of privilege) discovered in the nature of the statement complained of rather than in the mind of the defender gives the lie to that impression. In fact, unintentional defamation is as actionable as intentional defamation, and it is no defence for most defenders to show that they did not or even could not intend to cause injury to the pursuer. The essence of the wrong of defamation is its effect on the pursuer rather than the intention of the defender, and it is an intentional delict only in the highly recondite sense that intent to injure must exist but is nearly always irrebuttably presumed. Intention must, of course, be averred and proved by the pursuer in a case of verbal injury[1].

Circumstances of unintentional defamation

There are a number of different circumstances in which a defender may be entirely innocent of harmful intent but nevertheless liable in damages for his or her acts (apart altogether from the normal delictual rules of vicarious liability when a defender can be liable for the delicts of another[2]). Defenders may for example, intending to refer to one person, use a name which belongs also to another person who takes offence; or they may innocently create fictional characters in whom pursuers see themselves; or they may disseminate, propagate, broadcast, distribute or merely deliver the statements of others without knowledge that these statements are defamatory. Each form of unintentional defamation gives rise to different considerations.

---

1 See further, Chapter 3.
2 See above at pp 74–75.

Use of pursuer's name

That the use of the pursuer's name can lead to liability even when the use was not intended to refer to the pursuer can be illustrated by a number of cases, the most famous of which is that of *Hulton & Co v Jones*[1]. Here, a newspaper had published a fictitious, but apparently genuine, article about a character called 'Artemus Jones', which contained statements that, had they been made against an actual person, were defamatory. Unfortunately for the newspaper, there did exist in real life a Mr Artemus Jones – a barrister – and he sued the publisher claiming that he had been defamed. The defence was that, since the newspaper writer had no knowledge of the existence of the real Mr Jones, he could not be said to have any intent to injure or, in other words, that his lack of intention amounted to lack of malice. That defence was rejected, unanimously, by the House of Lords on the ground that if reasonable readers could take the statements to refer to the plaintiff then the plaintiff had been defamed. The Lord Chancellor, Lord Loreburn said:

'What does the tort [of defamation] consist in? It consists in using language which others knowing the circumstances would reasonably think to be defamatory of the person complaining of and injured by it. A person charged with libel cannot defend himself by shewing that he intended in his own breast not to defame, or that he intended not to defame the plaintiff, if in fact he did both. He has none the less imputed something disgraceful and has none the less injured the plaintiff. A man in good faith may publish a libel believing it to be true, and it may be found by the jury that he acted in good faith believing it to be true, and reasonably believing it to be true, but that in fact the statement was false. Under those circumstances he has no defence to the action, however excellent his intention[2]. If the intention of the writer be immaterial in considering whether the matter written is defamatory, I do not see why it need be relevant in considering whether it is defamatory of the plaintiff[3] . . . Just as the defendant cannot excuse himself from malice by proving that he wrote it in the most benevolent spirit, so he cannot shew that the libel was not of and concerning the plaintiff by proving that he never heard of the plaintiff. His intention in both respects equally is inferred from what he did. His remedy is to abstain from defamatory words'[4].

This reasoning was accepted in Scotland very shortly after *Hulton* was decided. In *Wragg v DC Thomson & Co Ltd*[5] a Scottish newspaper, reprinting an article taken from an American magazine, published a headline saying: 'George Reeves Shoots Wife'. A music-hall artiste, who worked in Glasgow under that name, sued for defamation. On the question of whether it was necessary for the pursuer to show that the defenders actually intended to refer

---

1 [1910] AC 20.
2 Note this: malice in the legal sense is irrebuttably presumed to exist 'however excellent his intention'.
3 This may well be so, but it does not explain why the defender should be held liable for the defamation. In the law of negligence a person may injure another but be not liable because there is no *culpa*, or breach of a duty of care. This indicates that defamation is different from all other forms of delict, where *damnum* without *culpa* is usually legally innocuous.
4 [1910] AC 20 at 23 and 24.
5 1909 2 SLT 315, 409.

to the pursuer, the Lord Ordinary accepted the Court of Appeal decision in *Hulton* and the Inner House accepted the affirming decision of the House of Lords. Lord Anderson later used *Hulton* as authority for the proposition that, 'as a general rule, innocence, that is absence of malice – the non-existence of any intention to defame – is no defence to the publication of a slander'[1].

This was not, however, new law in Scotland. In *Finlay v Ruddiman*[2] a newspaper reported that one John Finlay, shoemaker, had been incarcerated on a charge of rape. The pursuer was a quite different shoemaker of that name and it was held to be no defence that the defender intended not to defame any particular person but only to report a fact[3]. Similarly, in *Outram v Reid*[4] the *Glasgow Herald* published a list of bankruptcies, including that of 'John Reid, wine and spirit merchant, Glasgow'. Such a wine and spirit merchant had indeed been declared bankrupt, but there was another John Reid of the same vocation and from the same city who had not been declared bankrupt, and who claimed that his business had suffered by this publication. Damages were awarded[5].

Creation of fictional characters

It is one of the most common conceits that people consider themselves interesting enough for others to write about them. It not infrequently happens that individuals see themselves in characters apparently created by the imagination of novelists, playwrights or filmmakers, and decide to take offence[6]. If a novelist has genuinely invented a character, but coincidentally it does bear some resemblance to a real person, and reasonable people see the resemblance and identify the character with the person, then any derogatory comments about the character might found an action for defamation by the person notwithstanding the novelist's lack of intention to injure. The defamation lies in the nature of the allegation and not in the intent of the defender and it follows that the pursuer's case (in defamation) is no stronger if he or she alleges that the novelist actually did intend to injure. In *Cuthbert v Linklater*[7] the pursuer, an SNP activist known as Wendy Wood, sued Eric Linklater on the basis that a disreputable character in his novel *Magnus Merriman* was clearly drawn from her: the character was an SNP activist called Beattie

---

1 *Gibson v National Citizens' Council* 1921 1 SLT 241 at 242.
2 (1763) Mor 3436.
3 Hume, *Lectures on the Law of Scotland* III, 152 thought that this decision 'was too strong', and in *Craig v Hunter & Co* 29 June 1809, FC a similar published mistake which was immediately retracted and apology given was held not to give rise to liability unless the pursuer could show either intent to injure or negligence.
4 (1852) 14 D 577.
5 See also *Harper v Provincial Newspapers Ltd* 1937 SLT 462, another case of two individuals with the same name, and *Harkness v Daily Record* 1924 SLT 759, where the names were similar.
6 See eg *Ross v Hopkinson* (1956) CLY 5011.
7 1935 SLT 94.

Bracken. The case was held relevant (rather surprisingly[1]) but later settled. Not only may the author be sued for this type of defamation, but publishers and broadcasters responsible for putting the work into the public domain may also be sued, notwithstanding that they may be even more innocent of intent to injure than the author. In *Boyd v BBC*[2] the defenders were the broadcasters of a play written by the pursuer's estranged husband. It contained a character called Julia who led a grossly disreputable and immoral life and the pursuer alleged that the character recognisably portrayed her. The Sheriff Principal held that she had made out a *prima facie* case of defamation and granted interim interdict[3].

This puts broadcasters, publishers, and writers in a very difficult position. It is clearly impossible for a publisher or a novelist to check that every character created does not resemble a real person[4]. The remedy, said Lord Loreburn, LC[5], 'is to abstain from defamatory words'. Freedom of the press would clearly suffer immense and unacceptable restriction if nothing derogatory were ever to be published, and artistic and cultural endeavour would be quickly destroyed[6]. That 'remedy' is clearly insufficient and indeed contrary to public policy.

Distributing the statements of others

As has already been seen[7] the repetition or dissemination of someone else's words is actionable against the repeater or disseminator if the words convey defamatory imputations, and this is so even when the defender is not responsible for the contents of the statements, or cannot in any practical way check the accuracy of every derogatory fact repeated, published or delivered. Particular difficulties are caused to newspapers who often have a duty to carry the words of others, or who publish letters from their readers, or who accept

1 There were other similarities between Wood and Bracken, and the defender's contention that he had not intended to refer to the pursuer, it is submitted, spurious. Much stronger was the argument that he had not defamed her by alleging that she had entered a public urinal and by doing so had 'lacked womanly delicacy'.
2 1969 SLT (Sh Ct) 17.
3 The defenders were, after proof, assoilzied.
4 An interesting example is *Youssoupoff v MGM Pictures* (1934) 50 TLR 581, in which the Russian Princess Irina Alexandrovna, who was the wife of one of the murderers of Rasputin, alleged that the character 'Princess Natasha' in the MGM film *Rasputin, the Mad Monk* was in fact she, and that the scene in which the Princess is seduced or ravished by the monk was defamatory. Her award of £25,000 was upheld on appeal. In that case, though some names had been changed, the film was alleged by the defendants to be based on fact – but the film-maker's view of 'fact' is notoriously suspect.
5 *Hulton & Co v Jones* [1910] AC 20 at 24.
6 Try removing the unpleasant characters from Dickens, or Scott, or Murdoch, or even Wodehouse and see the quality of what remains. It is well-known that *Jarndyce v Jarndyce* was based on a real case; it is said that the magistrate Mr Fang in *Oliver Twist* was based on a notorious magistrate called Mr Laing (pronounced Lang). The father of *The Bride of Lammermoor* is noticeably unpleasant, and his professional and home life bears a remarkable similarity to that of our own James Dalrymple, First Viscount of Stair.
7 Above at pp 29–31.

advertisements and notices. Others who distribute statements, such as bookshops and libraries may also find themselves liable for the defamatory content of these statements. In *Morrison v Ritchie & Co*[1] an unknown person placed a notice in *The Scotsman* to the effect that twins had been born to the pursuers. This was considered defamatory (at that time) since the pursuers had been married for only one month. It was held that the action against the newspaper was relevant, notwithstanding that the newspaper had no knowledge of the pursuers nor intent to injure them. In this sort of case the newspaper is innocent in the sense that there is nothing derogatory on the face of what it publishes, and it is only by taking account of extraneous facts, which the publisher does not know nor can be expected to know about, that the statement becomes defamatory[2]. The innocence of libraries and bookshops is even more readily apparent.

Defences to unintentional defamation

The harshness of the above rules is mitigated to a certain extent – though not entirely – by the existence of two separate defences, one statutory and one common law, which can be called in aid by defenders who are technically guilty of defamation but not guilty of any intention to injure the pursuer.

Statutory offer of amends

Section 4 of the Defamation Act 1952[3] provides a statutory defence which, in some circumstances, will protect the person who defames unintentionally. The wording of that section clearly indicates that the defence is designed for newspaper publishers and other professional publishers, but it is nowhere limited to these categories[4]. The section is lengthy and, it must be said, opaque. In summary, its provisions are as follows. If there has been an 'innocent' publication[5] then it is open to the publisher to make an 'offer of amends'[6]. If this offer is accepted then no proceedings for defamation can be taken or continued[7]. If the offer is rejected then it is a defence to any action for defamation that the offer was made as soon as practicable and that it has not been withdrawn[8]; but if the defender has published words that were not

---

1 (1902) 4 F 645.
2 Cf *McLean v Bernstein* (1900) 8 SLT 31 (p 42); *Cassidy v Daily Mirror Newspapers Ltd* [1929] 2 KB 331; *Hough v London Express Newspapers Ltd* [1940] 2 KB 507.
3 As applied to, and amended for, Scotland by s 14.
4 Section 16(1), defining 'words' to include pictures, visual images, gestures and other methods of signifying meaning, applies to this section as to others.
5 Defined in s 4(5).
6 Defined in s 4(3) with further particulars in s 4(2).
7 Defamation Act 1952, s 4(1)(a).
8 Ibid, s 4(1)(b).

written by him then the defence is available only if the words were written by the author without malice[1]. The onus lies with the defender to prove that the publication was innocent, that the offer of amends had been made as soon as practicable[2], and, if applicable, that the author of the words acted without malice. These provisions may now be looked at more closely.

Innocent publication

Section 4 applies only if the publication complained of has been published innocently, and this is defined in the following terms[3]:

'For the purposes of this section words shall be treated as published by one person (in this section referred to as the publisher) innocently in relation to another person if and only if the following conditions are satisfied, that is to say –
(a) that the publisher did not intend to publish them of and concerning that other person, and did not know of circumstances by virtue of which they might be understood to refer to him; or
(b) that the words were not defamatory on the face of them, and the publisher did not know of circumstances by virtue of which they might be understood to be defamatory of that other person,
and in either case that the publisher exercised all reasonable care in relation to the publication; and any reference in this subsection to the publisher shall be construed as including a reference to any servant or agent of his who was concerned with the contents of the publication.'

Paragraph (a) deals with cases such as *Hulton v Jones, Finlay v Ruddiman, Outram & Co v Reid*, and *Wragg v DC Thomson*. Each involved situations in which the publisher meant to refer to either a fictitious character or another person of the same name. It would also cover the case of the novelist who invents a character in whom the pursuer sees him or herself. Paragraph (b) deals with cases like *Morrison v Ritchie & Co*, for the notice of the birth of twins in that case was not on the face of it defamatory. It is to be noted in relation to this paragraph that the defender must prove merely that he 'did not know of circumstances' which would make the publication defamatory, rather than that he could not be expected to know of such circumstances.

On the satisfaction of either paragraph, it must further be shown that all reasonable care had been taken in relation to the publication. So while *Outram & Co v Reid*[4] would today come within paragraph (a), the same result would ultimately be reached since the court held there that the newspaper had not taken reasonable care to ensure that there was not confusion[5].

---

1 Defamation Act 1952, s 4(6).
2 See *Ross v Hopkinson* [1956] CLY 5011.
3 1952 Act, s 4(5).
4 (1852) 14 D 577.
5 The newspaper had omitted to publish the address of the bankrupt, which it knew, and which would have served to distinguish the bankrupt from the defender.

Offer of amends

Section 4(1) provides, in part, that 'A person who has published words alleged to be defamatory of another person may, if he claims that the words were published by him innocently in relation to that other person [as defined above], make an offer of amends'. This is defined[1] as follows:

'An offer of amends under this section shall be understood to mean an offer –
(a) in any case, to publish or join in the publication of a suitable correction of the words complained of, and a sufficient apology to the party aggrieved in respect of those words;
(b) where copies of a document or record containing the said words have been distributed by or with the knowledge of the person making the offer, to take such steps as are reasonably practicable on his part for notifying persons to whom copies have been so distributed that the words are alleged to be defamatory of the party aggrieved.'

It is further provided[2] that:

'An offer of amends under this section must be expressed to be made for the purposes of this section, and must be accompanied by a written declaration specifying the facts relied upon by the person making it to show that the words in question were published by him innocently in relation to the party aggrieved; and for the purposes of the defence under paragaph (b) of subsection (1) of this section[3] no evidence, other than evidence of facts specified in the written declaration, shall be admissible on behalf of that person to prove that the words were so published.

Nothing in this subsection shall be held to entitle a defender to lead evidence of any fact specified in the declaration unless notice of his intention to do so has been given in the defences.'

Acceptance of offer of amends

If the offer of amends is accepted by the party aggrieved and it is duly performed, no proceedings for defamation can be taken or continued by that party against the person making the offer in respect of the publication in question (but without prejudice to any cause of action against any other person jointly responsible for that publication)[4]. It is further provided[5] that:

'Where an offer of amends under this section is accepted by the party aggrieved –
(a) any question as to the steps to be taken in fulfilment of the offer as so accepted shall in default of agreement between the parties be referred to and determined by the Court of Session or, if an action of defamation is depending in the sheriff court in respect of the publication in question, the sheriff, whose decision thereon shall be final;
(b) the power of the court to make orders as to expenses in proceedings by the party aggrieved against the person making the offer in respect of the publication in question, or in proceedings in respect of the offer under paragraph (a) of this subsection, shall include power to order the payment by the person making the offer to the party

1 1952 Act, s 4(3).
2 Ibid, s 4(2).
3 Below, at p 86.
4 1952 Act, s 4(1)(a).
5 Ibid, s 4(4).

aggrieved of expenses on an indemnity basis and any expenses reasonably incurred or to be incurred by that party in consequence of the publication in question; and if no such proceedings as aforesaid are taken, the Court of Session or, if an action of defamation is depending in the sheriff court in respect of the publication in question, the sheriff may, upon application made by the party aggrieved, make any such order for the payment of such expenses as aforesaid as could be made in such proceedings.'

Rejection of offer of amends

It is provided[1] that:

'if the offer is not accepted by the party aggrieved, then, except as [provided by section 4(6)], it shall be a defence, in any proceedings by him for defamation against the person making the offer in respect of the publication in question, to prove that the words complained of were published by the defender innocently in relation to the pursuer and that the offer was made as soon as practicable after the defender received notice that they were or might be defamatory of the pursuer, and has not been withdrawn'.

The onus is on the defender to establish (1) that the publication was made 'innocently' as defined above; (2) that the offer has been rejected; (3) that it was made as soon as practicable[2]; and (4) that it is still open.

Publishing the words of others

In addition to proving these conditions, a publisher who publishes another person's words, such as a newspaper which publishes the words of a reporter, or a book publisher who publishes the words of an author, or a bookshop or library which makes these words available to the general public, is further obliged by section 4(6) to prove that the words were written by the author without malice. 'Malice' is not defined in the Defamation Act 1952. Its normal meaning in the law of defamation, which arises primarily in cases of privilege, involves oblique or indirect motive other than the fulfilment of a duty, but that cannot be applicable here since there is generally no duty to publish. If malice is taken to mean direct ill-will towards the pursuer then it is not clear why the law should presume this in cases of admittedly unintentional defamation. Proof of the lack of spite is probably a good deal more difficult than proof of its existence, and it is difficult to know what proof is needed to satisfy this condition. This problem is compounded by the fact that it is lack of malice in the writer that the defender has to prove rather than lack of malice in the defender. Another difficulty is that while 'words' is defined to include pictures, visual images, gestures and other methods of signifying meaning[3] it is not clear how, say, a gesture can be 'written' either with or without malice. It may well be that this requirement to prove malice applies only to words in the

---

1 1952 Act, s 4(1)(b).
2 On which, see *Ross v Hopkinson* [1956] CLY 5011 (an offer seven weeks later was considered too late).
3 1952 Act, s 16(1).

narrow sense; alternatively, the word 'written' should be interpreted *mutatis mutandis* with the making of pictures and gestures.

Effectiveness of section 4

There have been few court decisions on section 4, though perhaps this is not surprising. The aim of the section is to prevent cases from getting to court and the lack of judicial discussion may well serve to indicate its success[1]. Certainly the provisions of the section could have prevented lengthy and expensive litigation in *Hulton v Jones* and in *Wragg v DC Thomson*. However, the effectiveness of the section is clearly limited by its unhelpful structure, and by some of the limitations which do not have obvious merit. For example the provision whereby a publisher must prove that the writer wrote without malice is difficult to justify. This provision would prevent the defence being used in a case like *Morrison v Ritchie*, where the writer of the birth notice sent to the newspaper for publication was never identified and it was therefore impossible to show that the writer acted without malice[2]. And the requirement to show lack of malice makes reliance on section 4 almost impossible for bookshops and libraries. Yet it is in just such cases that innocent defenders most deserve to be protected: luckily, there is a common law defence, about to be discussed, available to them.

Innocent dissemination

As we have seen, the general rule in defamation is that every person responsible for passing on a defamatory idea is as liable in damages as the original defamer[3]; we also saw that lack of intention to defame is, generally speaking, no defence[4]. To apply these two rules strictly would result in the law moving into the realms of fantasy. It would be ludicrous to suggest that the Royal Mail could be sued for delivering a letter with defamatory content, or that every newspaper boy delivering the morning papers could be sued for any defamatory statement contained therein, or that every library, newsagent or book store could be sued for any defamatory statement in a book or magazine that it happens to have on its public shelves. English law has developed a defence which is available to newsagents, booksellers, libraries, and other persons who are in the business of distributing communicable matter but who have no control over the content of that matter nor practical means of discovering whether the matter is defamatory. This is known as the defence of 'innocent dissemination'. There are few cases on the subject, but the matter was summed up in respect of English law by Carter-Ruck as follows:

1 Carter-Ruck, *Libel and Slander* (4th edn, 1992) pp 155 and 156.
2 Clive, Watt & McKain, *Scots Law for Journalists* (5th edn, 1988) p 183.
3 Above, at pp 29–31.
4 Above, at p 79.

'The law will excuse a mere distributor of a libel who is neither the author, nor the printer, nor the original publisher, provided he is able to satisfy the court:
(a) that he did not know that the document in question contained a libel and that he did not know that it was likely to contain one; and
(b) that his ignorance was not due to any want of care on his part'[1].

The matter has been little discussed in the Scottish courts, but there is no doubt that the defence, or something similar, is part of our law. Lord Moncreiff in *Morrison v Ritchie & Co*[2], in discussing the English cases[3] does not deny the applicability in Scotland of similar principles and indeed seems to apply the English principles to the present case[4]. Lord Anderson in *Gibson v National Citizens' Council*[5] is more explicit. He holds that innocence is a defence pleadable by 'mere messengers', or the mechanical instruments by which the slander is published. Further, he holds that defenders who are not responsible for the form or content of the material in which the defamation is contained will be *prima facie* liable for defamation but will not be liable if they can show (and the onus is on them) that they did not know that the material contained a libel and that this ignorance was not due to any negligence on their part. In other words, in cases of mere messengers or those not responsible for the contents of the material complained about, the presumption of intent to injure is not, as it usually is, irrebuttable. This can be seen in the judgment of Lord Stormonth Darling in *McLean v Bernstein*[6]. There the pursuer sued both a person who placed an allegedly defamatory advertisement in a newspaper and the publishers of the newspaper which carried it. Lord Stormonth Darling held that both could be liable, though he pointed out that the type of malice required was different for each defender. He further opined:

'The pursuer will probably not get a verdict against the newspaper unless he can satisfy the jury that there was on the part of the newspaper a certain recklessness in inserting the advertisement . . . The further . . . that you get from the original source of the slander it may, according to reason and common sense, be necessary to say that the person who does not publish in the direct sense of the word, but merely propagates the slander, is not to be liable unless he does it consciously'.

Recklessness or some other fault on the part of the defender, or responsibility for the contents, will disable him or her from proving innocence. In England it has been held to be a matter of fact for the determination of the jury whether the defendant ought to have known of the defamatory content of the material he or she is responsible for disseminating. A library, for example, is not expected to check every single book that it possesses and cannot therefore be held to be aware of the contents of them all[7], but any organisation ought to

---

1 *Carter-Ruck* p 63.
2 (1902) 4 F 645.
3 (1902) 4 F 645 at 651–652.
4 The *Report of the Committee on Defamation* (the Faulks Committee) 1975 (Cmnd 5909) assumed that innocent dissemination was a recognised defence in Scotland and recommended (in common with most of their recommendations) no change in the law: para 316.
5 1921 1 SLT 241.
6 (1900) 8 SLT 31 (p 42).
7 *Weldon v Times Book Co Ltd* (1911) 28 TLR 143.

have some procedure for picking up and acting upon calls for withdrawal from publishers[1]. As soon as a person claims that material defames him or her, disseminators are put on their notice that the material might contain defamatory matter, at least when it is reasonable to expect that the disseminator should know about the claim. It is no excuse for a distributor to say that the mass and volume of its business precludes it from checking the material it distributes[2]. The nature of the publication will affect the likelihood of its containing defamatory material, and the more salacious the publication the less chance the defence has of succeeding. It is, for example, well known that the magazine *Private Eye* is frequently sued for libel[3], and a distributor of that magazine ought to be on greater guard than he would be with a magazine such as, for example, the *People's Friend*. However, as Lord Denning MR pointed out[4], just because a magazine has a bad reputation does not mean that no distributor can handle it safely, otherwise freedom of the press would be destroyed. Rather, with magazines which have reputations for carrying defamatory content, distributors should keep a closer eye on whether claims are being made against it. If they take reasonable care in all the circumstances, distributors will not be liable for the defamations they innocently propagate.

There is no authority for extending the defence to the initial publisher or broadcaster, and it is limited to defenders who have no control over the content of the material they are distributing or disseminating. So in *Morrison v Ritchie & Co*[5] the defence did not apply since the newspaper which accepted the birth notice was held to be responsible for whatever appeared in its own columns and was therefore expected to take care to ensure that it printed nothing defamatory. In the facts of that case[6], it is difficult to see how the defenders could have protected themselves and it is not self-evident that the law is satisfactory in not allowing the defence in such circumstances. Lord Moncreiff[7] clearly did not want the defence extended to cover those who have or ought to have some control, editorial or practical, over the material being published. Nevertheless, it might consist better with the principle of freedom of the press if Scots law were to hold that both innocent repeaters and original broadcasters are not liable for the defamatory remarks of others unless they act intentionally, negligently or recklessly. It is a quirk in the law that damages can be obtained for defamation against an entirely innocent defender and that quirk should be limited to situations in which it is essential to give protection to reputation: it is not needed in circumstances in which its only effect is to give the pursuer a choice of defenders. To extend the defence of innocent dissemination to the original publisher or broadcaster would not unduly prejudice pursuers, for the original defamer whose words are

---

1 *Vizetelly v Mudie's Select Library Ltd* [1900] 2 QB 170.
2 *Sun Life Assurance Co of Canada v WH Smith & Co Ltd* (1933) 150 LT 211.
3 See for example *Sutcliffe v Pressdram Ltd* [1990] 1 All ER 269; *Maxwell v Pressdram Ltd* [1987] 1 All ER 656; *Herbage v Pressdram Ltd* [1984] 2 All ER 769; *Goldsmith v Sperrings Ltd* [1977] 2 All ER 566.
4 *Goldsmith v Sperrings Ltd* [1977] 2 All ER 566 at 573.
5 (1902) 4 F 645.
6 See above at p 83.
7 (1902) 4 F 645 at 652.

published or broadcast far and wide can be held liable for the full consequences if the full publicity is the natural and probable consequence of his original wrong[1]; it would on the other hand provide a significant boost to the notion of freedom of the press. Some support for this suggestion can be found in Article 10 of the European Convention on Human Rights, which has been interpreted by the European Court of Human Rights to permit limitations on freedom of expression only in so far as this is necessary in a democratic society to protect, *inter alia*, the reputation of others[2]. If it is open to the pursuer to sue the original defamer it can hardly be argued that it is 'necessary in a democratic society' to protect his reputation to allow him also to sue the innocent publisher or reporter of the statements complained about[3]. Freedom of expression should be limited only when the desired protection cannot otherwise be achieved and on that test innocent dissemination would be given far wider scope than it has been given hitherto.

1 See below at pp 171–173.
2 See *Lingens v Austria* (1986) 8 EHRR 407; *Barford v Denmark* (1989) 13 EHRR 493; *Thorgeirson v Iceland* (1992) 14 EHRR 843; *Castells v Spain* (1992) 14 EHRR 445.
3 Though the European Convention on Human Rights is not part of the domestic law of Scotland, and the Scottish courts will not – unlike their English counterparts – use it to interpret or apply domestic law (see *Kaur v Lord Advocate* 1981 SLT 322; *Moore v Secretary of State for Scotland* 1985 SLT 38) the point remains good. The Scottish courts balance the public policy in encouraging free speech with the rights of individuals when applying the rules of privilege and when defining defamation in relation to public characters. There is no reason why they should not perform the balancing act in other aspects of defamation too.

CHAPTER SEVEN

Absolute privilege

Introduction

Absolute privilege is the protection given to communications made in circumstances in which public policy requires that the maker of the communication should be able to speak his or her mind freely without regard to the consequences, this irrespective both of whether the statements are true and of whether the statements are made maliciously. A statement protected by absolute privilege cannot in any circumstances be made the basis of an action for defamation or verbal injury, or indeed any other delict. The aim of absolute privilege is not to allow the person protected to defame others with impunity, though it may have this effect, but to prevent actions being raised on the basis of statements which are not, as well as those which may be, defamatory. Absolute privilege is to be distinguished from qualified privilege[1] in that a claim based on defamation made in circumstances of absolute privilege is always irrelevant while a claim for defamation made in circumstances of qualified privilege is relevant, but – as we will see – only if malice is sufficiently averred. It is a question of law whether or not a communication is protected by absolute privilege, and a failure to establish absolute privilege will result in no privilege being granted unless there are also averments sufficient to establish a case of qualified privilege. While absolute privilege, being a defence, will normally be for the defender to establish, it nearly always arises in circumstances in which it is clear from the record that it may apply (ie that the claim may be irrelevant) and it will therefore be for the pursuer to aver and prove that the circumstances of the particular case fall outwith the protection of the defence. There are certain well-recognised circumstances in which a communication will attract the protection of absolute privilege. The category of circumstances in which absolute privilege applies is not closed, but it will be extended only if it satisfies the irresistible demands of the policy it is designed to achieve.

Statements in Parliament

The most complete form of absolute privilege, and the one that has been subject to least challenge, concerns statements made in Parliament. There are

---

1 See below, Chapter 8.

at least two reasons for this. First, constitutionally, the courts have no jurisdiction over acts done or statements made in Parliament[1], and people are protected from harmful attacks by the control that each House has over its own affairs and the behaviour of its own members. Secondly, it is a matter of the highest public interest that members of both the House of Commons and the House of Lords should be able to speak freely on any matter they desire, without fear of incurring civil or criminal[2] liability therefor. Our parliamentary system is designed to operate through the medium of adversarial debate.

This form of absolute privilege is the most complete in the law since unlike, say, judicial privilege[3], it is not limited to relevant or pertinent remarks: members of Parliament are free to say anything on any matter whether related or not to an issue currently being or to be discussed in the House. The protection applies to anything said on the floor of either House, or in a committee thereof (such as in the Scottish Grand Committee) or in any other parliamentary proceeding over which either House exercises control. It applies also to persons not members of either House but who are acting for or on the authority of either House: so for example the officers of both Houses are protected, as are witnesses giving evidence to a Select Committee. Also protected are persons responsible for statements in a petition addressed to Parliament[4].

Judicial proceedings

Most, but not all, active participants in the judicial process are protected in what they say (and do) by absolute privilege. Again, the major justification for this is the public interest in encouraging freedom of expression in circumstances in which that is more important than the protection of reputations.

'The overriding public interest in free statement of facts, beliefs and opinions in the course of the administration of justice justifies absolute privilege for all statements made in judicial proceedings and complete immunity for the makers of such statements'[5].

'The motive of the law is not to protect corrupt or malevolent Judges, malicious advocates, or malignant and lying witnesses, but to prevent persons acting honestly in discharging a public function from being harassed afterwards by actions imputing to them dishonesty and malice, and seeking to make them liable in damages'[6].

1 Bill of Rights 1688, article 9.
2 For example for conspiracy or, in England, criminal libel: see *Ex Parte Wason* (1869) LR 4 QB 573.
3 See below at pp 108–109.
4 Though there is no absolute privilege protecting letters to MPs: *Rivlin v Bilainkin* [1953] 1 All ER 534.
5 Walker, *Delict* (2nd edn, 1981) p 800.
6 *Williamson v Umphray and Robertson* (1890) 17 R 905 at 911 per Lord President Inglis.

Court officers, for example sheriff clerks, are not granted the protection of absolute privilege[1]. Neither are the parties to a civil suit[2]. While the over-riding consideration is that of public policy, different factors are relevant to each of the several parties to the judicial process.

Judges

There are early decisions in which it was held that a judge will be liable for his actions as a judge if it can be proved that he has exceeded his authority[3] or had acted from motives of private malice[4]. These decisions are no longer regarded as good law, and since the case of *Haggart's Trustees v Hope*[5], in which the House of Lords affirmed the decision of the Court of Session, it has been the law of Scotland that a judge cannot be sued for defamation or verbal injury even when he acts with malice: in other words, he is absolutely privileged in what he does or says judicially[6]. In a later case, Lord Moncreiff justified the rule as follows:

'the absolute privilege of Judges is founded on the public policy that it is essential to the ends of justice that persons in such positions should enjoy freedom of speech without fear of consequences in discharging their public duties in the course of the judicial inquiry'[7].

He went on,

'The reason for the wideness of the protection is simply this: If a judge were liable to be sued in respect of words uttered in his judicial capacity, on the averment that what he said was irrelevant or not pertinent to the case or in excess of the occasion, or even that he uttered the words maliciously, experience tells us that although he might after trial succeed in clearing himself of the imputation he would be exposed to being called on to answer what *ex facie* of the summons was apparently a relevant charge'[8].

The remedy against a judge, if such be needed, is his removal from office for misconduct.

The privilege of judges is, however, rather more limited than that discussed above in relation to statements made in Parliament. As we have seen, a member of Parliament can say in a parliamentary debate anything he or she likes and he or she will be answerable only to the discipline of the House: he can in other words take the opportunity to depart from the issue being

1 *Watt v Thomson* (1870) 8 M(HL) 77. In performing their official functions such officers will be pro-tected by qualified privilege.
2 See below at pp 108–109.
3 So in *Leitch v Fairy* (1711) Mor 13946 an inferior judge was held liable after pronouncing decree in a case in which he had a personal interest; and in *Pitcairn v Deans* (1715) Mor 13948 a justice of the peace who had exceeded his jurisdiction was found liable to compensate for the imprisonment he had ordered.
4 *Band v Clerk & Scott* 31 May 1797, FC; *Oliphant v McNeil* (1776) 5 Mor Supp 573.
5 (1824) 2 Shaw App 125.
6 Accepted, without citation of authority, by Lord Justice-Clerk Boyle in *Hamilton v Hope* (1827) 5 S 569.
7 *Primrose v Waterston* (1902) 4 F 783 at 793.
8 Ibid. See also *Harvey v Dyce* (1876) 4 R 265.

considered by the House to defame a person in a manner that has no relevance whatsoever to the matter at hand. A judge will not be protected if he acts in this way and he cannot use his office to cloak the expression of personal grudges against persons entirely unconnected with the case before him. A judge can claim absolute privilege only for so long as he is acting judicially and if he takes himself outwith the judicial role he will lose his protection and will be as liable as any other person for his defamatory remarks[1].

The question of when does a judge act outwith his judicial role was discussed in a number of nineteenth-century cases, and the dicta suggest that a great leeway is given to Scottish judges. A judge does not stop acting as a judge just because he gets the law wrong[2], even in a question of the extent of his own jurisdiction[3], and unless his error is such that no judge of reasonable competence would have made it, his exercise of a jurisdiction that he does not have will nevertheless remain absolutely privileged[4]. The fact that statements made by a judge are defamatory and untrue is irrelevant to the question of whether they were uttered in judicial proceedings[5]. In the case cited, a magistrate, dealing with a nine-year-old boy charged with theft, called the boy's father, who was clubmaster at premises which sold alcohol, to attend the hearing, and lectured the father on the evils of drink, suggesting that the father's upbringing of the boy was the cause of the boy's getting into trouble with the police. The father sued the magistrate for defamation. The Second Division held that the magistrate was acting within his authority as magistrate, and indeed Lord Moncreiff stated that a judge could be held to have moved out of his judicial function only if, 'it can be demonstrated – that is, shewn so clearly that no man of ordinary diligence and judgment could honestly dispute it – that the words used had no connection with the case in hand'[6]. In another case, Lord Cowan said that before the court could hold that a judge had acted extra-judicially, 'we must be prepared to hold the sentence or interlocutor to have been either *ultra vires*, or so extravagantly absurd, and out of all bounds, as to be undeserving of the name of a judicial act'[7]. These dicta suggest a strict test for taking a judge outwith the judicial role and a heavy onus on a pursuer complaining of defamation or verbal injury by a judge: it would seem that any action against a judge would be irrelevant unless the pursuer can show that the judge's statements had no connection whatsoever with the matter at hand and

1 *Hamilton v Anderson* (1856) 18 D 1003; *Allardice v Robertson* (1830) 4 W & S 102; *Watt v Thomson* (1870) 8 M(HL) 77.
2 *Hamilton v Anderson* (1856) 18 D 1003 at 1021 per Lord Wood.
3 *McPhee v Macfarlane's Ex* 1933 SC 163 per Lord President Clyde (an action for wrongful imprisonment brought against a magistrate exercising a statutory jurisdiction the extent of which he had misinterpreted).
4 Lord Justice-Clerk Boyle in *Haggart's Trustees v Hope* (1824) 2 Shaw App 125 at 139 considered that a judge might be liable if he acted 'palpably ultra vires'.
5 *Primrose v Waterston* (1902) 4 F 783 at 791 per Lord Justice-Clerk Macdonald.
6 (1902) 4 F 783 at 793.
7 *Hamilton v Anderson* (1856) 18 D 1003 at 1023. See also *Mackellar v Duke of Sutherland* (1862) 24 D 1124 in which Lord Justice-Clerk Inglis said that the (qualified) privilege of a litigant would be lost if he talks about matters 'altogether irrelevant'.

that any connection, even one created by the judge himself, would be sufficient to confer absolute privilege[1].

While malice is normally relevant only in cases of qualified privilege, it may nevertheless be relevant here also, in the sense of being evidence that a judge has taken himself outwith his judicial role. If the pursuer can show that a judge acted not to advance the proceedings at all but for motives of personal spite or malice, this will be relevant evidence in helping to establish that the judge is acting non-judicially[2].

Many judges have administrative as well as judicial functions to perform, but it is only the latter that give rise to absolute privilege. In *Beaton v Ivory*[3] a sheriff acting as justice of the peace ordered the arrest of any person found in a particular locality, and an action for wrongful arrest was dismissed because of the absence of any relevant averments of malice: in other words the privilege available to the defender performing an administrative duty was qualified rather than absolute. On the other hand, the action of a sheriff in ordering a solicitor to leave his court was considered judicial since it was concerned with the administration of justice and it was therefore protected by absolute privilege[4]. And when the first Lord Hope, when Lord Justice-Clerk, strongly censured an advocate for the inadequacy of his preparation of a case, the advocate was unsuccessful in his claim for damages, being met with a plea of absolute privilege which was upheld by both the Court of Session and the House of Lords[5].

There is no distinction today drawn between judges of superior and judges of inferior courts, and both are entitled to the same protection[6]. It may however be that a superior court judge is less likely to be held to have taken himself outwith his judicial role, since his jurisdiction is much wider. An inferior judge, with more clearly defined boundaries of jurisdiction, may more easily find him or herself acting outwith his or her judicial function.

Pleaders

Advocates and solicitors pleading a case before a court are absolutely privileged in what they say, and they therefore cannot be sued for defamation or

---

1 That this protection is rather wider than that granted in other jurisdictions is shown by Carey Miller in 'Defamation by a Judge? Fixing the Limits' 1980 JR 88. Most jurisdictions in the USA require that the judge's statement be 'relevant' or 'pertinent' to the case at hand before it can attract absolute privilege, while in South Africa the judge's privilege is qualified in every case. Carey Miller makes a cogent argument that the test for absolute privilege should be one of 'reasonable relevance' of the judge's statement to the matter at hand.
2 *Hamilton v Anderson* (1856) 18 D 1003 at 1019 per Lord Justice-Clerk Hope.
3 (1887) 14 R 1057.
4 *Farrell v Walker* (1962) 79 Sh Ct Rep 61.
5 *Haggart's Trustees v Hope* (1824) 2 Shaw App 125.
6 *Primrose v Waterston* (1902) 4 F 783, disapproving *Allardice v Robertson* (1830) 4 W & S 102. *Allardice* was decided by the House of Lords and could not be overruled in *Primrose*. However, the distinction drawn in *Allardice* between superior and inferior judges would now be inconsistent with the extension of absolute privilege to quasi-judicial proceedings and tribunals, which has House of Lords approval: see below at pp 99–101.

verbal injury which they commit while pleading a case. The basis of this privilege seems to be that the pleader is acting on behalf of the client and may have had no opportunity himself to check the truth or otherwise of what he may be obliged to say in pursuance of his duty to his client. Counsel (and the same applies to a solicitor pleading a case in court, whether as a solicitor or as a solicitor-advocate) 'has duties of a representative kind to perform; he would not undertake these, and at least could not perform his duties with that freedom essential to the ends of justice, if he were not to have protection'[1].

'The principle of the rule so laid down is not that the law will deliberately protect a wrong of that kind [an impertinent slander uttered maliciously], but that the expediency of protecting an advocate in the exercise of his function is so high, that the Court will not entertain any question as to whether what he has said was irrelevant or impertinent and malicious'[2].

The privilege extends to written pleadings drawn up by the pleader. Originally only qualified privilege seems to have been given to written pleadings[3], but at least since the case of *Rome v Watson*[4] the law has granted absolute protection[5].

Like judges, pleaders are protected by absolute privilege only for statements that are made while they are acting within their proper role in the judicial process, and counsel who, during the course of a court hearing, steps out of that role and defames a person in circumstances in which the statement has no connection at all with the matter at hand will be liable for that defamation and will have no privilege to protect him. However, because our court system is adversarial, and designed to encourage the widest possible debate in the search for truth, the court will not enter into a close and minute examination of whether particular statements are relevant or irrelevant to the case being dealt with by the pleader[6], for counsel must be left free to develop their own arguments in their own way. Again like judges, for a pleader's statement to be actionable it would have to be shown (and the onus would be on the pursuer) that no reasonable person could consider that it had any connection at all with the matter at hand. In *Clark v Haddon*[7] it was held that one solicitor appearing in the sheriff court did not take himself outwith the protection of absolute privilege when he accused another solicitor similarly appearing of being unqualified to appear, as having been struck off the rolls.

Witnesses

The position of witnesses remained in some doubt in Scotland rather longer than the other participants in the judicial process[8], though the matter was

1 *Williamson v Umphray and Robertson* (1890) 17 R 905 at 914 and 915 per Lord Shand.
2 *Rome v Watson* (1898) 25 R 733 at 738 per Lord President Robertson.
3 See *Yeats v Ramsay* (1825) 4 S 275; *Manson v Macara* (1839) 2 D 208.
4 (1898) 25 R 733.
5 *Cunningham v Scotsman Publications Ltd* 1987 SLT 698 at 699H per Lord Clyde.
6 *Rome v Watson* (1898) 25 R 733 at 738 per Lord President Robertson.
7 (1895) 3 SLT 128 (p 85).
8 See cases discussed by Cooper *Defamation and Verbal Injury* (2nd edn, 1906) pp 140–141.

settled in England by the case of *Dawkins v Lord Rokeby*[1]. Here, it was not until 1904 that the matter was authoritatively settled in favour of absolute privilege. In *AB v CD*[2] a medical practitioner gave evidence in an action for separation between spouses and was sued for, inter alia, defamation alleged to be contained in some of his statements. It was held that so long as his evidence was pertinent to the matter at issue, he was protected by absolute privilege. Lord Justice-Clerk Macdonald said, 'Nothing is, I think, more clearly settled in our law than this, that a witness is absolutely privileged in giving his evidence, pertinent to the issue, and cannot be subjected in damages for slander for what he says in the Court of Justice'[3]. In the House of Lords Lord Halsbury LC, upholding that part of the Inner House's decision, said that that position 'is absolutely unarguable – it is settled law and cannot be doubted'[4]. The reason for the rule was given by Lord Young in the Inner House:

'It is in the interests of justice, and the public for whom justice is administered, that [the witness] should not give his answers under any apprehension of being liable to an action of damages should his evidence be defamatory of anyone . . . It is in the interests of the public that the truth should be ascertained in a Court of Justice, and that witnesses should give their evidence without any such apprehension or fear'[5].

This absolute privilege does not allow the witness to tell lies with impunity, for all witnesses are subject to sanction through the law of perjury. And the adversarial system itself contains an in-built protection against false evidence: as Lord Wilberforce put it, 'the trial process contains in itself, in the subjection to cross-examination and confrontation with other evidence, some safeguard against careless, malicious or untruthful evidence'[6].

The privilege of witnesses covers not only what they say in court, but also statements they make in precognition during the preparation of the court case by the parties or their agents. As Lord Halsbury LC put it in *AB v CD*[7],

'It is very obvious that the public policy which renders the protection of witnesses necessary for the administration of justice must as a necessary consequence involve that which is a step towards and is part of the administration of justice, namely, the preliminary examination of witnesses to find out what they can prove. It may be that to some extent it seems to impose a hardship[8], but after all the hardship is not to be compared with that which would arise if it were impossible to administer justice, because people would be afraid to give their testimony'[9].

---

1 (1873) LR 8 QB 255.
2 (1904) 7 F 72, affirmed by the House of Lords, sub nom *Watson v McEwan* (1905) 7 F(HL) 109.
3 (1904) 7 F 72 at 81.
4 (1905) 7 F(HL) 109 at 110.
5 (1904) 7 F 72 at 82.
6 *Roy v Prior* [1971] AC 470 at 480.
7 Sub nom. *Watson v McEwan* (1905) 7 F (HL) 109 at 111, overruling the Court of Session (Lord Young dissenting) on this point.
8 Ie the lack of any sanction such as indictment of perjury against a person defaming another at this stage.
9 The same principle protects statements made in documents which have been the subject of an action of recovery, and so it has been held in England: *Riddick v Thames Board Mills Ltd* [1977] 3 All ER 677.

Witnesses may lose the protection of absolute privilege if they take themselves outwith the role of witness and give expression to thoughts wholly irrelevant to the case they are involved in. In *AB v CD* Lord Justice-Clerk Macdonald limited his proposition to the giving of evidence 'pertinent to the issue'; and Lord Trayner in the same case said:

'I think it is well settled that what is stated by a witness in the witness-box is absolutely privileged, except in the case where the witness gives expression to a calumnious statement altogether irrelevant to the subject-matter of the case in which he is being examined, or to questions put to him'[1].

It should, however, be noted that, as Lord Young pointed out[2], questions allowed by the court are presumed to be proper questions, and therefore answers to questions allowed to be put to a witness ought always to attract absolute privilege. The test therefore seems to be whether the statement made by the witness can properly be described as an answer to a question put to him by counsel or the judge. If it is not, but is rather an entirely extraneous statement, then the privilege is lost and the statement, if defamatory, will be actionable[3].

Jurors

Lord Shand stated in *Williamson v Umphray and Robertson*[4] that 'A judge and jury must have an absolute privilege on grounds of public policy'. The policy Lord Shand had in mind was clearly the encouragement to jurors to perform their function properly and according to the evidence presented to them, and to prevent them from being influenced in their findings by the fear of attracting civil liability. Thus any findings of fact made by the jury relative to the case being tried in front of them are absolutely privileged and cannot found an action for damages. Because the jurors' role in making statements in court is limited, there will be few situations in which it could be argued that they had taken themselves outwith their role and thus had lost their protection[5]. Though there are no decisions on this point, it is scarcely to be doubted that statements made by a juror in the jury room in the course of the jury's deliberations cannot found an action for damages.

Parties

Contrary to the position in England and many other jurisdictions, the law of Scotland does not confer absolute privilege on the parties to the action, but

---

1 (1904) 7 F 72 at 85.
2 (1904) 7 F 72 at 82.
3 See the Lord Ordinary's opinion in *McDonald v McLachlan* 1907 SC 203 (overruled by the First Division on another point).
4 (1890) 17 R 905 at 914.
5 It is not, however, difficult to imagine awkward hypothetical problems: eg is a juror privileged when he shouts out to a witness that his evidence is a pack of lies (ie an allegation of perjury)? Such an allegation may well be pertinent to the case, but it is hardly within the province of the juror to make it publicly.

allows them only qualified privilege, with the result that statements made in judicial proceedings by one or other of the parties thereto can found an action based on verbal injury if there are sufficient averments of malice. The wrong is known, if somewhat misleadingly, as 'judicial slander', and is considered more fully in the following chapter[1].

Statements made in quasi-judicial proceedings and tribunals

Similar to the absolute privilege granted to most participants in the judicial process is the absolute privilege granted to the equivalent participants in quasi-judicial proceedings and tribunals such as public inquiries, courts-martial, church courts[2], arbitrations[3], social security appeal tribunals, employment appeal tribunals, child support appeal tribunals, children's hearings[4] and the like. In England it was decided last century that the privilege of witnesses applies not only to witnesses in courts but to witnesses before an inquiry which, though not a court of justice, nevertheless has 'similar attributes'[5], though what these attributes are cannot be defined with precision. A tribunal acting merely administratively is not one that attracts absolute privilege[6]. The matter was extensively considered in relation to Scots law in the case of *Trapp v Mackie*[7]. In that case the Secretary of State established an inquiry under the Education (Scotland) Act 1946 into the dismissal of a school rector. At the hearing a witness gave evidence which the rector considered to be maliciously false and he raised an action for malicious falsehood against the witness. The defender claimed absolute privilege, and all the judges who heard the case accepted that the defence was applicable in the circumstances. The Inner House found that because of the strong element of public interest involved in the inquiry, together with the fact that the inquiry had statutory authority, the inquiry could be said to have the attributes of a court and therefore absolute privilege applied. In the House of Lords, Lord Diplock said:

'To decide whether a tribunal acts in a manner similar to courts of justice and thus is of such a kind as will attract absolute, as distinct from qualified, privilege for witnesses when

---

1 Below at pp 108–109.
2 *A v B* (1895) 22 R 984.
3 In *Neill v Henderson* (1901) 3 F 387 arbitration proceedings were described by Lord Justice-Clerk Macdonald as 'a practically judicial proceeding' and by Lord Trayner as 'a judicial or quasi-judicial proceeding'. The case was one of qualified privilege only because the alleged slander had been uttered by a party. See also *Slack v Barr* 1918 1 SLT 133, in which Lord Anderson held that absolute privilege attached to a witness at arbitration proceedings. Whether the particular arbitration is suffi-ciently close to a court of law will depend on the factors mentioned in the text above.
4 See Kearney, *Children's Hearings and the Sheriff Court* (1987) p 13.
5 *Royal Aquarium Society v Parkinson* [1892] 1 QB 431.
6 *O'Connor v Waldron* [1935] AC 76. Cf Lord Anderson in *Slack v Barr* 1918 1 SLT 133 at 136, who envisaged a much wider application for absolute privilege. A Scottish court would today follow *O'Connor* rather than *Slack* since the House of Lords, in a Scottish case, has held that the law of Scotland is identical to the law of England on this point: *Trapp v Mackie* 1979 SLT 126.
7 1977 SLT 194 (OH), 1979 SLT 126 (IH and HL).

they give testimony before it, one must consider firstly, under what authority the tribunal acts; secondly the nature of the question into which it is its duty to inquire; thirdly the procedure adopted by it in carrying out the inquiry; and fourthly the legal consequences of the conclusion reached by the tribunal as a result of the inquiry'[1].

Lord Diplock identified ten areas of similarity between the present inquiry and a court of law, and concluded that the present inquiry had sufficiently similar attributes to a court to be granted the same protection. Lord Fraser was careful to point out that 'provided the tribunal is one recognised by law[2], there is no single element the presence or absence of which will be conclusive in showing whether it has attributes sufficiently similar to those of a court of law to create absolute privilege'[3]. The facts considered by both judges to be of particular importance in the present case were the adversarial nature of the proceedings, their constitution by statute, the fact that evidence was given on oath, and the fact that the outcome would have a significant (though not determinative) influence on the ultimate decision of the Secretary of State.

Though the cases have mostly involved witnesses, it is clear that the extent of the protection afforded to quasi-judicial proceedings and tribunals is the same as that afforded to judicial proceedings, ie it covers all the active participants except the parties[4], and it covers the preparations for the proceedings, as well as statements made in the course of the hearing. On the other hand, and perhaps illogically, statements that instigate proceedings seem to be covered by qualified rather than absolute privilege. So a complaint to the police that leads to an investigation and a criminal trial will be covered by qualified privilege, while the preparation of the case and the trial itself will be covered by absolute privilege. And complaints against policemen will be covered by qualified privilege[5] while disciplinary proceedings against the policeman will be absolutely protected[6]. This approach may, however, be inconsistent with that taken by the English Court of Appeal in *Hasselblad (GB) Ltd v Orbison*[7]. In this case, the defendant had written to the European Commission alleging that the plaintiffs had breached Article 85 of the Treaty of Rome. The Court of Appeal accepted that direct evidence given to the Commission during its investigations would be covered by absolute privilege, and, significantly, went on to hold that absolute privilege also covered the letter that instigated the Commission's investigation, if the letter was sufficiently closely connected to that investigation. Now, it is certainly to the public good that complaints to relevant authorities are not discouraged and for this reason there is an argument to the effect that allegations instigating such complaints

1 1979 SLT 126 at 129 and 130.
2 A tribunal does not require a statutory basis to be one 'recognised by law'.
3 1979 SLT 126 at 134.
4 *Neill v Henderson* (1901) 3 F 387.
5 *Anderson v Palombo* 1986 SLT 46; *Fraser v Mirza* 1993 SLT 527.
6 See Styles, 'Two Flaws in the Law of Defamation' 1991 SLT (News) 31.
7 [1985] 1 All ER 173.

should be covered by absolute privilege[1]. However, that argument is not strong. The law should have some way to deal with spurious and malicious complaints, and granting qualified privilege strikes the balance of protecting genuine complaints as well as providing a sanction against spurious complaints. A complaint is not like litigation, for it can be made easily and cheaply and can immediately have deleterious consequences for those complained against. It is submitted that to leave a person without a remedy who has lost financially because of a spurious complaint maliciously made against them would be unjust. Qualified privilege meets the case, and *Hasselblad*, if it reflects the law of Scotland at all, ought to be taken no further than its own facts.

Reports authorised by Parliament

It has been statutorily provided that all reports, papers, votes and proceedings published by or under the authority of either House of Parliament are absolutely privileged, and that any action for defamation thereupon can be brought to an end by the production of a certificate to that effect by the Lord Chancellor or the Lord Keeper of the Great Seal, or of the Speaker of the House of Commons or the Clerk of the House of Commons[2]. This provision overrules the well-known case of *Stockdale v Hansard*[3], in which the plaintiff had successfully sued the parliamentary reporter Hansard for reporting defamatory allegations made in a debate in the House of Commons (which were themselves, of course, absolutely privileged)[4].

Other circumstances of absolute privilege

The Lord Advocate is absolutely privileged in what he does or says in connection with prosecutions on indictment, and this protection extends to procurators fiscal and depute procurators fiscal acting on the authority and instructions of the Lord Advocate[5], and probably to advocates depute also. These officers of the Crown are protected by qualified privilege in other departments of their duties and responsibilities, which involves that both malice and want of probable cause be averred and proved by the pursuer[6]. Other officers of state, like ministers of the Crown and permanent secretaries,

---

1 *Styles*, above.
2 Parliamentary Papers Act 1840.
3 (1839) 9 Ad & E 1.
4 The circumstances indeed were rather more fraught with constitutional difficulty since the House of Commons considered Stockdale's action to be a contempt of Parliament and imprisoned both him and his solicitor as well as apprehending the sheriff who attempted to execute the decree against Hansard. Gilbert and Sullivan could hardly have bettered the comic potential of the situation.
5 *Hester v MacDonald* 1961 SC 370.
6 *McLaren v Procurator Fiscal for the Lothians and Borders* 1992 SLT 844.

are also absolutely privileged, so long as they are acting in the proper exercise of their functions[1]. For reasons of international law, a communication between (high) officials of a foreign embassy has been held to be absolutely privileged[2]. It was held in England that a military officer making an official report concerning a subordinate was absolutely privileged[3], but in the same jurisdiction it was doubted whether absolute privilege attached to communications between senior police officers[4]. The distinction may lie in the fact that there are constitutional implications in questions of army discipline which are lacking in questions of police affairs.

Statute has granted absolute privilege to certain reports and publications connected with the work of the Parliamentary Commissioner (the Ombudsman)[5], the local authority Ombudsman[6], the National Health Service Ombudsman[7], and the Pensions Ombudsman[8]. In England, though not, curiously, in Scotland, the Legal Services Ombudsman is similarly protected[9]. Reports of the Monopolies and Mergers Commission and its Director are also given absolute privilege[10]. All these reports are given absolute privilege in 'the law of defamation' or 'the law relating to defamation', and an interesting question arises whether this covers actions based on verbal injury, or on negligence[11], as well. Other statutes that intend to cover verbal injury do so expressly[12], suggesting that granting absolute privilege in cases of defamation does not carry with it such a grant in cases of verbal injury. Yet qualified privilege is meaningless in cases of verbal injury since its effect is to require proof of malice, which is required in any case of verbal injury; and to deny absolute privilege to such cases is to deny all privilege, which is probably not what the statutes intend. Given this, the courts may well interpret 'the law relating to defamation' to include both defamation and the related actions of malicious falsehood, slander of title and slander of goods. On the other hand, an action raised in negligence, being a quite separate type of claim, cannot be regarded as an 'action relating to defamation' and statutory absolute privilege will not apply.

1 *Chatterton v Secretary of State for India* [1895] 2 QB 189.
2 *Fayad v Al Tajir* [1987] 2 All ER 396.
3 *Dawkins v Paulet* (1869) LR 5 QB 94.
4 *Merricks v Nott-Bower* [1965] 1 All ER 717.
5 Parliamentary Commissioner Act 1967, s 10(5).
6 Local Government (Scotland) Act 1975, s 30.
7 Health Service Commissioners Act 1993, s 14(5).
8 Pension Schemes Act 1993, s 151(7).
9 Courts and Legal Services Act 1990, s 23(5). Cf the Law Reform (Miscellaneous Provisions) (Scotland) Act 1990. Protection may be afforded on the basis that the Scottish Ombudsman's reports are 'reports authorised by Parliament': see above at p 101.
10 Competition Act 1980, s 16.
11 See *Spring v Guardian Assurance plc* [1994] 3 All ER 129.
12 See for example the Legal Aid (Scotland) Act 1986, Sch 2, which excludes legal aid from 'defamation and verbal injury' and the Prescription and Limitation (Scotland) Act 1973, s 18A(4)(a) which defines 'defamation' to include verbal injury.

CHAPTER EIGHT

Qualified privilege

Introduction

'There is no such thing as slander without malice. Slander is a defamatory statement maliciously made to the injury of another. If the statement, however defamatory, is not malicious, it is not slander'[1]. The strict necessity in all cases for malice to exist is often overlooked, because in most cases it is unnecessary to libel malice. The defamatory nature of the communication justifies the court in presuming, rebuttably, the falsity of the statements complained about, and also justifies the court in presuming, irrebuttably, that the statements were made *animus injuriandi*. 'The law holds every man . . . to intend the injury his words or acts are naturally calculated to inflict'[2], and it is no defence for the defender to show that he lacked the intention to injure[3]. However, there are some situations in which the court is not justified in drawing the presumption of malice and in these circumstances the pursuer must, to state a relevant case, plead that the defender acted maliciously in making the statements complained about; and to succeed the pursuer must expressly prove malice on the part of the defender. Such situations are said to give rise to qualified privilege.

The basis of qualified privilege is, like absolute privilege[4], that there are some situations in which it is to the good of society as a whole that a person be free to speak his or her mind, regardless of whether or not this defames another person: the interest of society is put before the interest of the individual[5]. However, qualified privilege is quite different from absolute privilege which, once established, brings the case to an end by rendering the action irrelevant; qualified privilege is a defence which, once established, throws an extra burden onto the pursuer, that is to say the burden of showing that the defamatory statement was made maliciously[6]. In other words, the normal

---

1 *Shaw v Morgan* (1888) 15 R 865 at 870 per Lord Young; see also Lord Justice-Clerk Macdonald in *Nelson v Irving* (1897) 24 R 1054 at 1059.
2 *Drew v Mackenzie & Co* (1862) 24 D 649 at 663 per Lord Deas.
3 See further, Chapter 6.
4 See above at p 91.
5 *Nelson v Irving* (1897) 24 R 1054 at 1060 per Lord Justice-Clerk Macdonald; *Adam v Ward* [1917] AC 309 at 349 per Lord Shaw of Dunfermline; *Perera v Peiris* [1949] AC 1 at 20 per Lord Uthwatt.
6 In *Shaw v Morgan* (1888) 15 R 865 at 870 Lord Young suggested that the effect of a plea of qualified privilege was to throw onto the pursuer the burden of showing not only that the statement was made maliciously but also that the statement was false. This cannot be regarded as good law.

presumption of malice is displaced by an alternative presumption that the statement was made in *bona fide* response to a duty rather than in response to a desire to injure, and as such qualified privilege normally arises in situations in which the defender had a duty to speak his or her mind[1].

It is the circumstances in which a person makes a communication rather than the nature of the communication or the status or situation of the person who makes it that creates the privilege. The maker and the receiver of the communication and their relationship in all the circumstances may converge to create an occasion of qualified privilege. Whether such an occasion exists or not is a matter of law[2], and if it does the issue to be put to the jury must contain, to be relevant, an averment of malice. Whether there is a relevant averment of malice is also for the judge, but whether or not malice is proved is a matter for the jury or fact finder[3]. Occasionally, it will not be possible to say, before the finding of certain facts, whether a situation of privilege exists, and in that case malice will not be put in the issue, but the judge can instruct the jury accordingly if privilege is found in the course of the evidence[4].

Qualified privilege in the related actions

Qualified privilege is a defence that has practical relevance only in cases of defamation and not also in cases of verbal injury, though the circumstances and the policy considerations might well be the same in both. This is because with verbal injury malice has to be averred and proved in any case[5] and the privilege imposing that obligation on a pursuer adds nothing more to such a case. This again distinguishes qualified privilege from absolute privilege for the latter is as applicable to verbal injury as to defamation. It has been held by the House of Lords in an English case[6] that qualified privilege provides no defence in an action for negligence, even in cases in which the action could have been raised as one of defamation. Lord Keith dissented on the ground that the policy considerations that found qualified privilege apply to the situation no matter the nature of the claim made. However, the law is now clearly to the effect that a plea of qualified privilege can be avoided by the pursuer raising the case in negligence rather than in defamation, for malice is not relevant to the law of negligence.

---

1 *Hamilton v Hope* (1827) 5 S 569 at 587 per Lord Pitmilly; *Watson v Burnet* (1864) 24 D 494 at 497 per per Lord Deas.
2 *James v Baird* 1916 SC 510 at 517 per Lord President Strathclyde; *Adam v Ward* [1917] AC 309 at 378 per Lord Dunedin; *Hayford v Forrester-Paton* 1927 SC 740 at 745 per Lord Ordinary Fleming.
3 *Hayford v Forrester-Paton* 1927 SC 740 at 759 per Lord Hunter.
4 See eg *Reid v Coyle* (1892) 19 R 775 (though the finding that there was no averment sufficient to raise privilege was rather surprising in the circumstances – a doctor informed a patient's husband that the midwife was poisoning the patient).
5 See above at pp 34–35.
6 *Spring v Guardian Assurance plc* [1994] 3 All ER 129.

Circumstances of qualified privilege

The categories of absolute privilege, though not closed, are limited and will not readily be expanded[1]; the categories of qualified privilege are more open and more amenable to expansion, but they are also less easy to classify and delineate. The classes usually listed in the textbooks overlap each other to a substantial degree, and have few legal differences between them. With that qualification, the following is suggested, for illustrative purposes only, as a classification of the broad circumstances that attract qualified privilege: (1) statements made in response to a duty, whether legal, moral or social or in the protection of an interest; (2) fair and accurate reports of judicial and parliamentary proceedings; and (3) specified newspaper and broadcast reports given statutory protection by section 7 of and the Schedule to the Defamation Act 1952.

Privilege from duty or interest

Legal, moral or social duty

If a person makes a statement in response to a legal, moral or social duty to speak, then he will be protected in what he says to the extent that he has been motivated by that duty rather than by malice. If the statement is made in such circumstances then the law presumes that he has not been motivated by malice or intent to injure, with the result that the pursuer must aver malice to state a relevant case and to be successful in his action he must prove that it was the defender's malice rather than his duty that motivated him to speak.

It is generally easy for the court to determine whether a legal duty to speak exists or not, and if it does then, almost by definition, the response to that duty is protected by qualified privilege[2]. More difficult are the cases relating to moral or social duties. The concept is clearly a wide one, but it is to be determined on common sense principles. It has been held in England, in a case concerning an allegation of theft made against a servant to his master by a friend with whom the master was staying, that,

'The question of moral or social duty being for the judge, each judge must decide it as best he can for himself. I take moral or social duty to mean a duty recognised by English people of ordinary intelligence and moral principle, but at the same time not a duty enforceable by legal proceedings, whether civil or criminal. My own conviction is that all, or at all events, the great mass of right minded men in the position of the defendant would have considered

---

1 Above at p 91.
2 Some legal duties are statutorily protected by qualified privilege: see eg the Public Bodies (Admission to Meetings) Act 1960, which protects statements made in agendas or other documents which have to be distributed prior to certain meetings open to the public.

it their duty, under the circumstances, to inform Stanley of the suspicion which had fallen on the plaintiff[1].

The final arbiter is the judge, and he will apply an objective standard in determining whether the defender did have a moral or social duty to speak. The duty must be found to exist in fact, and it does not create privilege that the defender believed, mistakenly, that he was under such a duty. This is so however reasonable the belief and notwithstanding the defender's good faith.

The duty may be a public or a private one, that is one for the good of the public at large (eg the reporting of crime or the commenting upon public affairs) or for the good of an individual (eg warning about a person's associates or the passing of references about an employee between past and prospective employers), though the court may well be more inclined to accept that a duty to speak exists in the former case. So for example there is a strong public interest in the efficiency of the police force and complaints to the chief constable about junior officers are clearly privileged[2]. So too with elected bodies like local authorities: councillors have a duty to speak their minds on matters of public interest and council business and they are therefore privileged in doing so[3]. A good example of a social or moral duty is seen in the case of *Hayford v Forrester-Paton*[4]. In that case the pursuer, who carried out missionary work in the Gold Coast, came to Scotland to raise funds for his mission, and he formed a committee in whose name a public appeal for funds was issued. The pursuer visited the defender seeking a subscription, and the defender consulted a friend of his who was also a missionary in the Gold Coast. The friend sent a letter to the defender in highly pejorative terms against the pursuer, and the defender sent a copy of this letter to the committee. The pursuer sued the defender for defamation, but the occasion was held to be privileged and therefore the action was held irrelevant in the absence of averments of malice. Lord Justice-Clerk Alness said,

'I should have thought it plain that the defender had a right, if not indeed a duty, on the occasion in question, to communicate with the committee . . . Had the defender remained silent, then . . . he would have made himself and the committee participators in a fraud upon the public'[5].

Other situations of a social or moral duty include communications between directors of a company concerning the minutes of a board meeting[6]; statements by an employee to an employer concerning a fellow employee[7]; a television broadcast alleging that the pursuer had confessed to being involved in a murder, in the context of a programme designed to cast doubt on the

---

1 *Stuart v Bell* [1891] 2 QB 341 at 350 per Lord Justice Lindley.
2 *Cassidy v Connachie* 1907 SC 1112; *Anderson v Palombo* 1986 SLT 46; *Fraser v Mirza* 1992 SLT 740, 1993 SLT 527.
3 *Shaw v Morgan* (1888) 15 R 865 at 869 per Lord Justice-Clerk Moncreiff. See also *Mutch v Robertson* 1981 SLT 217.
4 1927 SC 740.
5 1927 SC 740 at 753. See also Lord Ormidale at 757.
6 *Chapman v Barber* 1989 SLT 830.
7 *Suzor v Buckingham* 1914 SC 299; *Sutherland v Turner* 1989 GWD 1–36.

conviction for that murder of the late Mr P Meehan[1]; a notice put on a notice board by the dean of a medical school that, in connection with recent thefts, a student had been suspended[2]; an allegation to a shooting tenant that the pursuer was a poacher[3]; statements made in court by counsel on instructions of an agent[4]; and a communication between a university principal and the patron of a chair concerning an appointment to the chair[5].

A social or moral duty to speak does not arise simply because the defender is asked to respond to a question or inquiry. The occasion is privileged only if the person responded to has a legitimate interest and it is this that imposes the duty to respond honestly, if it is decided to respond at all[6]. So while there is no duty on an ex-employer to supply references to a prospective employer, if he decides to do so then the occasion is privileged[7]. Whether a statement is made unsolicited or in response to a question may be relevant to malice[8], which may be more likely to be found if the statement is unsolicited.

Protection of interest

People are entitled to protect their own interests, and in doing so may speak or make communications that are defamatory, so long as their motivation is the protection of their own interests rather than intent to injure the person defamed. Such an interest must exist in fact and a person is not privileged when he defames another, believing that to do so is necessary to protect his own interests when, in fact, he is mistaken in that belief. This ground justifies a person in responding to criticism[9] or in correcting misleading statements. In *Chapman v Barber*[10] draft minutes of a board meeting were sent by one director of a company to another. The latter thought that they misrepresented his position and he accused the former of maliciously misleading the board. The former sued for defamation. The circumstances were held to give rise to qualified privilege, Lord Coulsfield saying,

'it seems to me to be clear that the defender had an interest, in the proper conduct of his own affairs, to correct a misrepresentation of his previous conduct, and that the members of the board of the company had a clear interest to be informed of matters in regard to which, it was alleged, the board was being deliberately misled'[11].

1 *Waddell v BBC* 1973 SLT 246. Mr Meehan was later pardoned for the crime.
2 *Rogers v Orr* 1939 SC 121.
3 *Nelson v Irving* (1897) 24 R 1054.
4 *Bayne v Macgregor* (1862) 24 D 1126.
5 *Auld v Shairp* (1875) 2 R 940.
6 *Notman v Commercial Bank of Scotland* 1938 SC 522.
7 *Farquhar v Neish* (1890) 17 R 716.
8 See below at pp 121–123.
9 *Campbell v Cochrane* (1905) 8 F 205; *Gray v Scottish Society for the Prevention of Cruelty to Animals* (1890) 17 R 1185.
10 1989 SLT 830.
11 1989 SLT 830 at 831.

Likewise a statement by an employer to employees as to why one of their number had been dismissed would be privileged[1], as protecting the employer's interests, and giving guidance to the employees as to what conduct might in the future lead to dismissal.

The most common example of qualified privilege arising from the right to protect one's own interests concerns the litigants in civil proceedings. A statement made by a litigant in the course of litigation may reasonably be presumed to be made with the intent of protecting the litigant's own interests rather than with the intent to injure the subject of the statement, and accordingly to make an action based on such a statement relevant the pursuer would have to aver and prove that intent to injure[2]. The parties are in a very different position from all other active participants in the judicial process, who are protected by absolute privilege[3], since while other participants are there to further the ends of justice and can therefore be presumed to be acting in good faith, the parties themselves are there for their own benefit and a presumption of good faith is far less defensible. The policy of the law indeed points in the opposite direction. If parties were absolutely privileged then they would have nothing to lose (except expenses) by raising frivolous and vexatious litigation, while if parties are not privileged absolutely then they will be inhibited from raising actions for merely malicious motives by the threat of themselves being sued[4]. In *Williamson v Umphray and Robertson*[5], in which both a pleader and a party in a previous action were sued, the case against the pleader was held irrelevant and that against the party relevant so long as sufficient averments of malice were made. Lord President Inglis said:

'[the party] does not come into Court in the discharge of any public function, or for any other purpose than to advance his own private interests. He is entitled to a certain freedom of speech, and may with impunity say many things which may be painful and injurious to his opponent or to third parties. But if he descends to false statements, known to himself to be false, and makes these not for the legitimate purpose of maintaining his suit but for the gratification of his own spite and malice, I am quite unable to see how any useful end of public policy can be promoted by a rule protecting him from an action for defamation. On the contrary, such a rule would in my opinion operate against sound public policy by encouraging evil-minded persons to raise or defend actions in which they are hopelessly wrong on the merits, for the mere purpose of gratifying their own malice, without fear of consequences'[6].

Walker suggests that parties conducting their own cases are in the position of pleaders and can rely on the absolute privilege granted to pleaders[7], but the

---

1 *Bryant v Edgar* 1909 SC 1080; *AB v XY* 1917 SC 15; *Sutherland v British Telecommunications* 1989 SLT 531 at 533 and 534 per Lord Justice-Clerk Ross.
2 An early recognition of this state of the law may be found in Lord Pitmilly's judgment in *Hamilton v Hope* (1827) 5 S 569 at 588.
3 See above at pp 92–99.
4 For another view, see Styles, 'Two Flaws in the Law of Defamation' 1991 SLT (News) 31.
5 (1890) 17 R 905.
6 (1890) 17 R 905 at 911. See also *Anderson & Stirling v Davidson* (1885) 1 Sh Ct Rep 351 (sheriff-substitute Dove Wilson and Sheriff Principal Guthrie Smith).
7 Walker, *Delict* (2nd edn, 1981) p 801. Cooper, *Defamation and Verbal Injury* (2nd edn, 1906) p 139 note 1, raises the issue as a query.

cases he cites are English or Irish, where parties are absolutely privileged in any case. Bearing in mind the reasons for the protection of pleaders and the lack of absolute protection for parties, it is submitted that parties cannot in Scotland clothe themselves with absolute privilege by conducting their own cases. On the other hand, a party who is called as a witness by his opponent is entitled to the absolute protection of any other witness, for the policy considerations are the same in both cases[1]. It is different if a party chooses to give evidence on his own behalf, in which case he remains in the position of a party[2]. An accused in a criminal case is in a very different position from a party in civil proceedings and ought to be regarded as absolutely privileged in what he or she says during the criminal proceedings since the need to encourage free speech in criminal cases is even stronger than in civil cases and accused persons have no control over whether the case is brought or not.

Requirement for reciprocity

It is the occasion rather than the communication that is privileged and an allegation made in circumstances of privilege may not be protected in other circumstances. A minister may well be privileged in telling an applicant for an eldership that he is unsuitable for the post[3] but he would not be privileged if he broadcast this assertion from the pulpit to the whole congregation. And a citizen will be privileged in the information he gives to the police, but will not be privileged in spreading the information to the public at large[4]. It will seldom, if ever, be an occasion for privilege when the defamatory communication is made to the pursuer alone. In *Suzor v Buckingham*[5] a cashier was dismissed from his employment, on an allegation of theft. The manager of the business went to the cashier's house and repeated the allegation. It was held that, the visit being entirely private and personal, there was no occasion for privilege.

The reason why privilege does not exist in these circumstances is that, while the speaker may have a duty or interest to speak, the listener has no interest in being spoken to. Privilege only arises if there is a reciprocity in the sense of the speaker having a duty or interest and the listener having a reciprocal interest[6]. This 'interest' must be more than base curiosity and it must amount to an actual connection with the matter at issue. This reciprocity is sometimes difficult to establish. In *Sutherland v British Telecommunications*[7] an employee who had been dismissed, he thought unfairly, after being accused of theft wrote to a television company hoping that it would make a programme about his case.

1 *Mackintosh v Weir* (1875) 2 R 877.
2 *Watson v Burnet* (1862) 24 D 494.
3 *Murray v Wyllie* 1916 SC 356.
4 *Douglas v Main* (1893) 20 R 793.
5 1914 SC 299.
6 *Adam v Ward* [1917] AC 309 at 334 per Lord Atkinson. See also Lord Ormidale in *Auld v Shairp* (1875) 2 R 940 at 953; *James v Baird* 1916 SC 510 at 517 per Lord President Strathclyde.
7 1989 SLT 531.

The television company wrote to the pursuer's ex-employers for their comments, and they replied that the pursuer had been dismissed for fraud and theft. The pursuer then sued his ex-employers for defamation, and they pleaded privilege. It was not doubted that the defenders had an interest in making the statement, but the pursuer denied that the television company had an interest to receive the statement. It was held that the employee's action in complaining to the television company had conferred an interest and a duty upon the latter to receive any communication from the employers relating to the employee's dismissal, with the result that the occasion of the communication from the employer to the television company was privileged and the case failed for lack of averment of malice. The interest of the defender (the maker of the statement) may be a personal one, or it may be mutual with the recipient, but in both cases the person receiving the communication must not be entirely disinterested. As Lord President Strathclyde put it in *James v Baird*[1], 'a communication honestly made upon any subject in which a person has an interest, social or moral, or in reference to which he has a duty, is privileged if made to a person having a corresponding interest or duty'. Like the interest or duty of the maker, the interest of the recipient must exist in fact and not simply in the belief, however honest or reasonable, of the maker.

'It is not sufficient for the person who makes the communication honestly to believe that a duty or interest exists. The defence of privilege fails even although the person making the communication reasonably believed that the person to whom he made it had some duty or interest in the subject-matter, if none such really existed'[2].

In this case, the president of a district nursing association sent to the parish council a letter stating that a parish medical officer had been negligent in the provision of services to one of his patients. The parish council did not have any responsibility for the (private) patient and the First Division held therefore that it had no interest in receiving the information: consequently it found that there was no privilege notwithstanding the pursuer's belief that the parish council did have an interest in the matter. The House of Lords overruled this[3] on the ground that the parish council had a duty to ensure that proper medical relief was afforded to all old-age pensioners: their interest in receiving the complaint rendered the occasion privileged.

Extent of protection

If the statement complained of goes beyond the legitimate interests of the parties, the privilege may be lost, at least in so far as extraneous matters are concerned. No-one is entitled to use a privileged occasion as 'a cover and cloak for malice'[4]. It has been said that the privilege of a litigant is lost if 'the statement were altogether impertinent to the issue depending between the

---

1 1916 SC 510 at 517.
2 1916 SC 510 at 518.
3 1916 SC(HL) 158.
4 *Hamilton v Hope* (1827) 5 S 569 at 584 per Lord Justice-Clerk Boyle.

parties'[1]. 'The existence of privilege on one matter gives no protection to irrelevant libels introduced into the same communication'[2]. In *Craig v Jex-Blake*[3] privilege was held to be exceeded when, during a discussion on whether female medical students should be admitted to lectures in an infirmary, a member of the court of the infirmary defamed one of the students who had taken part in a protest on the issue. It was held that there was no privilege. The case has since been doubted[4], and in more recent times it has become clear that the courts allow a fairly wide latitude to persons performing duties and protecting interests, and will not be too precise in delineating the limits of privilege. If a statement has a legitimate relationship, however remote, with the duty or interest involved it will be protected, even although it is not, strictly, relevant. The policy of the law in granting qualified privilege is to encourage free speech and this policy would be destroyed if speakers were forced to be on constant guard against straying from the logically, or legally, relevant. Likewise privilege covering a private letter will not be lost because, say, the secretary of the recipient opens it and sees the defamatory material contained therein[5]. This question was discussed in the English House of Lords case of *Adam v Ward*[6]. Here, the plaintiff had made, in the House of Commons, an allegation against an army officer. On the matter being investigated by the Army Council, a press release was issued, exonerating the army officer and making statements about the plaintiff which he considered to be defamatory. The occasion was clearly privileged, but the plaintiff alleged that the press release contained matter not necessary for its purpose, and also that it had been circulated too widely. After examining a number of previous decisions, Lord Atkinson said this[7]:

'These authorities, in my view, clearly establish that a person making a communication on a privileged occasion is not restricted to the use of such language merely as is reasonably necessary to protect the interest or discharge the duty which is the foundation of his privilege; but that, on the contrary, he will be protected, even though his language should be violent or excessively strong, if, having regard to all the circumstances of the case, he might have honestly and on reasonable grounds believed that what he wrote or said was true and necessary for the purpose of his vindication, though in fact it was not so'.

On the allegation that the press release had been circulated too widely, it was held that, given the original complaint had been made in the Imperial Parliament, its rebuttal was not too widely circulated[8]. This case was followed in *Horrocks v Lowe*[9], in which the plaintiff complained of the defendant's strong

---

1 *Mackellar v Duke of Sutherland* (1859) 21 D 222 at 226 per Lord Justice-Clerk Inglis.
2 *Adam v Ward* [1917] AC 309 at 318 per Lord Chancellor Finlay. See also *Rae v McLay* (1852) 14 D 988.
3 (1871) 9 M 973.
4 See particularly the comments of Lord Young (who, in fact, was losing counsel in *Craig*) in *Shaw v Morgan* (1888) 15 R 865 at 871.
5 *Chapman v Barber* 1989 SLT 830 at 831K and L per Lord Coulsfield.
6 [1917] AC 309.
7 [1917] AC 309 at 339.
8 [1917] AC 309 at 319 per Lord Chancellor Finlay, at 324 per Lord Dunedin, at 343 per Lord Atkinson.
9 [1974] 1 All ER 662.

language at a meeting of a town council, of which both parties were members. Lord Diplock said:

'The protection afforded by the privilege would be illusory if it were lost in respect of any defamatory matter which on logical analysis could be shown to be irrelevant to the fulfilment of the duty or the protection of the right on which the privilege was founded. As Lord Dunedin pointed out in *Adam v Ward* the proper rule as respects irrelevant defamatory matter incorporated in a statement made on a privileged occasion is to treat it as one of the factors to be taken into consideration in deciding whether, in all the circumstances, an inference that the defendant was actuated by express malice can properly be drawn'[1].

To lose the benefit of privilege, statements made on a privileged occasion must be shown to have gone 'beyond what was germane and reasonably appropriate to the occasion or [to have been given] a publicity incommensurate with the occasion'[2]. It is likely that privilege will be lost only if it can be shown that the alleged defamatory matter was utterly extraneous to the occasion or of no connection whatsoever thereto.

Reports of parliamentary or judicial proceedings

While the general rule is that a person who repeats or republishes a defamatory statement is as liable as the original utterer[3], this suffers an exception in cases in which the original statement was covered by absolute privilege, such as in parliamentary or judicial proceedings, for it is to the public good that reports of such statements are published. There are some circumstances in which newspaper reports, news broadcasts, or any other form of republication of statements made in such circumstances will be protected by qualified privilege.

Reports of parliamentary proceedings

Reports authorised by either House of Parliament are protected by absolute privilege[4]. This does not extend to reports, such as news items in newspapers or television broadcasts, concerning statements made in Parliament the publication of which is not authorised by either House. However, it has been held in England that the common law grants a qualified privilege to fair and accurate reports of proceedings in Parliament, the onus of proving fairness and accuracy being on the defender[5]. There is no Scottish authority directly in point to support this proposition but in principle privilege ought to be available. It has been suggested that the privilege is absolute rather than qualified[6].

---

1 [1974] 1 All ER 662 at 670.
2 *Adam v Ward* [1917] AC 309 at 321 per Earl Loreburn.
3 Above at pp 29–31.
4 Parliamentary Papers Act 1840; see above at p 101.
5 *Wason v Walter* (1869) LR 4 QB 73; *Perera v Peiris* [1949] AC 1 (PC).
6 *Cooper* p 143.

However, the analogy with reports of judicial proceedings, upon which there is much more authority (discussed below), is so strong that the same level of privilege (that is qualified privilege) ought to be granted to both.

Reports of statements made in a foreign Parliament are probably privileged to the same extent as reports of proceedings of the British Parliament[1]. Reports of any public proceedings of the legislatures of any of Her Majesty's dominions are statutorily granted qualified privilege[2]. The European Parliament is not covered by this provision, but reports of proceedings of that Parliament are almost certainly covered by the same common law principle that covers British parliamentary proceedings, for the same considerations that found the privilege apply to both bodies. Reports of proceedings of international organisations, such as the United Nations, may well be protected to the same extent.

Reports of judicial proceedings

In *Richardson v Wilson*[3] Lord President Inglis said:

'The publication by newspapers' [and the same would apply today in relation to the broadcasting of news bulletins by radio or television] 'of what takes place in Court at the hearing of any cause is undoubtedly lawful; and if it be reported in a fair and faithful manner the publisher is not responsible though the report contains statements or details of evidence affecting the character of either of the parties or of other persons . . . The principle upon which this rule is founded seems to be that, as Courts of justice are open to the public, anything that takes place before a judge or judges is thereby necessarily and legitimately made public, and, being once made legitimately public property, may be republished without inferring any responsibility'.

This has been interpreted by most textbook writers to mean that reports of judicial proceedings are absolutely privileged[4], and this is the position, though statutorily so[5], in England. However the Scottish cases are much more equivocal and indeed suggest, for the most part, that the privilege is merely qualified and that therefore it can be lost if malicious motive in the publication is averred and established.

This can be seen most clearly in the judgment of Lord Kyllachy, speaking in the Inner House in *Wright & Greig v Outram & Co*[6]. He said: 'A person

---

1 Reports of foreign judicial proceedings are subject to the same privilege as reports of Scottish court proceedings: see below at p 116.
2 Defamation Act 1952, s 7 and Schedule: see below at p 117.
3 (1879) 7 R 237 at 241.
4 *Cooper* p 143; Glegg, *Reparation* (4th edn, 1955) pp 177 and 178. Stewart, *Delict* (2nd edn) p 169 says that such reports are 'probably' absolutely privileged. Walker is self-contradictory. In *Delict* p 805 he says, 'In Scotland fair and accurate reports of judicial proceedings apparently enjoy absolute privilege in all cases at common law' and at p 834 he says, 'At common law a fair and accurate report of the proceedings in a public court of justice enjoys qualified privilege'. The fifth and earlier editions of *Scots Law for Journalists* (pp 185–189 in the fifth edition) say that the privilege is absolute, but the sixth edition states that the privilege is qualified: this takes account of the decision in *Cunningham v Scotsman Publications Ltd* 1987 SLT 698 (see below at pp 115–116).
5 Law of Libel Amendment Act 1888, as amended by the Defamation Act 1952.
6 (1890) 17 R 596 at 599, emphasis added.

reporting truly – that is fairly and accurately – the proceedings in public courts of justice is not answerable for the circulation thereby of defamatory matter – *at all events, in the absence of proof of express malice*'. Though the judges in the Inner House in this case are rather less clear, none of them expresses any disagreement with Lord Kyllachy. Lord Justice-Clerk Macdonald says that if the report is fair and accurate then this 'saves them [the newspapers publishing the report] from the presumption that their publication of such a report as this . . . is done to gratify malice', which suggests that fairness and accuracy, once established, puts the onus on the pursuer to prove malice (which is, of course, the effect of qualified privilege).

In *Pope v Outram & Co*[1], a newspaper carried a report of an action for divorce, which had been based on an allegation of adultery. The pursuer sued on the basis that the report repeated the allegation of adultery and it was held that the defender had the onus of proving the fairness and accuracy of the report of the court case and that the pursuer did not have to negative this defence in his averments. The fact that issues were allowed to go to the jury suggests that the defence was not one that rendered the action irrelevant but rather one in which, though relevant, the defence could be negatived by the pursuer's evidence (ie the privilege was qualified rather than absolute). That an averment of malice could have that effect is recognised, though *obiter*, in *Riddell v Clydesdale Horse Society*[2]. This was an action seeking to interdict the publication of the result of a court case and Lord President Inglis said: 'I think it entirely irrelevant to inquire whether there was an *animus injuriandi* in anything that was said or done'. However here he was referring to anything said or done in the court proceedings themselves and he was not suggesting that the absolute privilege attaching to court proceedings attaches also to reports thereof. He continued as follows,

'In the course of legal proceedings many things may be said or done that would have been better left unsaid and undone, but the publication of a fair and accurate report of these things cannot be prevented. If this is a fair and accurate report of proceedings in a court of competent jurisdiction, *reported for a legitimate purpose*, I do not see that it is possible to entertain the application for interdict'[3].

The qualification in italics suggests that the privilege is not absolute and that a different result would be reached if the publication were for an illegitimate purpose, such as, presumably, express intent to injure. The Lord President refused to decide whether an averment of malice would be relevant in an action for damages, but he said '*prima facie* the publication of a fair and accurate report will not [found an action for damages], but if the action is accompanied with averments of malice it may be that it will'. Lord Shand is more explicit that an averment of malice would be necessary to found an action for damages for a fair and accurate report of proceedings in a court of

1 1909 SC 230.
2 (1885) 12 R 976.
3 (1885) 12 R 976 at 983, emphasis added.

justice[1]. On the other hand, in *Thomson v Munro & Jamieson*[2] the privilege was expressly described by Lord Kincairney in the Outer House as absolute.

The most recent judicial discussion of the matter is found in the Outer House decision of *Cunningham v The Scotsman Publications Ltd*[3], in which the primary question was whether the privilege attaching to reports of court proceedings applied to documents founded upon in open court even although not read out. That question was answered affirmatively, but the general rules of law were accepted by counsel and summarised by Lord Clyde as follows:

'In general anyone who repeats a defamatory statement may himself be liable for defamation. But an exception is recognised in relation to the reporting of what took place on a privileged occasion such as the proceedings in a court of law . . . The exception is to the effect that if what is said publicly in open court is reported fairly and accurately, then the person so reporting may be protected by a qualified privilege, that is to say that he is not answerable for the circulation of defamatory material in the absence of proof of express malice'[4].

After an exhaustive examination of the authorities Lord Clyde repeated this proposition: 'The Scottish cases disclose the general principle that a fair and accurate report of what takes place in court may be protected by qualified privilege'[5]. The result of these cases seems to be this. The primary question is whether the report is fair and accurate. If, on the one hand, it is fair and accurate then the report is privileged: privilege being a defence the onus of proof is on the defender to establish fairness and accuracy and the pursuer is not obliged, in stating his case, to aver unfairness and inaccuracy[6]. As, however, the privilege is qualified, a case based on reports of judicial proceedings is relevant only when the pursuer avers malice, and he is entitled to a verdict only if he can prove malice: malice may be proved by showing that, notwithstanding that the report is a fair and accurate account of the proceedings, nevertheless it was published for some illegitimate reason such as deliberately to injure rather than to inform the public. The less contemporary the report the easier this will be to establish[7]. If, on the other hand, the report is not fair and accurate then it is entitled to no privilege and the normal rules apply. The material is presumed false and it is presumed that it was published maliciously: the defender is entitled to prove the truth of the material contained in the report, ie to plead *veritas*, but he cannot plead lack of malice[8]. In summary, a pursuer can seek redress for the publication of a report of court proceedings only if the report is not fair and accurate (ie if it is not privileged) or, if it is fair and accurate (and

---

1 (1885) 12 R 976 at 984.
2 (1900) 8 SLT 255 (p 327).
3 1987 SLT 698.
4 1987 SLT 698 at 699I.
5 1987 SLT 698 at 703G.
6 Subject to what is said below, at p 128.
7 Though it is to be remembered that reports may legitimately be made for reasons other than the newsworthiness of the contents: see for example *Buchan v North British Railway Co* (1894) 21 R 379, in which convictions for travelling on a railway without payment were published as warnings to others.
8 Unless the defence of innocent dissemination applies: see above at pp 87–90.

therefore privileged), when it was published with malicious intent to injure him.

Extent of the defence

The defence of qualified privilege applies to reports of all statements made in open court, as well as reports of documents read out. And it is rather wider than that, covering documents founded upon in open court even although these are not read out[1]. In the case cited Lord Clyde said:

'The test in my view is not what is actually read out – although all that is read out is published – but what is in the presentation of the case intended to be published and so put in the same position as if it had been read out. If it is referred to and founded upon before the court with a view to advancing a submission which is being made, it is to be taken as published'[2].

The privilege may cover information never mentioned in court but which is essential to the case[3]. The privilege does not cover reports of statements made in the open record, nor, probably, the closed record[4]. It will not cover proceedings held in private[5]. Children's hearings, which are not courts and to which the public are not admitted, are in a special position and bona fide journalists cannot be excluded from attending[6], though confidentiality of the child is protected. Clive, Watt & McKain, who otherwise regard the privilege to report court proceedings as absolute, say 'it can hardly be doubted that [reports of children's hearings] would enjoy at least qualified privilege'[7]. The privilege will cover reports of foreign court proceedings, if there is a sufficient public interest in their being published in this country[8].

It is not necessary that the report be full and exhaustive[9], so long as it is a correct and true report and does not, by omitting some important fact, give a false impression[10]. In *Duncan v Associated Scottish Newspapers*[11] a newspaper reported that a pursuer in a previous action for defamation had failed to prove facts and circumstances as a result of which the defender was assoilzied. In reality the pursuer had failed to prove facts and circumstances from which malice might be inferred, which was necessary since the occasion of the alleged defamation was one of qualified privilege. It was held that this report

---

1 *Cunningham v Scotsman Publications Ltd* 1987 SLT 698.
2 1987 SLT 698 at 706C and D.
3 *Harper v Provincial Newspapers Ltd* 1937 SLT 462.
4 *Macleod v Justices of the Peace of Lewis* (1892) 20 R 218 per Lord Young.
5 Cf *Thomson v Munro & Jamieson* (1900) 8 SLT 255 (p 327).
6 Social Work (Scotland) Act 1968, s 35(3). Referrals before the sheriff, which are heard in chambers, are different and journalists can be excluded if the sheriff so decides. If permitted to attend, journalists may report what occurs fairly and accurately and if they do their reports are protected by qualified privilege.
7 Clive, Watt and McKain *Scots Law for Journalists* (5th edn) p 187.
8 *Riddell v Clydesdale Horse Society* (1885) 12 R 976; *Webb v Times Publishing Co* [1960] 2 All ER 789.
9 *Wright & Greig v Outram & Co* (1890) 17 R 596 at 600 per Lord Justice-Clerk Macdonald.
10 *Harper v Provincial Newspapers Ltd* 1937 SLT 462.
11 1929 SC 14.

was fair and accurate, even although it had suggested there was no defamation rather than that there was no malice, and that consequently the report could not found an action for defamation.

Comment upon the report is not privileged[1], though the defence of fair comment, based on very different principles, might be available[2]. The report is to be read as a whole, and if a headline gives a misleading impression then the report as a whole might not be held to be fair and accurate[3].

Statutory privilege of newspapers and broadcasts

In addition to the above common law categories of qualified privilege, it is also statutorily provided that newspapers[4] and broadcasts from a broadcasting station within the United Kingdom[5] are protected by qualified privilege in relation to certain types of reports that they publish. The relevant reports are listed in the Schedule to the Act, which is in two Parts, to which different degrees of privilege attach. Part I reports are protected by qualified privilege in the normal way and are not actionable unless the publication is proved to have been made with malice[6]. Part II reports are treated rather differently, and it is provided that qualified privilege will not apply to the reports listed if it is proved that the defender has been requested by the pursuer to publish in the newspaper in which or in the programme service in which the original publication was made, a reasonable letter or statement by way of explanation or contradiction, and has refused or neglected to do so, or has done so in a manner not adequate or not reasonable having regard to all the circumstances[7]. In these circumstances malice does not have to be proved by the pursuer. 'Newspaper' means any paper containing public news or observations thereon, or consisting wholly or mainly of advertisements, which is printed for sale and is published in the United Kingdom either periodically or in parts or numbers at intervals not exceeding 36 days[8].

The reports listed in Part I of the Schedule, and therefore subject to the normal qualified privilege, are as follows:

(1) A fair and accurate report of any proceedings in public of the legislature of any part of Her Majesty's dominions outside Great Britain.

(2) A fair and accurate report of any proceedings in public of an international organisation of which the United Kingdom or Her Majesty's

---

1 *Drew v Mackenzie & Co* (1862) 24 D 649.
2 See below at Chapter 10.
3 *Clive, Watt and McKain* p 186; Carter-Ruck, *Libel and Slander* (4th edn, 1992) p 141.
4 Defamation Act 1952, s 7.
5 Ibid, s 9(2).
6 Ibid, s 7(1).
7 Ibid, s 7(2), as amended by the Cable and Broadcasting Act 1984, s 28, and the Broadcasting Act 1990, s 166(3). See *Khan v Ahmed* [1957] 2 All ER 385.
8 Defamation Act 1952, s 7(5).

government in the United Kingdom is a member, or of any international conference to which that government sends a representative.

(3) A fair and accurate report of any proceedings in public of an international court.

(4) A fair and accurate report of any proceedings before a court exercising jurisdiction throughout any part of Her Majesty's dominions outwith the United Kingdom or of any proceedings before a court-martial held outside the United Kingdom under the Naval Discipline Act 1957, the Army Act 1955, or the Air Force Act 1955.

(5) A fair and accurate report of any proceedings in public of a body or person appointed to hold a public inquiry by the government or legislature of any part of Her Majesty's dominions outside the United Kingdom.

(6) A fair and accurate copy of or extract from any register kept in pursuance of any Act of Parliament which is open to inspection by the public, or of any other document which is required by the law of any part of the United Kingdom to be open to inspection by the public.

(7) A notice or advertisement published by or on the authority of any court within the United Kingdom or any judge or officer of such a court.

The reports listed in Part II of the Schedule, and which are therefore privileged only when an explanation or contradiction has not been refused by the publisher, are as follows:

(8) A fair and accurate report of the findings or decision of any of the following associations, or of any committee or governing body thereof, that is to say –

  (a) an association formed in the United Kingdom for the purpose of promoting or encouraging the exercise of or interest in any art, science, religion or learning, and empowered by its constitution to exercise control over or adjudicate upon matters of interest or concern to the association, or the actions or conduct of any persons subject to such control or adjudication;

  (b) an association formed in the United Kingdom for the purpose of promoting or safeguarding the interests of any trade, business, industry or profession, or of the persons carrying on or engaged in any trade, business, industry or profession, and empowered by its constitution to exercise control over or adjudicate upon matters connected with the trade, business, industry or profession, or the actions or conduct of those persons;

  (c) an association formed in the United Kingdom for the purpose of promoting or safeguarding the interests of any game, sport or pastime to the playing or exercise of which members of the public are invited or admitted, and empowered by its constitution to exercise control over or adjudicate upon persons connected with or taking part in the game, sport or pastime,

being a finding or decision relating to a person who is a member of or is subject by virtue of any contract to the control of the association.

(9) A fair and accurate report of the proceedings of any public meeting held in the United Kingdom, that is to say, a meeting bona fide and lawfully held for a lawful purpose and for the furtherance or discussion of any matter of public concern, whether the admission to the meeting is general or restricted.

(10) A fair and accurate report of the proceedings at any meeting or sitting in any part of the United Kingdom of
   (a) any local authority[1] or committee of a local authority or local authorities;
   (b) any justice or justices of the peace acting otherwise than as a court exercising judicial authority;
   (c) any commission, tribunal, committee or person appointed for the purposes of any inquiry by Act of Parliament, by Her Majesty or by a Minister of the Crown;
   (d) any person appointed by a local authority to hold a local inquiry in pursuance of any Act of Parliament;
   (e) any other tribunal, board, committee, or body constituted by or under, and exercising functions under, an Act of Parliament,
   not being a meeting or sitting admission to which is denied to representatives of newspapers and other members of the public.

(11) A fair and accurate report of the proceedings at a general meeting of any company or association constituted, registered or certified by or under any Act of Parliament or incorporated by Royal Charter, not being a private company within the meaning of the Companies Act 1948.

(12) A copy or fair and accurate report or summary of any notice, or other matter issued for the information of the public by or on behalf of any government department, officer of state, local authority, or chief officer of police[2].

Notwithstanding that a report comes within the terms of one of the above paragraphs, it will be denied privilege if (1) the publication is prohibited by law, or (2) the matter is not of public concern and the publication is not for the public benefit[3]. It is a matter for the judge to determine under the first ground whether the publication is prohibited by law; but under the second ground it is a question of fact for the jury or fact finder to decide whether the defender has shown that the publication dealt with a matter of public concern or public benefit[4].

---

1 Defined in para 13 of the Schedule (as amended).
2 In *Blackshaw v Lord* [1983] 2 All ER 311 it was held that not every statement of fact made by a government official in the course of his employment was covered by this provision. In particular, a statement made by a government press officer in response to a journalist's question was not covered because the word 'issued' suggested that the initiative must come from the government department and in the present case it could not be said that the statement was a formal statement released to the press on the initiative of the government department concerned.
3 Defamation Act 1952, s 7(3). This was a rule of English common law: *Pankhurst v Sowler* (1887) 3 TLR 193.
4 *Kingshot v Associated Kent Newspapers Ltd* [1991] 2 All ER 99.

Malice

As we have already seen, the effect of a successful plea of qualified privilege by the defender is not to bring the case to an immediate end, but rather to shift the burden of proof back to the pursuer to prove that the communication complained about had been made maliciously. While malice is normally taken to mean intent to injure, or *animus injuriandi*, it is in fact far wider than that. Malice is:

'such animosity, ill-temper, love of scandal and gossip, or mere rash and thoughtless loquacity, as induces a man to forget what is due to the fair fame of his neighbour; and to use words by which his feelings and reputation may be injured'[1].

The defence of qualified privilege attaches to circumstances in which the court may fairly presume that the defender was speaking out of duty or in defence of an interest, and malice is in essence the reverse of this. So malice is proved by showing that the defender was motivated not by duty or interest, but by either intent to injure or any other intention that is not referable to the fulfilment of the duty or the protection of the interest. Malice does not in this context connote bad intent, but more lack of good intent. Lord Gifford said that in situations of privilege the defender,

'must be protected in an action for slander, unless it can be established that he acted maliciously and *in mala fide*, not in the honest discharge of what he believed to be his duty, but under the influence of personal and unjustifiable motives . . . I think malice . . . has this wide meaning, that it includes every motive except the honest and pure wish fairly and sincerely to discharge a duty'[2].

In other words, the important issue in establishing malice in the face of the defence of qualified privilege is more misuse of an occasion than intent to injure. As Lord Diplock said in *Horrocks v Lowe*[3],

'to destroy the privilege the desire to injure must be the dominant motive for the defamatory publication; knowledge that it will have that effect is not enough if the defendant is nevertheless acting in accordance with a sense of duty or in *bona fide* protection of his own legitimate interests'.

Recklessness as to whether the statement will injure or not can in some circumstances amount to malice, so long as the pursuer can show that the defender had not been motivated by duty or interest[4]. In the words of Lord Deas:

---

1 *Adam v Allan* (1841) 3 D 1058 at 1073 per Lord Jeffrey (Lords Fullerton and Cuninghame concurring).
2 *Auld v Shairp* (1875) 2 R 940 at 958.
3 [1974] 1 All ER 662 at 662.
4 *Finburgh v Moss' Empires Ltd* (1908) 16 SLT 61 (p116) at 120 per Lord Ardwell; *Hayford v Forrester-Paton* 1927 SC 740 at 754 per Lord Justice-Clerk Alness; *Horrocks v Lowe* [1974] 1 All ER 662 at 669 per Lord Diplock.

'Malice in the legal sense does not necessarily imply actual personal malice, but only such recklessness or gross carelessness and (it may be) ignorance as the law holds to be utterly inexcusable, and consequently applies thereto the maxim *culpa lata equiparatur dolo*'[1].

Proof of malice

Notwithstanding the wide meaning to be given to 'malice', it is notoriously difficult for pursuers to establish and due to inability or failure to plead malice many cases come to an end when the defender establishes that the situation discloses qualified privilege. While the meaning of words used is determined by an objective test by reference to their ordinary and natural meaning[2], the question whether the words were used maliciously depends upon the subjective state of mind of the maker of the statement at the time it was made[3]. Malice, being a state of mind, can only ever be inferred from the facts and circumstances of the case. Sometimes, though rarely, malice can be inferred from the strength of the language used, or the circumstances in which the communication is made[4], and in these cases it may be sufficient for the pursuer to make a general averment of malice. In such a case,

'there must be something so extreme in the words used as to rebut the presumption of innocence and to afford evidence that there was a wrong, and an indirect, motive prompting the publication'[5].

'If . . . malice is to be inferred from the form of language used on the occasions complained of, from its intensity, its violence, virulence or recklessness, then the language itself is the fact and circumstance from which malice must be inferred'[6].

The defender must always, however, be made aware of the case he is being asked to answer, and this will require in most cases that facts and circumstances from which the court may infer malice must be averred. A general averment of malice will be sufficient only in those rare cases when malice can be inferred from the defamatory statement itself, otherwise facts and circumstances must be specified. 'The degree and character of the specification which is required for the purpose of relevancy must vary with the circumstances of each case, but the standard must always be such as to make the charge of malice *prima facie* reasonable'[7]. The more clearly the case is one of privilege, the stronger the facts and circumstances must be to show malice[8].

---

1 In *Urquart v Grigor* (1864) 3 M 283 at 288. Recklessness as to whether the statement is true or not will have the same effect: *McLean v Adam* (1888) 16 R 175 at 182 per Lord Lee. See also *Ritchie & Son v Barton* (1883) 10 R 813.
2 Above at pp 8–17.
3 *Fraser v Mirza* 1993 SLT 527.
4 *Lyal v Henderson* 1916 SC(HL) 167 at 183 per Lord Kinnear; *Adam v Ward* [1917] AC 309 at 318 per Lord Chancellor Finlay.
5 *Lyal v Henderson* 1916 SC(HL) 167 at 175 per Lord Chancellor Buckmaster.
6 *Suzor v McLachlan* 1914 SC 306 at 313 per Lord President Strathclyde. See also *Anderson v Palombo* 1986 SLT 46 at 48G per Lord McDonald.
7 *Elder v Gillespie* 1923 SLT 32 at 34 per Lord Morison.
8 See *Cooper* pp 198–202.

The circumstances may be intrinsic or extrinsic. Intrinsic circumstances,

'mean the whole circumstances surrounding and directly leading up to the utterance of the slander, including the grossness of the charge, its undue publicity, its unnecessary repetition, the impropriety of the language, the failure to make previous inquiries when inquiries would have been natural, and the absence of reasonable grounds for making such an accusation'[1].

In *Lyal v Henderson*[2] Lord Kinnear said that malice may sometimes be proved by showing that there was something in the method of communication, or in the terms of the communication itself, which necessarily inferred ill-will or a dishonest use of a privileged occasion. So to give the communication much wider publicity than it ought to have, or to use extremely vituperative language, may well infer malice. Lord Buckmaster in the same case said[3]:

'If once the privilege be established, unless there be extrinsic evidence of malice, there must be something so extreme in the words used as to rebut the presumption of innocence and to afford evidence that there was a wrong, and an indirect, motive prompting the publication'.

Extrinsic evidence of malice might take the form of events showing antecedent ill-will on the part of the defender, the repetition of the slander[4], previous unfounded allegations of the same nature[5], an unexplained contradiction in references concerning the same person[6], or want of probable cause in making the allegation[7]. However, the best evidence of malice, and the most conclusive, is proof that the defender knew the statement to be false[8]. So in *McTernan v Bennett*[9] it was a sufficient averment of malice on the part of two policemen who had accused the pursuer of assaulting them that they knew him and therefore knew the allegation to be false[10]. As Lord Diplock put it in *Horrocks v Lowe*[11]:

'If it be proved that he did not believe that what he published was true this is generally conclusive evidence of express malice, for no sense of duty or desire to protect his own legitimate interests can justify a man in telling deliberate and injurious falsehoods about another, save in the exceptional case where a person may be under a duty to pass on, without endorsing, defamatory reports made by some other person'[12].

However, conversely, if it is found that the defender truly believed what he said, then while this may sometimes be evidence of a lack of malice it will not be conclusive, for a person can as easily use the truth for a bad motive as a good

1 *Suzor v McLachlan* 1914 SC 306 at 316 per Lord Skerrington.
2 1916 SC(HL) 167 at 183.
3 1916 SC(HL) 167 at 175.
4 *Elder v Gillespie* 1923 SLT 32; *Douglas v Main* (1893) 20 R 793.
5 *Anderson v Palombo* 1986 SLT 46.
6 *Macdonald v McColl* (1901) 3 F 1082. Cf *Auld v Shairp* (1875) 2 R 940.
7 See below at p 124.
8 *Mitchell v Smith* 1919 SC 664 at 674 per Lord Sands; *Hayford v Forrester-Paton* 1927 SC 740 at 754 per Lord Justice-Clerk Alness; *Fraser v Mirza* 1992 SLT 740 at 748E per Lord Murray.
9 (1898) 1 F 333.
10 After conviction for the assault the pursuer was liberated when his alibi came to light.
11 [1974] 1 All ER 662 at 669.
12 Cf Lord Young in *McLean v Adam* (1888) 16 R 175 at 181: 'No occasion will justify wilful falsehood spoken to a neighbour's prejudice'.

one, and on a privileged occasion may use what he believes to be the truth for a malicious motive rather than for the fulfilment of a duty[1].

It is not in itself proof of malice that the statement is defamatory[2] (unless, perhaps, the allegation is so gross or outrageous that a presumption of malice can reasonably be drawn). Likewise, the fact that the defender is guilty of an error of judgment in making the statement complained of is not in itself evidence of malice[3], nor is acting on insufficient inquiry[4], or pleading *veritas* in the action[5]. A difference of opinion, coupled with a fair, though strong, criticism of an opponent's position is no evidence of personal rancour or ill-will[6]. Nor is it conclusive of malice that the statement has gone beyond what is strictly necessary for the privileged occasion, and privilege is not lost just because the person speaks further than is necessary for the protection of his interest or performance of his duty[7]:

'To submit the language used on privileged occasions to a strict scrutiny and to hold all excess beyond the actual exigencies of the occasion to be evidence of express malice, would greatly limit, if not altogether defeat, the protection which the law gives to statements so made'[8].

The incorporation of irrelevant defamatory matter in a statement made on a privileged occasion is to be treated as only one of the factors to be taken into account in determining whether, in all the circumstances, an inference of malice can properly be drawn[9].

Malice is a personal attribute, with the result that a master is not liable for the malice of his servant unless it is shown that in acting maliciously the agent was carrying out the wishes of the principal[10], and an agent is not liable for the malice of his principal[11]. A newspaper cannot plead qualified privilege when it publishes a letter but refuses to disclose the name of the writer, because that refusal denies the pursuer the chance to prove malice on the part of the writer: in these circumstances it would be appropriate to presume malice on the part of the newspaper[12].

Want of probable cause

In actions for abuse of process, or against public officials for abuse of office, it is necessary for the pursuer to aver and prove not only malice but also want of probable cause. For example an action for wrongful arrest or wrongful

---

1 *Horrocks v Lowe* [1974] 1 All ER 662 at 666 and 667 per Viscount Dilhorne, and at 670 per Lord Diplock.
2 *Adam v Ward* [1917] AC 309 at 330 per Lord Dunedin.
3 *AB v XY* 1917 SC 15; *Hayford v Forrester-Paton* 1927 SC 740 at 756.
4 *Suzor v Buckingham* 1914 SC 299; *Murray v Wyllie* 1916 SC 556; *Hayford* 1927 SC 740.
5 *Hayford* 1927 SC 740.
6 *Lyal v Henderson* 1916 SC(HL) 167 at 176 per Lord Chancellor Buckmaster.
7 *Adam v Ward* [1917] AC 309; *Lyal v Henderson* 1916 SC(HL) 167; *Horrocks v Lowe* [1974] 1 All ER 662; see above at pp 110–112.
8 *Lyal v Henderson* 1916 SC (HL) 167 at 175 per Lord Chancellor Buckmaster.
9 *Adam v Ward* [1917] AC 309 at 328–329 per Lord Dunedin. See also Earl Loreburn at 321. For earlier, more equivocal, authority, see *Cooper* p 206.
10 *Mackellar v Duke of Sutherland* (1862) 24 D 1124.
11 *Adam v Ward* [1917] AC 309; *Egger v Viscount Chelmsford* [1964] 3 All ER 406.
12 *Brims v Reid & Sons* (1885) 12 R 1016.

prosecution will not be available against, say, the Lord Advocate or a procurator fiscal unless the defender has acted maliciously and without good or probable cause[1]. Such actions often contain defamatory implications and sometimes the alleged defamation is the most significant element of the claim: a wrongful arrest amounts to an innuendo of criminal behaviour[2]. Though in a claim for wrongful arrest the pursuer will be obliged to aver both malice and want of probable cause, it is not to be supposed that want of probable cause is an element in an action for defamation[3]. Lord Justice-Clerk Aitchison in *Notman v Commercial Bank of Scotland*[4], delivering the judgment of a Court of Seven Judges, listed the classes of actions in which want of probable cause must be put in issue: '(1) actions for abuse of process; (2) actions for malicious prosecution or denunciation; and (3) actions directed against public officers for words spoken or written, or acts done, in the discharge of their public duties'. The real cause of complaint in the third class is not the defamation but the abuse of process or the abuse of office and except in this type of case qualified privilege obliges the pursuer to aver and prove only malice and not also want of probable cause. In *Fraser v Mirza*[5] a pursuer who had been prosecuted (unsuccessfully) for reset wrote to the Chief Constable complaining about the officers who had investigated the case and charged him. He alleged that the officers were motivated by racism and other bad motives. Earlier cases[6] had suggested that the effect of privilege in cases of complaints about the police to senior officers was to require the pursuer to establish both malice and want of probable cause in making the complaint, but in the present case Lord Justice-Clerk Ross founded on *Notman* and held that such complaints do not come within the three classes specified by Lord Justice-Clerk Aitchison, and accordingly want of probable cause did not have to be averred and proved by the pursuer[7].

Though it does not need to be averred and proved as a separate element of the claim, want of probable cause is not entirely irrelevant in ordinary actions for defamation, for it may amount to good evidence of malice, which of course is what does have to be proved. This was recognised by Lord Justice-Clerk Aitchison in *Notman*, when he said, '"want of probable cause" has no place in issues of defamation. But this does not mean that in actions of defamation a defender may not prove probable cause as negativing or tending to negative malice, or that a pursuer may not prove want of probable cause as showing or tending to show malice'[8].

1 *Hester v MacDonald* 1961 SC 370.
2 See above at p 14.
3 *Tytler v Macintosh* (1823) 3 Mur 236 at 244 per Lord Chief Commissioner Adam (quoted by Lord Justice-Clerk Aitchison in *Notman v Commercial Bank of Scotland* 1938 SC 522 at 530); *Webster v Paterson & Sons* 1910 1 SLT 176 per Lord Dunedin (a case of judicial slander). Any authority to the contrary, such as the statements of Lord President Strathclyde and Lord Skerrington in *Murray v Wyllie* 1916 SC 356 must now be taken to be overruled by *Notman*.
4 1938 SC 522 at 531.
5 1992 SLT 740.
6 *Cassidy v Connachie* 1907 SC 1112; *Anderson v Palombo* 1986 SLT 46.
7 This part of the judgment was not challenged when the case went to the House of Lords: 1993 SLT 527.
8 1938 SC 522 at 535. See also *Cooper* p 205.

CHAPTER NINE

Veritas, or the defence of truth

Introduction

In early cases some confusion is evident as to whether or not the maxim *veritas convicii non excusat* (literally, 'the truth of the defamation does not excuse') represented the law of Scotland. This confusion is frequently explained by the embarrassment caused by the Court of Session having assumed a jurisdiction over a matter which was at least partly criminal[1], and it was often asserted that while the maxim applied in the criminal action it did not apply in the civil action, which is, of course, all that is left in the law of Scotland today[2]. The distinction, at least in the older law, is easy to understand. The criminal action was designed to punish the *animus injuriandi*, which might exist irrespective of the truth or falsehood of the allegation made. With the civil action however the primary purpose of the action was to restore the *fama* of the person who had been defamed, and to achieve this the original remedy was palinode, that is a public retraction of the words complained of by an acceptance that they were untrue: the courts could not order the defender to state as untrue that which was true and the truth of the statement therefore amounted, if for reasons of procedure rather than of principle, to a complete defence. The distinction became less easy to maintain when damages took over from palinode as the primary civil remedy. It was possible to argue that damages to compensate for loss of character would not be available when no character legally worth protecting was lost (ie that when the allegations were true there was *damnum absque injuria*)[3], but many judges maintained a need to 'punish' with civil damages all allegations made *animo injuriandi*, whether true or not. There are therefore conflicting decisions in the period before 1816, some holding that the *veritas convicii* was a complete defence[4], and some in which the maxim *veritas convicii non excusat* was upheld[5]. In *Dyce v Kerr*[6] the Second Division was equally divided on the question of whether the maxim *veritas*

---

1 See Lord Justice-Clerk Inglis in *Mackellar v Duke of Sutherland* (1859) 21 D 222 at 228 – 229. On the criminal antecedents to the action for defamation, see above at pp 1–4.
2 See particularly Lord Auchinleck in *Hamilton v Rutherford* (1771) Hailes 441, Mor 13924. See also the pleadings for the defender in *Chalmers v Douglas* (1785) Mor 13939.
3 See for example the third plea in law of the defender in *Hamilton v Rutherford* (1771) Mor 13924 at 13931.
4 See eg *Gordon v Pain* (1738) Mor 6080; *Chalmers v Douglas* (1785) Mor 13939; *Macdonald v Macdonald* 2 June 1813, FC.
5 See eg *Hamilton v Rutherford* (1771) Hailes 441, Mor 13924.
6 9 July 1816, FC.

convicii non excusat did or did not represent the law of Scotland, and the Lord Ordinary in the case, Lord Pitmilly, was brought in to decide the issue. Holding to his judgment at first instance, he held that in some cases *veritas* would entirely exculpate: these were cases in which the defamation had arisen from a public motive[1]. In other cases *veritas* would either exculpate or mitigate the damages due, and in yet other cases *veritas* would merely mitigate the damages due, and proof of the truth could have only that effect. If any consistency can be gleaned from these early cases, it is to the effect that truth was no defence if there was *animus injuriandi*, in the sense of malice which requires to be proved if the defamation occurred on a privileged occasion. The later development of privilege as a defence and the bringing in of *animus injuriandi* in that way takes away, it is submitted, the authority of the early cases which accepted the maxim *veritas convicii non excusat*. They are, in any case, clearly superseded by later decisions.

The idea that the maxim applied to criminal defamation died, of course, with the death of the criminal aspect of defamation. The Jury Court, which took over actions of defamation, allowed the Lords Commissioners the opportunity to establish the principle that the defender is entitled to have a counter-issue put to the jury that the libel averred by the pursuer is in its essential points true, this providing a 'justification' (the term still used in English law for the defence) for the making of the statements complained about. So in *Scott v McGavin*[2] a Roman Catholic priest claimed damages for an allegation that he extorted money from the poor, and the defenders were held entitled to prove instances of extortion in justification of their claims: the Lord Chief Commissioner said that this was the first case in which the *veritas convicii* had been pleaded as a defence[3]. *Veritas* was by 1830[4] at the latest seen as an absolute defence to the civil action, on the principle that defamation is the taking away of that repute to which a person is entitled: if a person is not entitled to the reputation he has (because it is based on false knowledge), he cannot complain when it is damaged by the publication of the truth.

There has been no case since the establishment of the Jury Court in which it is held that *veritas* is not a complete defence to an action of defamation[5]. The matter has been unquestioned since the decision in *Mackellar v Duke of Sutherland*[6] in which Lord Justice-Clerk Inglis expressed surprise and regret that the question should have been raised at all, considering that it had been

---

1 *Veritas* as a defence is thus seen at this stage almost as qualified privilege is understood by the later law.
2 (1821) 2 Mur 484.
3 See also *Hamilton v Hope* (1827) 4 Mur 222.
4 The date on which the Jury Court was absorbed into the Court of Session: Court of Session Act 1830.
5 The Lord Ordinary expressed the opinion *obiter* in *Friend v Skelton* (1855) 17 D 548 at 551 that 'truth is not always a justification of libel', but the sort of 'libel' he was talking about was that which would now be regarded as an example of verbal injury, to which different considerations apply: see above at pp 40–41.
6 (1859) 21 D 222. See also *McNeill v Rorison* (1847) 10 D 15 in which truth was held to be a justification rather than a mitigation.

the practice for 40 years past to regard the *veritas convicii* as a good and complete defence. This position is unchallengeable today.

Veritas and the related actions

There has never been any judicial doubt but that the truth of the allegation absolutely prevents an action raised in verbal injury rather than in defamation, and all the cases of verbal injury specify that falsity is a requirement for actionability[1]. The difference with defamation is that *veritas* is a defence for the defender to establish in that action, while in verbal injury falsity is part of the definition of the wrong[2] and is for the pursuer to prove. Walker has argued that in relation to the public hatred cases falsity is not required to be shown[3] but, as explained above[4], this view is mistaken.

If the case is raised in negligence rather than in defamation or verbal injury, the question arises as to whether the defence of truth is as irrelevant as the defence of qualified privilege. In *Spring v Guardian Assurance plc*[5] the judges who addressed the issue accepted unequivocally but without explanation the proposition that an action for negligence could not be founded on a true statement. *Hedley Byrne v Heller & Partners*[6], upon which *Spring* was based, was, of course, concerned with negligent *mis*statements but the assumption that actionability is limited to misstatements requires justification and explanation. It would seem improbable that truth is to be regarded as a defence for the defender to prove, as in defamation, and it is more likely that falsity is part of the wrong of negligence, to be proved by the pursuer. Falsity may be required on the basis that one cannot be negligent in telling the truth (or, to put it another way, that one never has a duty to avoid telling the truth), but this reasoning is not persuasive in any legal system that permits actions for breach of confidence[7]. A more likely basis for the requirement of falsity in actions based on negligent misstatements is to say that telling the truth cannot cause any legally recognised loss: this approach consists with the view taken in the law of defamation itself[8]. The rest of this chapter will be limited to *veritas* as a defence to an action for defamation.

---

1 See above at pp 34–35, 40–41.
2 Cf in England, where the term used is malicious falsehood.
3 *Delict* (2nd edn, 1981) pp 736–740.
4 Above at pp 40–41.
5 [1994] 3 All ER 129.
6 [1964] AC 465.
7 See *AB v CD* (1851) 14 D 177; *AB v CD* (1904) 7 F 72.
8 In *Balfour v Attorney General* [1991] 1 NZLR 519 the plaintiff sought damages for a statement in his employment file that he was a 'long standing and blatant homosexual'. The statement was apparently true – if expressed somewhat pejoratively – but the case failed due to the plaintiff's inability to show that the statement rather than the fact itself had caused the loss he was suing for, that is diminution of promotion prospects.

The place of *veritas* today

A person is only entitled to that reputation which he or she deserves and the law will not protect an ill-founded reputation. A person who has derogatory or demeaning characteristics is not entitled, in our system, to have them hidden, or to prevent their publication. There is no right of privacy in this sense and the law still holds to the view expressed in 1826 that, 'the grand preservation of morals is the censorship of public opinion, and that opinion can never operate wholesomely, if people are to be restrained from telling the truth of each other'[1]. A pursuer seeking civil damages must come to the court with 'clean hands'. It follows that a statement is actionable as being defamatory only if it alleges something that is false. A statement that is true is not defamatory because it is not able to harm a justified repute and though it may of course harm an unjustified repute that is regarded by the law as *damnum absque injuria*[2]. It is therefore part of the definition of defamation that the statement complained of is false. If it appears on the record that the facts communicated are true the pursuer's claim will be held irrelevant[3]. Further, the pursuer must state in his issue that the imputation is false, both in order to indicate to the jury his assertion of innocence and also because, though presumed, falsity is part of the definition of the wrong[4].

However, just as the criminal law presumes the innocence of the accused, so the law of defamation presumes the freedom from derogatory attributes of the pursuer. The result of this is that, though falsity is part of the definition of the wrong, it is presumed by the law from the defamatory nature of the communication that it is false, with the result that *veritas* is a defence which the defender has the onus of proving. Truth is presumed just as malice is presumed, but, unlike with malice, it is open to the defender to disprove truth and so defeat the pursuer's whole case.

In the older cases the defence of *veritas* was referred to as 'justification', and this is still the term used in England today: it is 'justifiable' to publish abroad imputations about an individual simply because they are true. This is not an appropriate way to express the matter today and a better analysis would be to regard the truth of the statement as one that takes away the defamatory nature of, rather than one that justifies or makes acceptable, the publication of hurtful or harmful material. In addition, truth takes away the loss, because

---

1 Brodie, Commentaries on Stair's *Institutions* (1826) I, 4, 4.
2 Green's *Encyclopaedia of Scots Law* vol 5, para 1128; *Walker* p 794.
3 So in *Carson v White* 1919 2 SLT 215, in which the allegation was one of insolvency the pursuer did not deny that he was notour bankrupt in his answers to the defender's statement of facts which contained this allegation. Lord Anderson, taking this as an admission of notour bankruptcy, held that this meant that the truth of the defamatory statement appeared on the record and that the action was therefore irrelevant: a counter-issue was not needed to reach that result since relevancy was a matter for the judge not the jury. See also *Campbell v Fergusson* (1882) 9 R 467.
4 So the action was dismissed in *Buchan v North British Railway Co* (1894) 21 R 379 when the pursuer sued the defenders who had posted his name on a list of passengers convicted of travelling without paying, since the pursuer had alleged in his issue only that the statement had been made maliciously, not that it was false.

the destruction of an unjustified reputation is seen as no loss in law. The terminology of justification may well be appropriate as a defence to criminal libel, but not, it is submitted, to the purely civil wrong that defamation is today in Scotland. That '*veritas*' in Scotland is the equivalent of 'justification' in England now has statutory sanction[1].

Facts to be proved

What facts require to be proved in order to establish *veritas* will depend upon the nature of the defamatory allegation and what is generally understood by the words used. The idea contained in the allegation is what has to be established as fact. Certain accusations can be proved true by showing a single disreputable act; others can be proved true only by showing a series of acts, or an inclination to act, or an aspect of character. To claim that a man is a liar suggests a habit of dishonesty and it is not therefore justified by showing a single instance of dishonesty. The same can be said for an allegation that the pursuer is a drunkard[2]. On the other hand, 'by common usage a person who has committed one murder is called a murderer and such an appellation would accordingly be justifiable by proof of one instance'[3]. Allegations that go to character rather than acts require proof of habit in order to establish the defence of *veritas*. Such cases require a number of instances to be proved which illustrate the pursuer's character, rather than only one instance[4]. As Lord Murray put it in *Brownlie v Thomson*[5], 'it is not a justification for calling a man an immoral character, to say that at some previous time he had been guilty of immoral acts'. The instant case was an action for damages by a pursuer complaining of being called a poacher in 1857 and the Second Division refused the defender a counter issue to the effect that the pursuer had committed an act of poaching in 1851 and had been frequently seen poaching between then and 1856. 'Poacher', at least at that time, did not suggest a character attribute from which the pursuer could not shake free but suggested rather that the pursuer was currently (and temporarily) guilty of the act of poaching[6]. More specific allegations of continuing acts cannot be met with a plea of *veritas* which seeks to prove only one or more actions in the past. So, an allegation that a person kept a mistress was not justified by proving that he had had adulterous intercourse with a woman on two previous occasions[7].

1 Defamation Act 1952, s 5, as applied to Scotland by s 14(d); Rehabilitation of Offenders Act 1974, s 8(3), as applied to Scotland by s 8(8).
2 *Hunter v MacNaughton* (1894) 21 R 850.
3 *Walker* p 796.
4 *McDonald v Begg* (1862) 24 D 685 at 686 per Lord Deas.
5 (1859) 21 D 480 at 483.
6 Whether an allegation is one of character or of act is sometimes difficult: can a woman who was once a prostitute ever rid herself of that epithet? Or a man who was (is) an adulterer? Surely.
7 *Burnet v Gow* (1896) 24 R 156.

In order for the defence of *veritas* to be successful the defender must establish the whole truth of the allegation and it is not sufficient for him to prove part only if another, defamatory, part remains. 'To establish a defence of *veritas* the respondents [defenders] would require to prove the truth of all the material statements in the defamatory matter complained of, justifying everything in the defamatory statement which is injurious to the pursuer'[1].

Cooper suggests that English law, describing the defence as 'justification' rather than '*veritas*', requires a less exact correspondence between the facts proved in justification and the terms of the slander complained of[2], but it is doubtful if there really is any substantive difference of approach on this point between the two systems. It is clear that in Scotland, as in England, the defender is not obliged to prove every factual detail in his statement, for some details may not be of a defamatory nature. The part that must be proved as fact is the 'sting' of the allegation. Thus in *Andrew v Penny*[3] an Aberdeenshire sheep farmer accused a neighbouring sheep farmer of stealing his sheep. The court held that in establishing the defence of *veritas* the defender had to prove that the pursuer took sheep that were not his, but that he did not also have to prove that the sheep taken belonged to the defender. The sting was the allegation of theft, not theft from the defender, and *veritas* would be established by proving the sting and not the surrounding circumstances.

If the communication complained of amounts to an innuendo, then *veritas* is established by proving the derogatory impression created, not by proving the factual accuracy of the words. So for example to allege that a person is homosexual would not be defamatory in itself[4], but it might innuendo hypocrisy if the person has publicly denied being homosexual or is known to have argued against gay equality. A defence of *veritas* must be directed towards showing that the pursuer is a hypocrite rather than showing that he is homosexual, though the latter may well be evidence of the former.

It does not matter if the defender makes mistakes in the facts surrounding the defamatory allegation: *veritas* is a defence if the truth of the defamation is established notwithstanding that other, non-defamatory, remarks are admittedly false[5]. Conversely, it is no defence to prove that the statements made are meticulously true in fact, but false in substance[5]. So for example in an action against a defender who accused the pursuer of theft by removing an item belonging to the defender and keeping it as his own, *veritas* will not be established by proving these facts if the pursuer removed the item mistakenly believing it to be his. The essence of an allegation of theft is the accusation that the pursuer acted with criminal intent, and not simply that he removed something not belonging to him. Bertie Wooster certainly removed Sir Watkyn Bassett's umbrella in *The Code of the Woosters* but Sir Watkyn's accusation of theft could not have been defended by a plea of *veritas*, for all that he could

1 *Fairbairn v SNP* 1980 SLT 149 at 153 per Lord Ross.
2 Cooper, *Defamation and Verbal Injury* (2nd edn, 1906) p 210.
3 1964 SLT (Notes) 24.
4 See above at p 20.
5 Per Lord Shaw of Dunfermline in *Sutherland v Stopes* [1925] AC 47 at 79.

prove was the removal rather than the theft[1]. Likewise, where a publication contains two or more separate and distinct defamatory statements and the pursuer sues on one only, the defender is not entitled to a counter issue concerning the truth of the others. It is different if there is a common 'sting' to all the allegations and they are not really separable one from the other[2].

It is statutorily provided that:

'in an action for defamation in respect of words containing two or more distinct charges against the pursuer, a defence of veritas shall not fail by reason only that the truth of every charge is not proved if the words not proved to be true do not materially injure the pursuer's reputation having regard to the truth of the remaining charges'[3]

The effect of this section is to allow the defender a complete defence even when he does not prove the truth of all the allegations he made against the pursuer, so long as, in the opinion of the jury, the allegations not proved to be true do not materially injure the pursuer's reputation. In determining whether reputation has been injured, the allegations that were proved true are clearly material and are to be taken into account. If the allegations are not distinct and separable but amount, in reality, to one defamatory imputation (whether this is so being a matter for the judge) then this statutory provision does not come into effect[4]. Nor does it come into effect if there are numerous allegations made by the defender concerning the pursuer, but the pursuer chooses to sue on only one of them[4].

The statements must be proved to be true in fact for the defence of *veritas* to succeed, and it is not sufficient for the defender to prove that he believed the statements true, or that he was merely repeating a report from a credible source[5]. The defence will be successful if the imputation was that the pursuer had committed or been charged with or prosecuted for or convicted of or sentenced for a criminal offence and this is proved to be so, even if the conviction is 'spent' under the Rehabilitation of Offenders Act 1974[6]. However, the defence cannot be relied upon in these circumstances if the defamation is proved to have been committed maliciously[7]. The principles to be applied in determining whether there is malice are the same as those applied in cases of qualified privilege[8].

Once the *veritas convicii* is established, there is no room for the defence of fair comment for the same statements, because the defence of *veritas* is absolute, and sufficient to end the case[9]. It is, however, competent for a defender to plead both that he did not make the statements alleged and also that even if he had done so the statements are true: the latter is not inconsistent with the

1 The defence would, on the other hand, be available when Bertie is later accused of stealing the cow-creamer – for that is exactly what he does.
2 *Polly Peck (Holdings) plc v Trelford* [1986] 2 All ER 84.
3 Defamation Act 1952, s 5, as applied to Scotland by s 14(d).
4 *Polly Peck (Holdings) plc*, above.
5 *Fairbairn v SNP* 1980 SLT 149 at 153 per Lord Ross.
6 Rehabilitation of Offenders Act 1974, s 8(3).
7 Ibid, s 8(5).
8 *Herbage v Pressdram Ltd* [1984] 2 All ER 769. On proof of malice, see above at pp 121–123.
9 *Sutherland v Stopes* [1925] AC 47, especially Lord Shaw of Dunfermline at 73.

former because it is hypothetical until proved and if proved will in all cases provide a complete defence[1]. The defender 'may have a legitimate interest in so providing for the possible event of the jury being of the opinion, contrary to his own assertion, that he did utter the slander'[2]. The same is true if the defender denies that his statement has the meaning innuendoed by the pursuer. The defender is not barred from pleading *veritas* by having previously apologised to the pursuer and at that time accepting the statements were false if further statements of the same nature are later made and are sued upon[3].

Burden of proof

The onus of proving the *veritas convicii* lies with the defender, and, since a claim for defamation is a civil claim, the standard of proof to be satisfied is the balance of probabilities. This is so both for allegations of immorality, bad character and the like, and for allegations of criminality. *Veritas* is established if the commission of a crime by the pursuer is proved on the balance of probabilities, even if it cannot be proved beyond reasonable doubt. So in *Andrew v Penny*[4], in which an allegation of theft was met by a plea of *veritas*, the first Lord Milligan held that the standard of proof applicable was the 'balance of probabilities' notwithstanding that the allegation was one of a criminal offence. He added, however, that in view of the seriousness of the allegation, a high degree of probability was required.

In a quite different context (that of finding established or not a ground for referral to the children's hearing) the Second Division has held that there are only two standards of proof in Scotland, and that even when the ground for referral is predicated upon the commission of a criminal offence[5], proof is on the balance of probabilities[6]. A statement by Lord Denning in very similar terms to that of Lord Milligan mentioned above, that 'the more serious the allegation the higher the degree of probability that is required'[7] was described as 'unfortunately phrased' and the better way of putting it described thus: 'The weight of evidence required to tip the scales may vary with the gravity of the allegation to be proved'. Counsel for the pursuer and for the defender in *Gecas v Scottish Television*[8] agreed that these statements represented the law in actions for defamation, and the second Lord Milligan accepted that he should

---

1 *Mason v Tait* (1851) 13 D 1347.
2 *Burnet v Gow* (1896) 24 R 156 at 157 per Lord Ordinary Kincairney.
3 *R v S* 1914 SC 193.
4 1964 SLT (Notes) 24.
5 By someone other than the child referred. If the ground for referral is that the child has committed an offence, then the standard is the criminal standard: Social Work (Scotland) Act 1968, s 42(6).
6 *B v Kennedy* 1987 SLT 765. The same was held in *Wilson v Price* 1989 SLT 484, when the pursuer in an action for damages for negligence was met with the defence that both the pursuer and the defender had been engaged in a joint criminal enterprise at the time of the negligence: this could be proved on the balance of probabilities.
7 In *Hornal v Neuberger Products Ltd* [1957] 1 QB 247 at 258.
8 1992 GWD 30–1786.

proceed upon these agreed principles. This is, of course, a principle of general application and is not limited to allegations of criminality. So the weight of evidence required to establish the truth of an allegation of gross sexual perversion may well be greater than that required to justify an allegation of, say, minor untruthfulness.

The pleadings

In a jury case it is important that the defender in pleading *veritas* makes plain not only on the record but also in a counter issue that he will attempt to prove the truth of the allegations made. In a non-jury case there must be a plea in law to the effect that the facts stated are true.

'The rule of our practice is that if the defender undertakes to prove the truth of words, spoken or written, complained of in an action of slander, he must undertake that in the record in distinct and positive terms. And not only so, but he must take a counter issue, putting to the jury the question, whether what is complained of is true in whole or in part; if it be in part, then specifying distinctly what part. And if such an issue is not taken it is not competent to prove the truth of the words spoken either in whole or in part, either for the express and direct purpose of showing the truth, or for the other purpose suggested of mitigating the damages. All that is so well settled that it is quite unnecessary to cite cases in support of it'[1].

The reason for this is explained by Lord Fraser in *Paul v Jackson*[2]: 'The object of the counter issue is indeed solely to advertise the pursuer of the defender's intention, so that he may be prepared with his evidence to shew that the statements contained in the libellous letter are untrue'. A counter issue or plea in law which is so vague that it does not give proper notice to the pursuer of what is intended to be proved against him will not be permitted[2].

The requirement for a counter issue in order to put truth to the jury cannot be avoided by raising truth merely as a matter to mitigate damages, and evidence of truth will not be permitted to be led in the absence of an issue in justification[3]. Nor is the defender entitled, without a counter issue, to lead evidence of the truth of the allegation in order to show provocation[4]. The pursuer can, however, if sufficient notice is given, be cross-examined about his or her general character in order to mitigate damages in any action in which it is claimed that character has been attacked, because the pursuer in such an action has necessarily put his or her character in issue[5].

If the counter issue or plea in law does not meet the statement the pursuer has put in issue, or does not take the sting out of the alleged defamation, it will not be allowed. So in *British Workman's and General Assurance Co v Stewart*[6] a

---

1 *Craig v Jex-Blake* (1871) 9 M 973 at 979 per Lord President Inglis.
2 (1884) 11 R 460 at 467.
3 *McNeill v Rorison* (1847) 10 D 15; *Craig v Jex-Blake*, above.
4 *Paul v Jackson* (1884) 11 R 460.
5 *C v M* 1923 SC 1. See further, below at pp 170–171.
6 (1897) 24 R 624.

counter issue was refused which sought to prove that an insurance company's accounts were intended to mislead the public, because the issue allowed was whether the accounts had been deliberately falsified by the pursuers. In *McDonald v Begg*[1], where the pursuer had moved from Dunfermline to Edinburgh, an allegation that the pursuer had a bad character in Dunfermline could not be justified by proving actions which took place after the pursuer had moved to Edinburgh[2]. And in *C v W*[3] a counter issue of professional misconduct was held irrelevant in meeting a charge of professional incompetence[4]. Similarly, the counter issue cannot be used to establish more disreputable facts than those complained about and alleged to be true. So in *Bookbinder v Tebbit*[5] the plaintiff, a local politician, raised an action against a national politician who had accused him of overspending public funds. The defendant was not permitted to prove a general charge of squandering public money but was limited to the specific allegation actually being complained about. And in *H v P*[6] where the defender had accused the pursuer of committing adultery with him, he was not permitted to prove that she had committed adultery with him and two others.

As always, relevancy is a matter for the court, which has to determine whether the plea meets the allegations complained of. 'To justify a libel or slander there must be a distinct substantive averment of a fact or facts which, if proved, will justify it, not in the opinion of the jury, but in the opinion of a court of law'[7].

It is competent to take a counter issue which justifies a separable part of the defamation complained of, even if this leaves other parts which the defender does not intend to prove the truth of. Success with such a counter issue may limit the damages awarded[8], even although it cannot, of necessity, exculpate completely[9].

---

1 (1862) 24 D 685.
2 See also *Fletcher v HJ & J Wilson* (1885) 22 SLR 433 in which *veritas* could not be put in the issue when the defenders had claimed that the pursuer had been convicted of theft seven times and they offered to prove that he had been convicted twice, 23 years ago when he was a boy of 14.
3 1950 SLT (Notes) 8.
4 The difference between professional misconduct and professional incompetence is explored above at pp 22–24.
5 [1989] 1 All ER 1169.
6 (1905) 8 F 232.
7 *Macleod v Marshall* (1891) 18 R 811 at 816 per Lord Young and Lord Justice-Clerk Macdonald.
8 *O'Callaghan v DC Thomson & Co* 1928 SC 532; *McNeill v Rorison* (1847) 10 D 15 at 25 per Lord Moncreiff.
9 Unless s 5 of the Defamation Act 1952 is applicable: see above at p 131.

CHAPTER TEN

Fair comment

Introduction

It is essential to our notions of democratic freedom that everyone is entitled to hold his or her own opinions and, however prejudiced or ill-considered or wrong they are, is entitled to express these opinions, in so far as doing so does not breach the criminal law[1]. This right to express opinions is one of the most important defences to the claim for defamation or verbal injury, for without it public debate, artistic and literary criticism, and political comment would all be severely circumscribed and our intellectual lives would be cruelly impoverished. It is to the good of democracy that we be free to comment upon the public acts of public men and women and to the good of art and literature that we be free to react openly and critically to whatever artists produce[2]. It is to the self-evident good of the legal system that legal writers be free to criticise – and to express disagreement with – court judgments and other judicial statements, even when this results in branding an acquitted person a criminal or an assoilzied defender a defamer. The defence of criticism, or comment, is most useful to publishers and broadcasters who, it may fairly be said, have a duty not only to report events but also to comment upon them. Reviews, whether of books or of films or of plays, and critiques of paintings and sculpures and buildings could seldom be published safely without this defence. It is, however, as well to note at the outset that however useful to the newspaper publisher or television or radio broadcaster, the right to make comment is a right that attaches equally to everyone, and the publisher or broadcaster has no greater or higher right to do so than a private individual[3]. The expression of opinion may of course damage an individual's honour, character and reputation just as much as a statement of fact, but due to the public interest in preserving the right of free speech it is open to the person

---

1 The Public Order Act 1986 is an example of the expression of opinion being a criminal offence, for s 18 of that Act makes it an offence to use or publish 'threatening, abusive or insulting words or behaviour intended or likely to stir up racial hatred'.
2 In an early case, *Jardine v Creech* (1776) Mor 3438, the publishers of the *Edinburgh Magazine and Review* published a criticism of a letter they had received and in reply to an action for defamation said 'the interests of literature requires that there should be a freedom of criticism, and their publication being a review, they plead the privilege of all their brethren'. Damages were awarded against the publishers, though the report does not indicate how the court responded to the defence.
3 *Longworth v Hope & Cooke* (1865) 1 SLR 53 at 55 per Lord Jerviswoode; *Langlands v John Leng & Co* 1916 SC(HL) 102 at 110 per Lord Shaw of Dunfermline; *Silkin v Beaverbrook Newspapers* [1958] 2 All ER 516 at 517 per Diplock J.

who expresses an opinion that has defamatory content to plead the defence which is normally today referred to, if somewhat misleadingly, as 'fair comment'. The defence would be equally applicable in an action for verbal injury, though it is far less likely ever to arise there. In its own terms it is unlikely to be an appropriate defence to a claim based on negligence, but the law may well hold that there is no duty of care to avoid making harmful comment.

The basis of the defence

There is some ambiguity as to the proper basis of this defence in law. Defamatory comments on the public acts of public persons might easily attract the defence of qualified privilege, on the basis of the democratic interest we all have in challenging and criticising such persons, and it seems clear that the defence of fair comment grew out of the defence of qualified privilege[1]. But if fair comment is no more than a subheading of qualified privilege, then that serves to limit its applicability and the defence will be defeated by proof by the pursuer of the defender's malice[2]. However, there are a number of judicial dicta suggesting that the defence, in Scotland at least, is rather more absolute than that. In *Müller v Robertson*[3] Lord Justice-Clerk Hope described an article in a medical journal which commented adversely upon a previous article in another journal as follows: 'This is not a direct accusation of falsehood against [the pursuer], but a comment upon a review in the Medical Gazette. I think that it is not a libel, but comes within the limits of fair controversy'[4]. If there is no libel then the existence or otherwise of malice is irrelevant. Lord McLaren in *Godfrey v W & DC Thomson*[5] is more explicit: 'The question is whether the article in this case is entitled to the *absolute* protection which the law extends to public criticism'[6]. A year later Lord McLaren gave what is generally regarded as the classic formulation of the defence in Scots law: 'The expression of an opinion as to a state of facts truly set forth is not actionable, even when that opinion is couched in vituperative or contumelious language'[7].

These dicta suggest that the effect of the defence of fair comment is to take away the actionable nature of the harmful statement, rather than, as with qualified privilege, to shift the onus onto the pursuer to establish that the statement has been made maliciously. This is not how the defence is presently applied in England, where proof of malice clearly defeats the defence[8], and it is

1 Cooper, *Defamation and Verbal Injury* (2nd edn, 1906) for example, discusses fair comment as a subheading within qualified privilege.
2 Above at pp 120–123.
3 (1853) 15 D 661.
4 See also Lord Neaves in *Auld v Shairp* (1875) 2 R 940 at 941: 'public criticism is no libel'.
5 (1890) 17 R 1108 at 1114 and 1115.
6 Italics added. Lord McLaren repeated his view of the law in *Gray v Scottish Society for the Prevention of Cruelty to Animals* (1890) 17 R 1185 at 1200.
7 *Archer v Ritchie & Co* (1891) 18 R 719 at 727.
8 See Carter-Ruck, *Libel and Slander* (4th edn, 1992) pp 113–118.

suggested that, though Scots law is not identical to English law, the above dicta are rather misleading for the law of Scotland too. The defence of fair comment is absolute in the circumstances in which it applies, that is when the statement complained of is shown by the defender to be a comment on rather than a statement of fact, and when it is not shown by the pursuer to be 'unfair' as hereinafter defined, just as qualifed privilege has the effect of an absolute defence when it cannot be shown that the statement complained of was made maliciously. There is a tendency, encouraged by unthinking reliance on English authority, to equate lack of 'fairness' with 'malice', and while the end result will often be the same the tendency should be resisted since fair comment is essentially distinct from qualified privilege. The defence of fair comment is available in all circumstances and to all defenders, while qualified privilege is available only in certain well-defined circumstances[1]. The difference with English law is that the motive with which comment is made is, in Scotland, irrelevant[2]: rather the limitation of the defence is the relevance of the comment to the facts being commented upon and a person may, with intent to injure (or, as the English would have it, with malice), give his true opinion on a statement of facts so long as the opinion is relevant to these facts, and in that sense is 'fair'. Lord McLaren qualified his 'absolute protection' proposition as follows: 'But newspaper critics are only privileged when they keep within the limits of public criticism, and when they exceed that limit, and touch upon matters affecting private character, they are responsible for what they say, like other members of the public'[3]. The defence is not absolute if that means that no comment can ever found an action for damages: rather, no 'fair' comment can found an action and a comment is not 'fair' when it is not relevant to the facts being commented upon. And it is for the pursuer to prove lack of fairness in this sense once the defender has established that the statement complained of is a comment on facts. It is this shifting of onus onto the pursuer that gives the superficial similarity to qualified privilege, but the similarity ends there.

One more question should be addressed in examining the basis of the defence: why should the law permit defamatory comments to be made when it does not permit defamatory statements of fact? There are two principal answers to this question. On the one hand, the democratic right to free speech and to take part in public debate, and the intellectual right to criticise works presented to the public, may be sufficient justification in themselves. If this is so then the defence should be given the widest possible scope. On the other hand, there are dicta suggesting that if the comment is based on fact which is brought to the attention of those to whom the comment was made, the comment will be unable to harm reputation since listeners and readers are thereby afforded the opportunity to make up their own minds about the validity

1 *Merivale v Carson* (1887) 20 QBD 275 at 280 per Lord Esher MR. The circumstances are listed in Chapter 8 above.
2 See further, below at pp 148–149.
3 *Godfrey v W & DC Thomson* (1890) 17 R 1108 at 1115. See also *Longworth v Hope & Cooke* (1865) 1 SLR 53 at 55 per Lord Jerviswoode.

of the comment. Lord McLaren in *Gray v Scottish Society for the Prevention of Cruelty to Animals*[1] said: 'If the facts be correctly stated the reader is in a position to form his own conclusions and the expression of opinion, if unfair, can injure no one but the writer himself'. And in *Bruce v Ross & Co*[2] Lord Trayner justified applying the defence because: 'The true facts were given to the public, who could judge whether they warranted the writer's opinion or not'. If this is the true basis for the defence of fair comment then it is limited to situations in which such facts are brought to the attention of the public as are sufficient to allow them to assess the comment.

This second approach appears to be the foundation of the majority speeches in *Telnikoff v Matusevitch*[3], in which the question was whether statements in a letter to a newspaper, written in response to an article previously published therein, were expressions of opinion or statements of fact. It was held that, since many people reading the letter would not have read the article, or would have forgotten its content, the question should be answered by having regard to the letter alone. This decision suggests, as Lord McLaren and Lord Trayner suggest, that the justification for allowing the plea of fair comment is that listeners and readers have the opportunity to make up their own minds as to the validity of the comment, by taking account of the facts available to the defender (which they could not do in the present case). Lord Ackner disputed this in a strong dissenting speech, and he based his decision purely on the right of any person to express views on a matter of public interest. He pointed out that,

'it would be absurd to suggest that a critic may not say what he thinks of a play performed only once, because the public cannot go and see it to judge for themselves. The defence of fair comment is available to a defendant who has done no more than express his honest opinion on publications put before the public'[4].

It would be similarly absurd to suggest that a literary critic could not comment on a book because most of those who read his or her review would not have read the book. Probably *Telnikoff* is to be limited to determining whether a statement is a comment or not and is not applicable in determining whether the comment provides a defence (ie whether it is 'fair' or not), and the Scottish dicta quoted above do no more than provide, when appropriate, an added justification for the defence over and above that based on public policy. Lord McLaren (again) puts the matter correctly:

'It is to be remembered that it is a privilege of every citizen to express his opinion freely regarding the public acts and utterances of his fellow citizens. It is sometimes said that everyone who occupies a public position invites criticism, and it will not, I think, make the criticism actionable that it is uncourteous, or even offensive or vituperative, provided it amounts to nothing more than an expression of opinion on a matter of public concern'[5].

1 (1890) 17 R 1185 at 1200.
2 (1901) 4 F 171 at 177 and 178.
3 [1992] 2 AC 343.
4 [1992] 2 AC 343 at 361.
5 *Godfrey v W & DC Thomson* (1890) 17 R 1108 at 1114.

COMMENT ON FACTS 139

The production of an artistic creation for public display, or a literary work for publication is also of necessity an invitation to comment, and when comment is made that is relevant to the creation or to the work, the creator cannot sue for damages thereupon.

The essentials of the plea: onus of proof

In order to succeed with the defence of fair comment, the defender must establish (1) that the statement complained of is a comment on fact or facts; (2) that the facts upon which the comment is made are truly stated; and (3) that the facts concern some matter of public interest. Once these three elements have been proved by the defender the onus is shifted onto the pursuer to show that the comment was not 'fair'. These elements may now be considered separately.

Comment on facts

A comment is an expression of opinion or of judgment or of criticism of known facts. It is an expression of what a person thinks rather than of what he knows. It is words that are judgmental rather than descriptive. However, the defence requires more than that a judgmental statement be made, for a mere expression of opinion can be used to innuendo a fact which can found an action. To say 'it is my opinion that X ought to be hung' will be defamatory if some derogatory allegation of fact can be drawn from the statement and it is no defence that it was dressed up as an opinion. If however the defender has truly stated the facts upon which he makes his judgment then the statement is entitled to protection, for giving the facts serves notice on his listeners and readers that the comment is his own opinion only and it allows the listeners and readers to make up their own minds as to whether the defender's comment is justifiable[1]. If it is not justifiable then only the defender's reputation will have been harmed and the pursuer has no case.

It follows that central to the notion of fair comment is the idea of an inference being drawn from underlying facts of which the listener or reader is made aware. Therefore, in order for the defence to be applicable, the statement complained of must contain two elements: fact and comment thereon[2]. Either on its own is not sufficient for this defence, nor may the comment be so mixed up with the facts that the listener or reader cannot distinguish between what is

<hr>

1 *Gray v Scottish Society for the Prevention of Cruelty to Animals* (1890) 17 R 1185 at 1200 per Lord McLaren; *Bruce v Ross & Co* (1901) 4 F 171 at 177 and 178 per Lord Trayner; *Kemsley v Foot* [1952] AC 345 at 356 per Lord Porter. And see *Telnikoff v Matusevitch* [1992] 2 AC 343.
2 'To raise this defence there must, of course, be a basis of fact on which the comment is made': *Sutherland v Stopes* [1925] AC 47 at 62 per Viscount Finlay.

report and what is comment[1]. It is for the defender to spell out, with sufficient precision to enable the pursuer to know the case he has to address, what part of the statement is comment that attracts the defence[2]. If the statement contains only facts, then the appropriate defence is that of *veritas* and the defender would have to prove that the whole statement is verifiably true. If the statement contains only comment then this is actionable if the pursuer proves an innuendo to fact, which is again susceptible to a plea of *veritas*. It is only if the comment is an inference clearly drawn from a fact that the defence of fair comment is applicable. So for example to say 'In my opinion this man is corrupt' is making a statement of fact because of the underlying innuendo of criminality. But to say 'this man gave a contract to his brother-in-law and is therefore corrupt' is making a statement of fact followed by an opinion inferred from that fact. The defence of fair comment would provide absolute protection if the fact is proved true, even although that fact alone does not justify the inference: the comment may be an invalid judgment but it is not for that reason alone 'unfair'[3].

It is often difficult to distinguish between a statement of fact and a statement of comment, and the same words may be one or the other depending upon the context in which they are used. To say 'Mitford is a racist' is a statement of fact, while to say 'Mitford denies the Holocaust and is therefore a racist' is a statement of, followed by a comment on, fact. Remove the 'therefore' in that statement and it might, however, amount to two facts. In *London Artists v Littler*[4] a theatre manager wrote letters to four actors, who had all given notice together, accusing them of being part of a plot to terminate a play. There was a clear statement of fact – that the actors had given notice together – and the manager claimed that the allegation of a plot was a comment on that fact. The Court of Appeal, however, held that the allegation of a plot was a statement of fact in itself rather than an expression of opinion on the accepted fact – with the result that truth (which in the event could not be proved) was the only defence. The role of the judge is to determine whether the statement can be so construed as to contain both fact and comment. If he is of the view that there is no doubt that only fact or only comment exists then the defence cannot be put to the jury[5]. If, however, the statement is reasonably capable of being considered as comment, then it is for the jury to determine whether it is indeed comment or fact[6]. If the jury decides that the

---

1 *Wheatley v Anderson & Miller* 1927 SC 133 at 147 per Lord Anderson, quoting with approval the well-known words of Fletcher Moulton LJ to this effect in *Hunt v Star Newspaper Co* [1908] 2 KB 309.

2 *London Artists v Littler* [1969] 2 All ER 193 at 201 per Lord Justice Edmund-Davies; *Control Risks Ltd v New English Library Ltd* [1989] 3 All ER 577.

3 For the meaning of 'unfair', see below at pp 148–149.

4 [1969] 2 All ER 193.

5 *London Artists v Littler* [1969] 2 All ER 193 at 201 per Edmund-Davies LJ; *Waddell v BBC* 1973 SLT 246 at 249 per Sheriff Principal Walker; *Fairbairn v SNP* 1980 SLT 149 at 152 per Lord Ross.

6 *London Artists* [1969] 2 All ER 193 at 199 per Lord Denning MR; *Telnikoff v Matusevitch* [1992] 2 AC 343 at 351 per Lord Keith of Kinkel.

statement contains both fact and comment, then the jury must go on to consider whether the comment is fair and on a matter of public interest.

Sometimes, particularly in relation to artistic criticism, the statement will be so clearly comment that little in the way of fact need exist. For example, to describe a painting as, say, 'childish daubs' is clearly a comment, and the only fact upon which it is based is the existence of the painting. It would not be necessary for the defender to establish as a fact that the painting was indeed 'childish'. This is opinion, not verifiable fact. It may, however, be incumbent on the critic to do more than simply make the assertion, but to go on to explain his opinion[1]. However, this is not in order to establish the fairness of the opinion but because otherwise the assertion might be taken by reasonable people to be an assertion of fact rather than of opinion.

Hidden facts

It is not necessary that the facts upon which the comment is made are spelt out in full in the statement that contains the comment complained about[2]. Rather, it is sufficient that facts are referred to or brought to the attention of the listeners and readers, whether directly or indirectly through inference or innuendo but with sufficient clarity that the listeners and readers are aware of the substratum of facts. This is so that the jury are aware of what was in the defender's mind and are thus able to come to a conclusion as to whether the comment was fair or not. Lord Anderson put the matter thus:

'The facts upon which the comment is based must be set out in the libel of which complaint is made. This seems to be essential in order to enable the jury to determine whether or not the comment is fair. The jury must know the facts as they existed at the time when the comment was made. But I am not prepared to assent to the pursuer's contention that only the facts set forth in the libel may be relied on by a defender. On the authorities, it seems to be competent and legitimate to particularise or expand these facts in the pleadings when the libel has contained mere generalities. This expansion however must, in my opinion, be germane to and supplementary of the facts set out in the libel'[3].

In *Kemsley v Foot*[4] an article was published in a newspaper attacking the Beaverbrook Press under the headline, 'Lower than Kemsley'. When the newspaper proprietor Lord Kemsley sued for defamation, he was met with a plea of fair comment, but he argued in reply that no sufficient facts had been spelt out upon which comment could validly be made. The House of Lords allowed the defence on the ground that, in the context of an article condemning the practices of one newspaper organisation, the headline clearly implied facts about the other organisation headed by the plaintiff. This substratum of fact was sufficient to justify making a comment. 'Lower than Kemsley'

1 *Johnston v Dilke* (1875) 2 R 836 at 838 and 839 per Lord Justice-Clerk Moncreiff.
2 *Wheatley v Anderson & Miller* 1927 SC 133 at 143 per Lord Justice-Clerk Alness; at 147 per Lord Anderson.
3 *Wheatley v Anderson & Miller* 1927 SC 133 at 147.
4 [1952] AC 345.

became a comment because derogatory facts about Lord Kemsley were clearly implied.

This case is probably the high-water mark for implied or hidden facts and it is unlikely to be applied in cases in which the hidden facts referred to are not of a sort that is well-known to any reasonably informed person (such as, for example, that Robert Maxwell was a crook and a fraudster, or that the Prince of Wales is an adulterer). *Kemsley v Foot* was not overruled, though clearly some judges were unhappy with it, in the more recent House of Lords case of *Telnikoff v Matusevitch*[1]. Here the defamatory statements were contained in a letter to a newspaper responding to a previously published article and the majority held, in determining whether the statements complained of were fact or were comment, that only the letter could be looked at and not the article also. Lord Ackner, who dissented from the majority, could not see how the majority's decision could be reconciled with *Kemsley*, and the basis of his dissent was the fear that every comment made on another's words would require to set out *verbatim* the words being commented upon. It was clearly this fear that motivated the decision of the Second Division in *Wheatley v Anderson & Miller*, and the portion of Lord Anderson's judgment quoted above should again be referred to[2]. It, and Scots law, seems to follow Lord Ackner in *Telnikoff* rather than the majority. Probably the law of Scotland is to the effect that it is not necessary that the defamatory statement sets out all the facts upon which comment is made, so long as there is sufficient to indicate to the reasonable listener or reader that the statement is a comment upon facts readily ascertainable[3]. 'Doris Lessing is a lousy writer' is a statement of opinion with sufficient indication within it of the fact being commented upon – that Doris Lessing writes. 'A N Wilson is a sanctimonious fool', on the other hand, contains no indication of facts founding the opinion and it could be actionable if an innuendo of fact could be drawn from it. In *Telnikoff* the real difficulty was that the letter could as easily be taken to be statements of fact as of comment. The case is probably to be explained by the majority's disquiet at the inaccuracies in – or at the very least false impression given by – the letter concerning the earlier article, though it might, if this is so, have been better to have decided the case on the basis that the facts were not truly stated[4].

That all the facts do not have to be set out in the statement making a criticism on the basis of these facts is perhaps best illustrated in the case of literary or artistic criticism. To say that 'this play is hopeless', or that 'this piece of sculpture is a meaningless blob' does not refer to any facts other than that a play has been written or that a sculpure exists, yet the criticism can be

---

1 [1992] 2 AC 343.
2 See also Lord Justice-Clerk Alness at 143.
3 In *Shanks v BBC* 1993 SLT 326 Lord Osborne refused to hold irrelevant averments concerning a conversation between the pursuer and a television reporter which formed no part of the subsequent broadcast which was complained about, this on the ground that the conversation may be relevant to the question of fair comment.
4 See below at pp 143–144.

made, even in the absence of an explanation as to why the critic comes to the view expressed. Again, it has been stated by Lord McLaren that it would be 'ridiculous' to suppose that a person writing in a legal periodical is exposing him or herself to liability whenever they comment on a court judgment and say that the judgment is erroneous or that the judge has disregarded authority or ignored precedent: 'if the facts be correctly stated the reader is in a position to form his own conclusions, and the expression of opinion, if unfair[1], can injure no one but the writer himself'[2]. A good legal article will, of course, specify those portions of a judgment that the writer takes issue with, but it would be wrong to suggest that there is a legal requirement to do so[3]. To write, in a legal periodical, something of the order that 'Lord X has, as usual, shown a lack of knowledge in the law in his latest opinion in the case of *A v B*' would found the defence of fair comment, the only facts commented upon being that Lord X decided the case of *A v B* and the comment being to the effect that he usually gives wrong decisions and did so in that case.

Facts truly stated

Once it is established or accepted that the statement complained of both contains comment and contains or sufficiently refers to facts, the next element that the defender must prove is that the facts upon which the comment has been made were truly stated[4]. Public policy has no interest in preserving the right to comment on facts that are misstated[5]. 'The comment must . . . not misstate facts, because a comment cannot be fair which is built upon facts which are not truly stated, and, further, it must not convey imputations of an evil sort, except so far as the facts, truly stated, warrant the imputation'[6]. The facts must be true in reality and not simply in the defender's mind, so the defence is not available just because the defender genuinely believes that the facts were as he stated them. Nor is the defence available if the facts do not exist at the time the statement is made, though they come into being later: in that situation the comment cannot logically be considered to be a comment on fact and it cannot change its nature after it is made[7]. The defender has to have knowledge of the fact before his statement can be considered to be a comment

---

1 By which he meant, unwarranted.
2 *Gray v Scottish Society for Prevention of Cruelty to Animals* (1890) 17 R 1185 at 1200 per Lord McLaren.
3 Of course judges do not sue academic critics, possibly because they realise that to do so would demean both their office and themselves. The English courts would be less cluttered with unworthy cases if more people took that commendable view.
4 *Wheatley v Anderson & Miller* 1927 SC 133 at p 143 per Lord Justice-Clerk Alness; at 145 per Lord Hunter.
5 *London Artists v Littler* [1969] 2 All ER 193 at 201 per Edmund-Davies LJ.
6 *Joynt v Clyde Trade Publishing Co* [1904] 2 KB 292 at 294 per Kennedy J. See also *Brent Walker Group plc v Time Out Ltd* [1991] 2 All ER 753.
7 *Wheatley v Anderson & Miller* 1927 SC 133 at 148 per Lord Anderson; *Cohen v Daily Telegraph Ltd* [1968] 2 All ER 407; *Cornwell v Myskow* [1987] 2 All ER 504.

on the fact. If the comment takes the form of a criticism of some work of art or literary creation, then the creation must not be misrepresented. For example to describe a work as 'immoral' because it is, say, 'an apology for adultery' would not be fair comment unless the work actually dealt with, whether expressly or by implication, adultery[1]. A certain leeway should, however, be granted to critics, who must be left free to read into works what they can see. A critic can lawfully damn David Hockney's latest painting as 'pornography' notwithstanding that no rational person would see any sexual content to the work. Free expression protects even prudery[2]. The fundamental test for the criticism is its relevance[3].

Though the general rule is that the facts upon which the comment is made have to be proved to be true, this is subject to two qualifications. First, it is provided in the Defamation Act 1952 that,

'In an action for defamation in respect of words consisting partly of allegations of fact and partly of expressions of opinion, a defence of fair comment shall not fail by reason only that the truth of every allegation of fact is not proved if the expression of opinion is fair comment having regard to such of the facts alleged or referred to in the words complained of as are proved"[4].

This reverses the common law position whereby failure to prove any fact contained in the statement complained of, however minor or incidental to the comment, destroyed the defence[5]. So for example for a literary critic to describe a book as Frankie Lyle's latest outpourings of trash in this, his third novel' would found the defence even if the book being commented upon is, in fact, the writer's fourth novel. Of course if any of the stated facts is itself defamatory the defender will be free from liability only by establishing the truth of such facts, whether or not connected to the comment.

Secondly, if the comment is being made upon a fact expressed in circumstances of absolute privilege, then the truth of the fact does not need to be established[6]. So for example if an allegation is made in the House of Commons and a newspaper comments upon that allegation, there is no necessity to prove the allegation correct and the defence of fair comment will still be available even although the allegation is later shown to be factually inaccurate. This rule applies so long as the comments were made on the basis of the facts as specified on the privileged occasion. It will, of course, be for the defender to prove that the allegation was made on a privileged occasion.

---

1 *Merivale v Carson* (1887) 20 QBD 275.
2 In the interesting Canadian case of *Planned Parenthood Newfoundland v Fedorik* (1982) 135 DLR (3rd) 714 the defendant had said that the plaintiffs' sex education film was 'pornographic'. The defence of fair comment failed because the defendant could not prove that she had ever seen the plaintiff's film. The court assumed that the description of something as 'pornographic' was a description of fact rather than a comment. This is, perhaps, not as obvious as the court assumed.
3 See further, below at pp 148–149.
4 Defamation Act 1952, s 6.
5 But see *Kemsley v Foot* [1952] AC 345 at 362 per Lord Tucker.
6 *London Artists Ltd v Littler* [1969] 2 All ER 193 at 201 per Edmund-Davies LJ.

'Truth' of the comment

The fact that the comment is not in fact true is neither here nor there[1]. If a comment is made which is a wholly invalid and unwarranted inference from a fact the defence is still available so long as the comment does not stray beyond the bounds of 'fairness', as later defined. To say 'the pursuer gave a contract to his brother-in-law and is therefore corrupt' will found the defence if the contract was in fact given to the brother-in-law, notwithstanding that this fact alone does not, on any reasonable assessment, mean that the pursuer is guilty of corruption. On the other hand, to say 'the pursuer gave a contract to his brother-in-law and is therefore a child abuser' would not found the defence because the comment is wholly irrelevant to the fact. Once a statement has been classified as a comment it is incompetent for the pursuer to draw an innuendo from it, otherwise the efficacy of the defence would be destroyed. So for example to claim that a person's acquittal at a criminal trial was wrong clearly implies an allegation of guilt, but this is not defamatory (even if false) since it is a comment upon facts truly stated: ie the acquittal[2].

Matters of public interest

Fair comment as a defence is available only if the comment is on a matter of public interest. This qualification is, however, of minimal force for it is to be remembered that the matter must be one *of* public interest, rather than one *in the* public interest. What is interesting to the public is extremely wide, and covers far more than the activities of members of public bodies like the government, army or monarchy, or artistic or literary endeavours put into the public domain, though these are all necessarily matters of public interest. Even the most serious newspapers daily carry stories concerning private individuals who, for one reason or another, have come to the attention of journalists. One might like to say that certain aspects of a private individual's personal life are of no legitimate interest to the public, but the level of sales of some newspapers (published in England but widely available in Scotland), and the nature of many of their stories, suggest little limit to the prurience of the public.

Lord Denning MR gave the following definition of matters of public interest:

'Whenever a matter is such as to affect people at large, so that they may be legitimately interested in, or concerned at, what is going on; or what may happen to them or to others; then it is a matter of public interest on which everyone is entitled to make fair comment'[3].

---

1 *Wheatley v Anderson & Miller* 1927 SC 133 at 147 per Lord Anderson; *Broadway Approvals v Odhams Press Ltd* [1965] 2 All ER 523 at 535 per Sellers LJ.
2 Per Lord McLaren in *Gray v Scottish Society for the Prevention of Cruelty to Animals* (1890) 17 R 1185 at 1200.
3 *London Artists Ltd v Littler* [1969] 2 All ER 193 at 198.

He went on to emphasise that fair comment can be made both on subjects in which the public is legitimately concerned, and those in which the public is legitimately interested. In the present case the internal politics within the London theatre world were held to be of public interest[1]. It has been said that 'where a person has done or published anything which may fairly be said to have invited comment . . . in such cases everyone has a right to make a fair and proper comment'[2]. So the publication of any work which can be expected to draw public comment in the form of reviews or criticism can be commented upon and the comments will be amenable to the plea.

Rebutting the defence: establishing unfairness

The defence of fair comment requires for its application that the defamatory statement complained of be a comment upon, rather than an allegation of, fact; and also that this comment be fair. It is to be emphasised that the defender's onus goes no further than establishing that the statement is comment upon fact truly stated and that once this onus is discharged it is for the pursuer to prove that the comment was 'unfair'[3]. For once the statement complained of is shown by the defender to contain a comment amounting to an inference from a true fact stated or apparent then the law will presume that the comment is fair, just as it presumes lack of malice when the statement is made on a privileged occasion[4]. The pursuer can therefore rebut the defence by showing that the comment was not 'fair'.

The definition of 'fair' in this context has been given little consideration in Scotland, and much in England, though it is not apparent that the two systems mean the same thing with the word. What is clear in both is that the word itself is misleading. The defence is not based on 'reasonableness', or 'justice', or 'moderation', or indeed 'fairness' in the ordinary meaning of that word and 'fairness' in the context of the defence of fair comment has nothing to do with reasonableness or justice[5]. The whole point of the defence is to preserve the right to hold and express opinions, however unreasonable, unjust or even unfair (in a moral sense) these opinions are[6]. Sheriff Malcolm put it thus: 'The opinion expressed may be wrong, misguided, foolish,

---

1 For a description of all the different situations which have been held to be matters of public interest, see Walker *Delict* (2nd edn, 1981) pp 842–847.

2 *Campbell v Spottiswoode* (1863) 32 LJQB 185 at 202 per Blackburn J.

3 'In alleging unfairness the plaintiff takes on him or herself the onus, also taken by an allegation of malice, to prove that the criticism is unfair either from the language used or from some extraneous circumstance': *Turner v MGM Pictures Ltd* [1950] 1 All ER 449 at 461 per Lord Porter, quoted with approval by Lord Keith of Kinkel in *Telnikoff v Matusevitch* [1992] 2 AC 343 at 355.

4 *Sutherland v Stopes* [1925] AC 47.

5 *McQuire v Western Morning News Co* [1903] 2 KB 100 at 109 per Collins MR.

6 Above at pp 137–138.

unfriendly, or have other characteristics, but so long as it is fair it is protected, and a very wide latitude indeed is allowed in deciding what is fair'[1].

'Fairness' in English law

It is well established that instead of reasonableness the concept of 'fairness' in the eyes of the English courts contains two distinct elements, the negativing of either one of which by the plaintiff will destroy the defence. These two elements were identified by Collins MR in *McQuire v Western Morning News Co*[2] when he said, 'I think "fair" embraces the meaning of honest and also of relevancy. The view expressed must be honest and must be such as can fairly be called criticism'.

A fair comment is one that has been honestly made on the facts, in the sense that it genuinely reflects the opinion held by the defendant. Lord Porter brings this out clearly:

'The question is not whether the comment is justified in the eyes of the judge or jury, but whether it is the honest expression of the commentator's real view and not mere abuse or invective under the guise of criticism . . . To a similar effect were the words of Lord Esher MR in *Merivale v Carson*[3] which are so often quoted – ". . . would any fair man, however prejudiced he may be, however exaggerated or obstinate his views, have [written] this criticism . . . ?" I should adopt [these words] except that I would substitute "honest" for "fair" lest some suggestion of reasonableness instead of honesty should be read in'[4].

The test in determining honesty is an objective test, that is 'whether any man, however prejudiced and obstinate, could honestly hold the view expressed'[5]. Extremity of position or harshness in expression are not in themselves evidence of dishonesty, but may take the comment outwith the bounds of fair comment in the sense of indicating to the jury whether the view propounded is such that an honest person could have held it. If the plaintiff proves that no person could honestly hold the view expressed the defence is defeated. Lack of honesty is often equated with malice[6] or a collateral improper motive.

As well as honesty, the comment must have been well-founded in the sense of being relevant to the facts upon which it is based. Criticism or comment that goes beyond the facts and into the realm of abuse cannot be protected by the plea of fair comment. So for example if a theatre critic were to criticise a play, his or her comments would be protected in so far as they referred to the play, but if they strayed into personal invective against the playwright the plea will not be available. This is so even when the personal invective is hidden or

---

1 *Caldwell v Bayne* (1936) 52 Sh Ct Rep 334 at 339. Cf Lord Esher MR in *Merivale v Carson* (1887) 20 QBD 275 at 280 and 281 and Diplock J in *Silkin v Beaverbrook Newspapers Ltd* [1958] 2 All ER 516 at 518.
2 [1903] 2 KB 100 at 110.
3 (1887) 20 QBD 275 at 281.
4 *Turner v MGM Pictures Ltd* [1950] 1 All ER 449 at 461. See also *Hunt v Star Newspapers Co Ltd* [1908] 2 KB 309 per Buckley LJ.
5 *Telnikoff v Matusevitch* [1992] 2 AC 343 at 354 per Lord Keith of Kinkel.
6 *Thomas v Bradbury, Agnew & Co Ltd* [1906] 2 KB 627; Carter-Ruck, *Libel and Slander* (4th edn, 1992) pp 113–118.

when a spurious connection with the facts is made. A theatre critic can say that a play is immoral, but he cannot continue with comments like 'that is not surprising since the playwright himself is immoral'. That would be a comment not on the play but on the playwright and to be protected such a comment would have to be backed up with facts concerning the playwright's personal life[1]. Often, of course, a comment on a work is inevitably a comment on the creator (such as, for example, 'this novel is badly written', or, as in the Scottish case of *Adam v Allan*[2], 'this infidel publication'). So long as the comment on the creator is relevant to the comment on the work the defence will be available. Comments may sometimes be so extreme that they cannot be taken to be comments on fact, and in that case too the defence will fail[3].

'Fairness' in Scots law

There has been much less discussion in the Scottish cases of what amounts to an unfair comment, but in the decisions there is noticeably less emphasis on the concept of 'honesty' as being part of 'fairness', and noticeably more on the notion of relevance. Lord McLaren, who had done so much to bring the defence into recognition in Scotland, laid down its classic definition as follows: 'The expression of an opinion as to a state of facts truly set forth is not actionable, even when that opinion is couched in vituperative or contumelious language'[4]. There is no qualification here that the opinion expressed be genuine or honestly held. Again, in *Godfrey v W & DC Thomson*[5] the only limit he specified was that of relevance: 'But newspaper critics are only privileged when they keep within the limits of public criticism, and when they exceed that limit, and touch upon matters affecting private character, they are responsible for what they say, like other members of the public'[6].

However, in the case in which the defence has received the most judicial consideration, *Wheatley v Anderson & Miller*[7], English decisions were heavily relied upon. Lord Anderson, after pointing out that there had been little discussion of the defence in Scotland, turned to the 'illuminative treatment' that it had received in England, and he quoted without comment English dicta to the effect that the statement complained of must be both fair and 'bona fide' (ie honest)[8]. This has been assumed to be the law ever since, but there is no

---

1 *Merivale v Carson* (1887) 20 QBD 275; *McQuire v Western Morning News Co* [1903] 2 KB 100.
2 (1841) 3 D 1058.
3 In *Sutherland v Stopes* [1925] AC 47 Viscount Finlay, having said at 63 that the defence would fail if the comment 'exceeded the bounds of fair comment', found it impossible at 68 to say that the epithet 'monstrous' passed the bounds of fair criticism.
4 *Archer v Ritchie & Co* (1891) 18 R 719 at 727. And see the same judge in *Boal v Scottish Catholic Printing Co Ltd* 1907 SC 1120 at 1122.
5 (1890) 17 R 1108.
6 *Godfrey v W & DC Thomson* (1890) 17 R 1108 at 1115. See also Lord Jerviswoode in *Longworth v Hope & Cooke* (1865) 1 SLR 53 at 55.
7 1927 SC 133.
8 1927 SC 133 at 147 per Lord Anderson. See also Lord Hunter to the same effect at 145.

subsequent judicial confirmation[1]. A quotation from an English case is not strong authority for suggesting that honesty is a condition recognised by Scots law in addition to those mentioned by Lord McLaren, and is clearly *obiter* in the context of *Wheatley*. It is difficult to see the justification for allowing the defence to be defeated by a pursuer showing lack of honesty in expression on the part of the defender. Just as one can lawfully tell the truth maliciously, or with intent to injure, so one ought to be able to opine relevantly on true facts, whether or not one actually holds the opinions expressed. If the basis of the defence is to protect free speech then the intent with which one exercises that right ought not to matter. So for a reviewer to comment harshly and adversely on a book deliberately in order to destroy its sales (say, in the hope of clearing the market for the reviewer's own book) may not be honest if the intent is to harm the book rather than to give expression to an opinion actually held[2]: but if the comment was relevant to the book the defence ought to be available because readers will have the opportunity to make up their own minds on the validity of the comment[3]. To rubbish a political opponent during an election is not unfair just because the person doing the rubbishing does not in truth believe that his opponent deserves it.

And there is a further reason why honesty ought not to be a requisite of fairness. Newspapers and broadcasters frequently publish other people's opinions rather than their own, and if honesty were required of the defender the defence of fair comment could seldom protect such publishers. This would be particularly apparent when, say, newspapers publish both sides of an argument and they logically are unable to claim honestly to hold both views concurrently. So long as the views are relevant to the debate then, notwithstanding the reliance on English law in *Wheatley*, the defence of fair comment ought to be available to all Scottish defenders who publish these views. It is submitted that in Scotland the defence of fair comment can be defeated by the pursuer showing only that the comment is not warranted by the facts, that is to say is not a relevant comment that can be made upon these facts. If the case is truly one of privilege rather than comment, but only then, malice or bad faith will destroy the defence.

---

1 An interesting discussion of fair comment can be found in *Caldwell v Bayne* (1936) 52 Sh Ct Rep 334 in which Sheriff Malcolm says at 339: 'So long as it is fair it is protected, and a very wide latitude indeed is allowed in deciding what is fair'.

2 In the English case of *Stark v Lewis* 6 February 1992, unreported (Court of Appeal) such a motive was held to be capable of founding a plea of malice, which was assumed to destroy the defence of fair comment.

3 Cf *Turner v MGM Pictures Ltd* [1950] 1 All ER 449.

CHAPTER ELEVEN

Miscellaneous defences

Introduction

Apart from the legal defences mentioned in the preceding five chapters there are defences of fact available to the defender, such as averments that he or she did not in fact make the statement or communication complained of, or that it did not refer to the pursuer. Matters of fact like these are to be determined by proof and, as always, it is for the pursuer to make sufficient averments to back up his or her case, which will include averments (and proof if they are denied) that the defender is the person responsible for the alleged defamation and that it was understood as being directed against the pursuer. There are a number of other defences which in essence are denials of the defamatory nature of the statements complained of and here again the onus rests with the pursuer to show that the statement is *prima facie* of a defamatory nature: the defence is, in other words, a plea to the relevancy of the case. The defences of *rixa*[1] and vulgar abuse[2] fall into this category. Other defences are to the effect that the presumption of malice cannot be made, with the result that, once the defender has established the circumstances in which that conclusion is justified, the onus reverts to the pursuer to show malice. Fair retort[3] and innocent dissemination[4] are examples. Finally, there are defences to the effect that the claim is not actionable for some reason, for example because it is out of time[5] or is not actionable according to the place where the harm occurred[6]: it is for the defender to establish one of these defences.

Statements made *in rixa*

In order to be actionable a statement or communication of idea must be capable of harming the subject's character, honour and reputation. That capacity is primarily determined by examining the defamatory quality of the

---

1 Below at pp 150–154.
2 Below at pp 154–155.
3 Below at pp 155–156.
4 Above at pp 87–90.
5 Below at pp 156–158.
6 Below at p 158.

statement[1], but even if a statement is on the face of it defamatory it will not be actionable unless it was made in circumstances in which the reasonable listener would take it seriously, for a statement not seriously understood will not be able to harm reputation, or cannot defame. One way of showing that a defamatory statement was not taken seriously is to show that the statement complained of was uttered *in rixa*, that is during the course of a quarrel, argument or brawl, or in the heat of a debate[2]. It would be wrong to say that words spoken in the course of an angry dispute are not defamatory: rather the occasion of anger may show the true sense in which the words were used and understood[3]. Anger alone does not found the defence: there must be a quarrel, strife or dispute between the parties in which their feelings become excited and their self-control weakened[4].

An early case illustrating this is *Reid v Scott*[5]. Here, the defender, in complaining to her servant that the latter was spending too much time in the company of the pursuer, called the pursuer 'a whore'. The majority of the court held that the circumstances did not amount to defamation since there was no more than hasty expressions used in the course of a scolding match and in the heat of passion. Again, in *Macdonald v Rupprecht*[6] a hotel proprietor, during an argument with a cook at the hotel over staffing levels in the kitchens, said of the cook that she was drunk. Lord Young said: 'If a cook gets into a squabble with her master in the kitchen and they both lose their temper, and the master, in order to browbeat the servant, says to her "you are drunk", I do not think that that constitutes a case of language which is actionable as being defamatory'[7]. Similarly, in *Christie v Robertson*[8] the parties were in dispute as to who had successfully bid for a horse at an auction and the defender, on being challenged by the pursuer to hand over the horse, declared that the pursuer was 'a bloody liar' who 'should have been in the hands of the police 20 times during the past five years'. It was held that because these words were neither intended by the defender nor were understood by the listeners to have a defamatory sense the action had to fail.

It would seem that there are two possible bases in principle to this defence. The first (and the one implied above) is that statements made in the heat of an argument will not be understood by the listeners to be meant seriously, and therefore will be incapable of harming the pursuer's character, honour and reputation. A statement takes on a defamatory quality only when, through the eyes of the reasonable disinterested observer, the statement *seriously* attributes something disparaging to the pursuer. But if the reasonable disin-

---

1 See above at pp 8–17.
2 Erskine, *Institute of the Law of Scotland* IV, 4, 80.
3 *Christie v Robertson* (1899) 1 F 1155 at 1157 per Lord McLaren. It follows that in other circumstances in which the law requires words to be seriously meant, a plea of *rixa* will be relevant to show lack of serious intent: see for example *Hunter v Hunter* (1883) 11 R 359.
4 *Hunter v Sommerville* (1903) 11 SLT 34 (p 70) at 71 per sheriff-substitute Strachan.
5 (1825) 4 S 5.
6 (1894) 21 R 389.
7 (1894) 21 R 389 at 391.
8 (1899) 1 F 1155.

terested observer would not believe that the words are meant to be taken seriously then they will not be regarded as defamatory. A listener to a heated argument may reasonably conclude that words spoken in haste and in anger are no more than abuse without serious content and the words, not being believed, will not be capable of harming the subject's reputation. So the jury's verdict was set aside in *Watson v Duncan*[1] because they 'were in error in attributing a serious meaning' to the statements complained of, which had been made during a noisy public meeting at which the pursuer had made an accusation against the defender and the defender had responded with the defamatory word 'liar'. It appears from this case, and consists with the general definition of defamation, that an objective test is to be applied to the words used: would the reasonable listener understand them to be serious allegations? And as Lord McLaren said,

'it is a condition of [the pursuer's] right to damages that the words complained of were applied to him in a defamatory sense, and the sense in which the words were really used is to be ascertained, as in any other case of construction, from the context and the history of the case or "surrounding circumstances"'[2].

If the defence succeeds on this approach then the pursuer's case necessarily fails since the essence of the defence is that there is no defamation[3].

A second possible basis to the defence, which some dicta support, is that words spoken in anger are not words from which malice can be inferred, even when the words themselves are calumnious and malice would therefore otherwise be inferred. The defence, on this basis, really amounts to this, that the anger rather than malice motivates the words[4]. So in *Mackintosh v Squair*[5] Lord Justice-Clerk Patton said that 'the words "scoundrel", "blackguard" and such like, used under irritation, do not carry in themselves evidence of intention to lower the character of the party as to whom they are used'. The affinity that this defence has with that of fair retort[6] also suggests this approach. If this is the true basis of the defence then its applicability does not finish the pursuer's case (as it would if *rixa* took away the defamatory nature of the statement): rather it would have the effect, like qualified privilege, of putting upon the pursuer the burden of establishing that the defender acted maliciously. However, to see the defence in terms of malice is not satisfactory since an angry dispute should not in itself be seen as an occasion that attracts, or has the same effect as, privilege. Privilege is based, by and large, on the public policy need to encourage free speech in certain circumstances[7], and there is no public interest in encouraging squabblers to abuse each other. If a statement is prima facie defamatory before the plea of *rixa* is applied then malice should be presumed, just as it is presumed in other cases of unintentional defamation. It

1 (1890) 17 R 404.
2 *Watson v Duncan* (1890) 17 R 404 at 408 per Lord McLaren.
3 See also *Fleming v Craig* (1939) 55 Sh Ct Rep 35, which adopts this approach.
4 See Lord Trayner in *Macdonald v Rupprecht* (1894) 21 R 389 at 391; *Ersk* IV, 4, 80.
5 (1868) 40 Sc Jur 561 at 562.
6 Below at pp 155–156.
7 Above at pp 91, 103–104.

is submitted that the true basis of the *rixa* defence is that reasonable listeners would not regard the words complained of as serious allegations and these words are, therefore, innocuous to the pursuer's reputation. The result is that the success of the defence necessarily involves the failure of the pursuer's case.

The extent of the defence is not the anger with which the words are spoken but the meaning attached to them by the listeners, and derogatory words spoken in the course of an angry dispute will be actionable if, in all the circumstances, a seriously meant allegation can reasonably be taken from the words. It would seem that the more specific the charge the more likely it is that seriousness will be inferred. Meaningless words hurled during a squabble, which are defamatory only by innuendo, are far less likely to be taken seriously than specific detailed charges. So in *Christie v Robertson*[1], Lord McLaren said:

'If a party, under whatever amount of provocation, makes a definite charge of crime or a charge of dishonest conduct against another, giving such point in regard to time and circumstances as to lead those who were present to believe that the charge was seriously made, it is no defence that the words were spoken in heat'[2].

It may be that the more serious the charge the less likely it is that the defence will succeed, for it is noticeable that the cases in which the defence has succeeded involve charges like 'liar'[3], 'drunk'[4] and 'whore'[5].

The defence has more chance of success if the defender has apologised as soon as the argument is over[6], or if there is no repetition and no attempt to spread the scandal[7]. It has less chance of success if the statement complained of is later repeated or if, as in *Grant v Mackay*[8], the defender deliberately calls upon bystanders to witness what he is saying: again, this suggests deliberation from which seriousness can be inferred. It would be very difficult to establish the defence in a case of written as opposed to spoken defamation (for writing suggests deliberation) but it is not, apparently, impossible[9].

Though the effect of the defence is to take away the defamatory quality of the words complained of, this does not mean that the onus is on the pursuer to disprove the plea. The pursuer has to establish that the words are prima facie capable of being defamatory or at least can be innuendoed as such, this in order to make his case relevant. It is then open to the defender to prove, if he can, that the words in fact lack defamatory effect because in the circumstances they were not meant to be and were not taken to be serious accusations. The

---

1 (1899) 1 F 1155.

2 (1899) 1 F 1155 at 1157.

3 *Watson v Duncan* (1890) 17 R 404; *Christie v Robertson* (1899) 1 F 1155; *Pybus v Mackinnon* (1908) 15 SLT 320 (p 846); *Fleming v Craig* (1939) 55 Sh Ct Rep 35.

4 *Macdonald v Rupprecht* (1894) 21 R 389.

5 *Reid v Scott* (1825) 4 S 5; *McKnight v Kelly* (1900) 16 Sh Ct Rep 30.

6 *Mackintosh v Squair* (1868) 40 Sc Jur 561.

7 *Reid v Scott* (1825) 4 S 5.

8 (1903) 11 SLT 216 (p 380).

9 *Lovi v Wood* (1802) Hume 613. See Cooper, *Defamation and Verbal Injury* (2nd edn, 1906) pp 94 and 95 for comment.

onus of proving the defence, therefore, rests with the defender, who should move for dismissal of the action as irrelevant.

Vulgar abuse or sarcasm

It is a defence to an action for defamation that the words complained of amount to no more than vulgar abuse or sarcasm[1]. There are two reasons for this. First, words falling into this category have no real meaning or are incapable of expressing a fact[2]. An example might be if the defender had said, 'the pursuer is a fucking bastard'. (It is, of course, different if an innuendo can be drawn[3] and sometimes, indeed, vulgar abuse has a perfectly well-recognised meaning such as, for example, the phrase 'bloody poof'.) In *Cockburn v Reekie*[4] Lord McLaren said:

'We have never gone so far as to hold that mere unmeaning abuse, mere vituperation, will give a right of action. We only give compensation for defamatory language – that is to say, language which conveys some definite imputation as to the character or conduct of the pursuer'[5].

Secondly, vulgar abuse or sarcasm is not generally regarded as having been meant seriously and is, therefore, akin to statements made *in rixa*[6]. So in *Hunter v Sommerville*[7] the sheriff described the phrase 'dirty sneak' as 'a mere term of abuse [which] contains no reflection on the pursuer's moral character or reputation as a business man'[8]. It is probably for this reason that satirical television and radio programmes which lampoon public figures, or political cartoons and caricatures doing the same, do not thereby commit defamation: they are not taken to be serious accusations, but expressions of wit, satire or sarcasm and are therefore incapable of injuring reputation[9]. In the late 1980s a satirical television puppet show continually portrayed the then Prime Minister, who was a woman, dressed in a man's suit. No reasonable viewer would regard this as a serious allegation of transvestitism. The same programme showed the Queen Mother continually drinking gin. There was no defamation because no reasonable viewer would take from that portrayal any seriously meant allegation likely to lower the woman in the estimation of right-thinking members of society.

1 *Cooper* p 46; Smith, *A Short Commentary on the Laws of Scotland* (1963) p 737.
2 *Christie v Robertson* (1899) 1 F 1155 at 1157 per Lord McLaren.
3 *Brownlie v Thomson* (1859) 21 D 480 at 485 per Lord Justice-Clerk Inglis; and *Jameson v Bonthrone* (1873) 11 M 703 at 704 per Lord Deas (the expression there was 'damned puppy').
4 (1890) 17 R 568.
5 (1890) 17 R 568 at 571.
6 *Cooper*, above.
7 (1903) 11 SLT 34 (p 70).
8 (1903) 11 SLT 34 at 71. See also *Fleming v Craig* (1939) 55 Sh Ct Rep 35.
9 Cf *Bell v Haldane* (1894) 2 SLT 317 (p 320) where an action was dismissed by Lord Kyllachy because the words used were 'plainly meant [to be] sarcasm, heavy indeed and laboured, but only sarcasm'.

The continual lampooning of an individual in a series of sarcastic or witty articles or programmes, which hold up the individual to public hatred, contempt and ridicule, has been held to amount to verbal injury[1], but satirical television or radio programmes that each week poke fun at, or even pore scorn over, individuals will not be held liable for verbal injury unless it can be shown that there is an intention to injure that person[2]: intent to amuse which causes injury is not sufficient.

Fair retort

A person is entitled to make a fair retort to charges made against him and if that retort contains matter that is defamatory of his accuser then that matter is not actionable unless it can be shown by the pursuer that the defender has acted maliciously, or with intent to injure[3]. In other words, the circumstances are such as will negative the presumption of malice, and in effect make the case one of qualified privilege[4]. So in the case cited the pursuer had been charged with cruelty to animals, having been reported to the procurator fiscal by the defenders. He was acquitted on a verdict of not proven but retained a feeling of grievance against the defenders. He brought this to the public notice by writing to a newspaper accusing the defenders of 'cruel injustice' towards him. In response to that letter the defenders wrote themselves to the newspaper, setting out the facts that they had reported, and pointing out the difference between the verdicts of not proven and not guilty. The pursuer sued for defamation. The court held that the defenders' letter amounted to fair retort with the result that malice had to be averred and proved. The accusation against the defenders was such that it demanded reply in order to protect their own reputation, and the fact that they replied was more readily explained by the desire to protect their own reputation than by a malicious intent to injure the pursuer[5]. In the absence of averment and proof of malice, the claim failed.

The retort, to be fair, must be kept within the bounds of relevancy[6] though what is or is not relevant is unlikely to be strictly construed[7]. In *Blair v Eastwood*[8] the defender was accused by the pursuer of being the father of her

---

1 *Sheriff v Wilson* (1855) 17 D 528; *Cunningham v Phillips* (1868) 6 M 926. See also *McLaughlan v Orr, Pollock & Co* (1894) 22 R 38 and *Burns v Diamond* (1896) 3 SLT 397 (p 256).
2 See above at pp 120–123.
3 *Gray v Scottish Society for the Prevention of Cruelty to Animals* (1890) 17 R 1185.
4 As such the defence will be inapplicable in an action for verbal injury, where intent to injure must be shown in any case. It is difficult to visualise how the defence could arise in a case raised in negligence.
5 See also *Laughton v Bishop of Sodor & Man* (1872) LR 4 PC 495.
6 *Milne v Walker* (1893) 21 R 155.
7 See also *Hamilton v Duncan* (1825) 4 S 414 and *NU Bank Employees v Murray* 1949 SLT (Notes) 25.
8 (1935) 51 Sh Ct Rep 304.

illegitimate child. He retorted by accusing her of having had sexual intercourse with at least two other men. This was held not to be a fair retort since it
was unnecessary for the defender to 'charge the pursuer with being free with
other men' to rebut her charge against him.

Prescription and limitation

Actions accruing prior to December 30, 1985

Prior to December 30, 1985 there was no specific statutory provision
governing the prescription and limitation of actions for defamation or verbal
injury. The result was that the law contained in the general provisions of the
Prescription and Limitation (Scotland) Act 1973 applied to these actions,
though how precisely these provisions affected defamation and verbal injury
was open to some doubt. It is clear that claims for damages for economic loss
were subject to the five-year prescription period laid down by section 6 of the
1973 Act, for such a claim was based on an 'obligation arising from liability
(whether arising from any enactment or from any rule of law) to make
reparation'[1]. Whether this provision applied to claims for damages for solatium for hurt feelings was, however, more doubtful and it might be that these
claims were subject to the three-year limitation period laid down by section
17[2] for actions for damages for personal injuries. Section 22 defines 'personal
injuries' for this purpose as including any disease and any impairment of a
person's physical or mental condition, but there is conflicting authority as to
whether the phrase was sufficiently broad to cover the hurt feelings that found
a claim for solatium. In *Barclay v Chief Constable, Northern Constabulary*[3]
Lord McDonald held that 'personal injuries' included injury to feelings such
as is claimed in an action for defamation; and in *Fleming v Strathclyde Regional
Council*[4] Lord Cullen held that the phrase 'personal injuries' was wide enough
to cover various forms of personal suffering, including distress and inconvenience. On the other hand, Lord Morton of Shuna expressly refused to
follow Lord McDonald in the case of *Smith v City of Glasgow District Council*[5]
on the ground that hurt feelings was not within the bracket Parliament
intended to include in its definition of personal injuries given in section 22,
with the result that claims for solatium arising from defamation were subject
to section 6 just as were actions for economic loss. This issue is unlikely now to
be resolved as the law has since changed but it is tentatively suggested that the
views of Lord Morton were more logical, if for no other reason than the

1 Sch 1, para 1(d), defining the obligations to which s 6 applies.
2 As amended by the Prescription and Limitation (Scotland) Act 1984.
3 1986 SLT 562.
4 1992 SLT 161.
5 1991 GWD 16–995.

inconvenience, inherent in the alternative approach, of having different periods governing different aspects of the same claim[1].

Actions accruing on or after December 30, 1985

Section 12 of the Law Reform (Miscellaneous Provisions) (Scotland) Act 1985 came into force on December 30, 1985 and introduced into the 1973 Act a new section 18A which specifically deals with all claims for defamation and verbal injury accruing thereafter. It is to be noted that 'defamation' in that new section is defined[2] to include '*convicium*[3] and malicious falsehood', which can be taken to mean verbal injury[4]. It is further to be noted that by specifying all actions for defamation and verbal injury with reference to their nature rather than to the type of damages claimed, section 18A has the effect of applying the same period to claims both for hurt feelings and for economic loss. Actions for negligence based on defamatory misstatements, in which only economic loss can be claimed[5], continue to be governed by the five-year prescription period contained in section 6.

Section 18A provides that no action for defamation or for verbal injury can be brought unless it is commenced within a period of three years after the date when the publication or communication in respect of which the action is to be brought first came to the notice of the pursuer[6]. Defamation and verbal injury are one-off events and not continuing wrongs which can found actions for howsoever long the wrong continues. In *Smith v City of Glasgow District Council*[7] the pursuer raised an action against his ex-employers for defamation more than three years previously. He argued that since the defamatory statements made by members of a council committee had entered the minutes of the council, the defamation he was suffering from was a continuing wrong for which the limitation period would not commence to run until the wrong (ie the defamatory statements in the minutes) ceased to exist. Lord Morton of Shuna rejected this argument and held that defamation consists of the uttering of a statement that is defamatory, and it is not continually repeated by being minuted in a permanent record.

In the computation of the period of three years there shall be disregarded any time during which the person alleged to have been defamed or verbally injured was under legal disability by reason of nonage or unsoundness of mind[8]. 'Nonage' is normally taken to refer to a minor (ie a person below the

---

1 It may be noted that since 1993 the Administration of Justice Act 1982 has defined 'personal injury' to include 'injury resulting from defamation or any other verbal injury or other injury to reputation' (s 13(1), as amended by Schedule to the Damages (Scotland) Act 1993).
2 Section 18A(4)(a).
3 That this word connotes a meaningless chimera is shown above in Chapter 3.
4 See above at p 36.
5 See above at p 6.
6 Section 18A(1) and (4)(b).
7 1991 GWD 16–995.
8 Section 18A(2).

age of majority, which is 18)[1]. However the age at which a young person may raise an action on his or her own behalf is now 16[2] and it would be anomalous to define 'nonage' for the purpose of raising an action as anything other than 16. A person is no longer under legal disability by reason of nonage once he or she has reached his or her 16th birthday, and it follows that the three-year period of limitation for actions for defamation and verbal injury allegedly committed against a person under 16 starts to run on the pursuer's 16th birthday.

The power of the court under section 19A to override the time-limits contained in section 17 was extended when section 18A was introduced and the court was given power to override the limits contained in section 18A also[3]. The court may, if it seems to it equitable to do so, allow the pursuer to bring an action notwithstanding that it is out of time under the terms of section 18A[4].

Prescription

All actions for defamation and verbal injury now prescribe after 20 years, and section 6 no longer provides a five-year prescription period when only economic loss is claimed[5].

Non-actionability by the law of the place of the delict

As is explained more fully later[6], defamation or verbal injury that occurs outwith Scotland is actionable in the Scottish courts only if it is actionable both by the domestic law of Scotland and by the domestic law of the place where it occurs. Because the pursuer can rely on the presumption that foreign law is the same as the law of Scotland, it falls on the defender to prove as a defence that the claim is not civilly actionable under the foreign law. The reason for non-actionability under that law is irrelevant and the defence is available whatever the reason for the inability to claim damages. The place of the defamation is for this purpose the place where the loss occurs[7]

---

1 See Thomson, Law Reform (Miscellaneous Provisions) (Scotland) Act 1985, *Current Law Annotations*, commenting on the word in relation to s 18A. See also *Forbes v House of Clydesdale Ltd* 1988 SLT 594.
2 Age of Legal Capacity (Scotland) Act 1991, s 1(1)(b) provides that a person of or over the age of 16 years shall have legal capacity to enter into any transaction. 'Transaction' is defined by s 9 as 'a transaction having legal effect and includes . . . (e) the bringing or defending of, or the taking of any step in, civil proceedings'.
3 Section 19A(1), as amended by the Law Reform (Miscellaneous Provisions) (Scotland) Act 1985, s 12(3).
4 Though there are no reported cases in which s 19A has been used in relation to s 18A, the principles will be much the same as when it is used in relation to s 17: see for example *Forsyth v AF Stoddard & Co Ltd* 1985 SLT 51; *Anderson v City of Glasgow District Council* 1987 SLT 279; *McCabe v McLellan* 1994 SLT 346.
5 Prescription and Limitation (Scotland) Act 1973, s 7 and Sch 1, para 2(gg), added by s 12(5) of the Law Reform (Miscellaneous Provisions) (Scotland) Act 1985.
6 Below at pp 186–191.
7 See p 191.

CHAPTER TWELVE

The remedies

Introduction

Actions for defamation and verbal injury are rare in Scotland, in comparison both to the equivalent actions in England and to other types of delictual claim recognised by Scots law. Legal practitioners may, however, be asked to advise either potential pursuers or potential defenders on these matters rather more often than the paucity of court actions might indicate and for that reason it is appropriate to consider briefly the extra-judicial 'remedy' of negotiation and settlement before examining in detail the two major delictual remedies of damages and interdict and their application to defamation and verbal injury. Also considered in this chapter will be the appropriate court process to be adopted in such actions.

Negotiation and settlement

It is well-known that legal aid is not available to fund court actions for either defamation or verbal injury[1] and an inevitable result of this is that few actions are taken to court by pursuers of modest means. However, rather less well-known is the fact that legal aid is available in the form of legal advice and assistance in defamation matters and both potential pursuers and potential defenders can be funded in their search for a settlement. A person who is affronted, say, by a newspaper article which he or she considers defamatory can therefore be legally aided in employing a solicitor to write seeking a retraction and apology or even seeking compensation. Also, not every person who has been defamed will be seeking monetary compensation: many will want nothing more than an apology and a correction of factually inaccurate statements. This can be achieved through negotiation without the necessity for court action. Though a claimant's hand will be strengthened by a willingness – and financial ability – to go to court if satisfaction is not received, negotiation and settlement is frequently all that the client wishes: it should of course always be the primary aim of the legal adviser to encourage a satisfactory settlement. This will be particularly so if the alleged defamation has been given only limited circulation and has caused no economic loss. The legal adviser ought

---

1 Legal Aid (Scotland) Act 1986, Sch 2, Pt II.

in the first instance to seek an apology from the alleged defamer, together with such correction of factual inaccuracies as is necessary to clear the person's name. Often the threat of taking the case to the Press Complaints Commission or the Broadcasting Complaints Commission will be sufficient to spur a media defender. Most newspapers published in Scotland will carry corrections and apologies and indeed may have strong incentive to do so in the form of section 4 of the Defamation Act 1952 which provides that a suitable correction and apology will give an innocent defamer an absolute defence to any subsequent action for defamation[1]. Even when the defamation is not 'innocent' within the terms of the statute, many people will be seeking no more and media defenders are usually willing to issue corrections of false derogatory statements. Many will also offer small monetary amounts as redress for affront. Spurious claims (that is, those concerning statements that no reasonable person would consider derogatory) are, quite properly, likely to get short shrift.

If economic loss is caused by the defamation then obviously the claimant will want something more than an apology, and whether the alleged defamer will be willing to offer monetary amends will depend on a number of factors. Foremost amongst these will be the likelihood that the claimant will take the matter further, the value of the claim, how confident the alleged defamer is that the statement complained of is not defamatory or that he can prove the accuracy of the statement, the availability of a defence, and the level of damages likely to be awarded by a court. This last-mentioned consideration will be strongly influenced by whether the case would be heard in Scotland or in England and the view has been expressed to the author by some media defenders that they are more likely to settle if the threat is to go to the English rather than the Scottish court. The reason for this is that the far higher level of damages available in England makes the financial risk greater for the defender, but it is, of course, to be remembered that the choice of going to England will not be open to everyone[2]. Actions for defamation or verbal injury are likely to be expensive for both parties and the relative unpredictability of the outcome makes these cases possibly more than any other appropriate for extra-judicial compromise, though clearly spurious claims can safely and should speedily be dismissed with the contempt that they deserve.

The court process

In cases in which the parties cannot settle or compromise, the claimant must decide whether to let the matter rest (in the hope that his or her reputation is sufficiently resilient to weather the attack) or to take the matter further to a court of law (and thereby risk far wider publicity with its potential for public ridicule greater than that caused by the defender). If the latter course is chosen then the action for defamation or verbal injury can be raised in either

1 For the details, see above at pp 83–87.
2 See further, below at Chapter 13.

the Court of Session or the sheriff court, and the choice of which court is appropriate will generally be made on the basis of the value of the claim. A less valuable claim may, however, be taken to the Court of Session if the legal issues are particularly complex.

Sheriff court

Cases of defamation can still be raised in the sheriff court, though this happens rarely[1]. Civil jury trials in the sheriff court had become increasingly rare and were never used in defamation actions. They were finally abolished in 1980[2] and the mode of inquiry today in all civil claims is by proof before the sheriff alone. Whether ordinary cause or summary cause procedure should be used depends upon the value of the claim (not taking account of interest and expenses) and summary cause procedure might be appropriate when the pursuer is simply seeking to clear his or her name. Actions for defamation cannot be raised using the small claims procedure[3] and though actions for verbal injury are not specifically excluded from that procedure they are highly unlikely to be considered appropriate.

Court of Session

Most cases of defamation and verbal injury come before the Court of Session, and there the mode of inquiry will be either proof or jury trial. Section 11 of the Court of Session Act 1988 enumerates certain actions that 'shall be tried by jury'[4]. One of the enumerated actions is 'an action for libel or defamation'[5]. This, however, is subject to section 9, which provides that the Lord Ordinary may allow a proof in any of the enumerated actions 'if the parties to the action consent thereto or if special cause is shown'. These have long been the rules[6]. It is a curious feature of the law that while jury actions for defamation became very rare in the second half of the twentieth century (indeed were non-existent, at least in the law reports, between 1950[7] and 1991[8]), it was not until 1992 that a reported decision actually discussed the issue of 'special cause'. Before then the practice had established itself of parties to an action for defamation invariably agreeing to a proof rather than a jury trial.

---

1 Apart from a counter-claim in an action for recovery of fees (*Mellicks v Anderson* 1993 GWD 27–1738) the last reported example was *Olsen v Keddie* 1976 SLT (Sh Ct) 64. Since 1945 there have been seven reported sheriff court cases of defamation (compared with over 30 in the Court of Session).
2 Law Reform (Miscellaneous Provisions) (Scotland) Act 1980, s 11 and Sch 3.
3 Sheriff Courts (Scotland) Act 1971, s 37(2) and Small Claims (Scotland) Order 1988, SI 1988/1999, para 2.
4 Procedure in jury trial is described in Maxwell, *The Practice of the Court of Session*, Chapter 9.
5 The 'or' in that phrase is exegetical. The phrase 'libel or defamation', which is today tautologous, can be traced to s 28 of the Court of Session Act 1825, from which s 11 of the 1988 Act is derived.
6 See previously the Evidence (Scotland) Act 1866, s 4.
7 *Moffat v London Express Newspapers Ltd* 1950 SLT (Notes) 46.
8 *Winter v News Scotland Ltd* 1991 SLT 828.

There have been many cases in other areas of the law, particularly in personal injury claims, in which the question has been discussed of what amounts to 'special cause' which justifies a proof rather than a jury trial. These cases[1] are of only limited assistance in relation to defamation, for each case has to be dealt with on its own facts, and 'special cause' must be a cause special to the particular case. The matter is to be determined, not by reference to any legal principle or category, but as a matter for sound judicial discretion[2]. Special cause means, 'some real ground of substance making the case unsuitable for jury trial. It must not be a mere hypothetical difficulty conjured up by the ingenuity of counsel. It ought to be something that is capable of articulate formulation, and not a mere generality'[3]. The format of the 1988 Act indicates that the onus of persuading the judge to grant a proof rests with the person seeking it, rather than the person relying on the statutory right to trial by jury. It follows that, even in the absence of agreement by the parties, if the case is straightforward and gives rise to no difficult issue of law then a jury trial will be granted. In *McCabe v News Group Newspapers Ltd*[4] the pursuer alleged that the defenders had defamed her by reporting her as having made a particular statement. The defenders submitted that the case was unsuitable for jury trial on the ground that it raised difficult and delicate questions of mixed fact and law. They submitted that the jury would have difficulty in understanding the interrelationship between the pleas of *veritas* and fair comment, which were both being pleaded. However, Lord Morison decided that the major issue in the case was whether the contentious statement had been made by the pursuer or not, which was a straightforward question of fact. Concerning the interrelation between *veritas* and fair comment, he found that any such complication would arise in every case in which both pleas are being made and that there was nothing special about this case which rendered the matter particularly difficult. Consequently, he held that special cause to justify withholding the case from a jury trial had not been shown, and issues were allowed[5].

The matter was discussed further and more fully in *Shanks v BBC*[6] in which Lord Osborne was persuaded that special cause had been shown to withhold the case from a jury and to proceed by means of a proof. In this case an accountant was claiming £900,000 for loss of business and affront allegedly caused by a television documentary about his business dealings. These dealings involved the winding up of companies in which the pursuer acted variously as accountant, director and shareholder. There were 27 different companies, eight inter-company transactions and nine changes of company name; there were nine innuendoes which the pursuer wished to establish, and various averments which might or might not be relevant. Lord Orborne held that a jury trial would be inappropriate because of the complicated nature of

---

1 Discussed fully in the opinion of Lord Osborne in *Shanks v BBC* 1993 SLT 326.
2 *Walker v Pitlochry Motor Co* 1930 SLT 367 at 373.
3 *Graham v John Paterson & Sons Ltd* 1938 SC 119 at 127 per Lord Justice-Clerk Aitchison.
4 1992 SLT 707.
5 The trial was never held as the case was thereafter settled.
6 1993 SLT 326.

the allegations made, which would involve a great deal of 'educational evidence' being put to the jury before they could understand the nature of the alleged defamation; because of the difficulties in assessing damages, which would have to be done by examining the profitability of the pursuer's business; because of the range and variety of the allegations being founded upon; because of the doubtful relevancy of many of the pursuer's pleadings; and because of the confused and unclear averments of the pursuer's loss. Lord Osborne disapproved a statement in Cooper[1] to the effect that 'it is extremely doubtful whether the Court would order proof before a judge instead of a jury trial if either party – and particularly if the pursuer – objected to its being so dealt with' in an action for defamation, on the ground that defamation cases are to be treated no differently from any other in determining whether there is 'special cause'.

It has been suggested[2] that a pursuer is likely to obtain more damages from a jury than from a judge sitting alone. Given the paucity of recent cases in Scotland it is difficult to provide empirical evidence to support this but there is little doubt that this belief can encourage pursuers to seek trial by jury. However, that encouragement is counteracted by the fact that juries are more expensive and this is a significant consideration to pursuers paying their own way in this risky action. Also, it is to be remembered that section 29 of the Court of Session Act 1988 allows the Inner House to order a new trial on the ground of inadequacy or excess of damages awarded by a jury[3].

Verbal injury

Section 11 of the Court of Session Act 1988, which deals with jury trials, is limited in its terms to 'an action for libel or defamation'. It is generally accepted today that an action for verbal injury is not an action for libel or defamation, but is something quite different in kind and is subject to very different rules[4]. Actions for personal injuries are within the enumerated causes in section 11 suitable for jury trial just as actions for defamation are, but in another context[5] there is a conflict of Outer House authority as to whether injury to feelings amount to 'personal injury'[6]. As has been seen, most claims for verbal injury will be claims for economic loss in any case and therefore will not be within one of the enumerated actions for jury trial. Even when only solatium is claimed and the claim is an enumerated cause, the distinction between defamation and verbal injury is sometimes so subtle that this alone will normally justify withholding the case from a jury. It is likely

---

1 *Defamation and Verbal Injury* (2nd edn, 1906) p 265.
2 McFadden (1994) 39 JLSS 24.
3 See below at pp 173–175 for details.
4 See above at pp 46–48.
5 That of prescription and limitation: see above at p 156.
6 Lord McDonald in *Barclay v Chief Constable, Northern Constabulary* 1986 SLT 562 and Lord Cullen in *Fleming v Strathclyde Regional Council* 1992 SLT 161 thought that 'personal injuries' includes injury to feelings, whereas Lord McDonald in *Smith v City of Glasgow District Council* 1991 GWD 16–995 thought that it did not. Section 13(1) of the Administration of Justice Act 1982 now defines 'personal injury' to include injury resulting from defamation and verbal injury.

that a jury trial would be thought appropriate for a claim for verbal injury only in very unusual circumstances. There is nothing to prevent an action for verbal injury being raised in the sheriff court, though only one example from the law reports can be traced[1].

Damages: general

Damages in the law of Scotland are awarded as reparation and not as punishment, vindication or example[2], and it follows that the level of damages to be awarded is determined by an assessment of the losses suffered by the pursuer that are legally recognised. Smith points out[3] that the law originally recognised two sorts of losses flowing from actionable words – first, the insult felt by the pursuer, for which an award of solatium was appropriate, and secondly the damage to reputation as an economic asset, for which damages by way of reparation was appropriate. It would appear that the element of insult was dealt with mainly by the commissary court which sought palinode (retraction of the insult[4]) and imposed solatium (a solace for the pursuer's hurt feelings) and that *animus injuriandi* was the basis of liability (because it had developed out of the *actio injuriarum*). The element of loss to reputation, on the other hand, was dealt with by the civil courts which provided the remedy of reparation, the basis of liability for which was *culpa* (having developed from the *lex aquilia*). Originally these two elements were quite distinct wrongs and were dealt with mainly by different courts, and while there was always much overlap each could exist independently of the other. The merging of the jurisdictions of the commissaries and the civil courts had the effect of merging the two bases of action, so that today an action for defamation is an action upon insulting words which may cause economic loss and for which damages may be due as both solace and reparation.

If the words are insulting the law will presume that a person who has feelings to hurt will indeed be hurt thereby and so entitled to solatium, even if the defamation (written or oral) is communicated to no-one other than the pursuer[5]. There is no such thing as *injuria sine damno* in cases of defamation of an individual[6], though the damages awarded will sometimes (though not

---

1 *Caldwell v Bayne* (1936) 52 Sh Ct Rep 334. The sheriff dismissed the claim here because it had not been pleaded with sufficient clarity, but he did recognise its competence.
2 *Gibson v Anderson* (1846) 9 D 1 at 6 per Lord President Boyle; *Black v North British Railway Co* 1908 SC 444 at 453 per Lord President Dunedin; *Winter v News Scotland Ltd* 1991 SLT 828 at 829E per Lord Morison.
3 *A Short Commentary on the Laws of Scotland* (1963) pp 724–727.
4 See for a clear example of palinode being extracted, *Symmond v Williamson* (1752) Mor 3435.
5 *Mackay v McCankie* (1883) 10 R 537; *Ramsay v MacLay & Co* (1890) 18 R 130. This is one of the fundamental differences between Scots and English law, where defamation is more strictly limited to reputation as an economic asset and requires, therefore, publication to a third party.
6 *Bradley v Menley & James Ltd* 1913 SC 923 at 926 per Lord Justice-Clerk Macdonald; *Cassidy v Connachie* 1907 SC 1112 at 1116 per Lord Stormonth-Darling.

always[1]) be merely nominal if, for example, the action was raised primarily to clear the pursuer's name and this has been achieved or the facts of the case, as established, are so unsatisfactory for the pursuer that the jury are of the opinion that little damage has been caused[2]. If economic loss has been suffered then this must be specified and quantified in the claim, for the law does not presume such losses. Indeed, if *only* economic loss is suffered, a claim for reparation without solatium will be competent, and there is not the difficulty in suing for pure economic loss flowing from an intentional delict such as defamation that exists, in some circumstances at least, in relation to negligence. Solatium may be claimed in a case of verbal injury as in a case of defamation, but in such a case the loss is not presumed and has to be averred and proved. In cases of verbal injury it is not necessary for the pursuer to aver or prove special damage if the words on which the action is founded are calculated to cause pecuniary damage to the pursuer[3]. Pursuers who have no feelings to hurt, such as corporations and other non-natural pursuers, cannot suffer insult and they can claim only economic loss[4]. As a consequence such pursuers must always specify and quantify their claim, and the measure of damages is the measure of the patrimonial loss. So in *Thomson v Fifeshire Advertiser*[5], a case of verbal injury (slander of business), it was held that the action was irrelevant in that there were no averments of damage of a patrimonial kind. If there is economic loss this may well be far greater than could ever be awarded to an individual by way of solatium. So in *Capital Life Assurance Society Ltd v Scottish Daily Record and Sunday Mail*[6] a sum of £327,000 (plus interest and expenses) was awarded, which by some way is the highest amount ever awarded in an action for defamation in a Scottish court. The bulk of that sum was made up of lost business which was proven to be a direct consequence of the defenders' defamatory allegation that the pursuers ran a 'disreputable' business.

Assessment of damages

In accordance with the general practice in Scottish pleadings, the pursuer must specify the amount being claimed, so the court does not have an entirely free hand and it cannot award a sum in excess of what is asked for. It also behoves the pursuer to justify the amount he or she claims, though this may be done in general terms. Within these limits, the question of assessment of damages is within the discretion of the jury in a jury case, and within the

---

1 See *Smith v Graham* 1981 SLT (Notes) 19.
2 See for example *Craig v Jex-Blake* (1871) 9 M 973; *Bonnar v Roden* (1887) 14 R 761; *Winn v Quillan* (1899) 2 F 322; *Bradley v Menley & James Ltd* 1913 SC 923; *Fraser v Finlayson* (1937) 53 Sh Ct Rep 97.
3 Defamation Act 1952, s 3.
4 See above at p 66.
5 1936 SN 56.
6 (1979) Scotsman, 6 January.

discretion of the judge otherwise. Few guiding principles can be laid down, except to state that each case depends upon its own facts. Patrimonial loss can usually be assessed (relatively) accurately and there is little difference between the quantification of such loss in defamation cases and in other cases. Such losses should, of course, be expressly averred and the basis of assessment given when this is not obvious, for example with lost profits, loss of goodwill, lost services[1], or, indeed, loss of reputation as an economic asset. Solatium is quite different, for it is entirely speculative in actions for defamation and can only be based upon what is considered to be fair and appropriate in the circumstances. In the wise words of Guthrie Smith[2],

'[the] jury are not expected to weigh in golden scales the precise sum which ought in justice to be given. Of the matter of *solatium* they have necessarily entire control; and all that they can be told is, to bear in mind that damages are given not for the purpose of gratifying private resentment, or of making a public example of the delinquent, but of restoring the person injured, as far as money can, to the position he would have occupied had the wrong never occurred . . . The only rule which can be laid down for the guidance of the jury is, that the sum to be given in name of *solatium* ought never to be such as will enable the party to make a profit of his misfortune'.

No guidance can be obtained from awards of solatium in other fields, in which very different considerations come into play. 'It is inappropriate to attempt to make a direct comparison between an award of solatium for pain and suffering caused by physical injury and an award of solatium for injury to feelings and reputation'[3]. It is, however, proper for the jury or the judge to take account of the level of awards made in other similar defamation cases in Scotland. So for example in *Winter v News Scotland Ltd*[4] the Inner House, in determining whether a jury award of £50,000 was so excessive as to justify the granting of a new trial[5], referred to *Thoms v Bain*[6] in which there were similar allegations and similar effects on the pursuer. £2,500 had been awarded in that case and the court in *Winter* held that the figure awarded in the present case over 100 years later was comparable to that. In this area more than any other little help can be gleaned from English cases since assessment of damages in that jurisdiction is based on very different principles and in particular punitive or exemplary damages are permitted[7]. Damages for solatium for defamation are,

---

1 It is conceivable that a pursuer can lose the services of a relative who is no longer willing to provide them as a result of the defamation. Defamation and verbal injury have been within the definition of 'personal injuries' for the purposes of the Administration of Justice Act 1982 since the enactment of the Schedule to the Damages (Scotland) Act 1993. For the different methods of assessing the value of services in personal injury claims, see Blaikie, 'Personal Injuries Claims: The Valuation of "Services"' 1994 SLT (News) 167.
2 *A Treatise on the Law of Reparation* (1864), pp 472–473.
3 *Winter v News Scotland Ltd* 1991 SLT 828 at 831A per Lord Morison.
4 1991 SLT 828.
5 See further, at pp 173–175.
6 (1888) 15 R 613.
7 *Winter v News Scotland Ltd* 1991 SLT 828 at 831D-E per Lord Morison; *Stein v Beaverbrook Newspapers Ltd* 1968 SC 272 at 278 per Lord Justice-Clerk Grant. On damages for defamation in English law, see Carter-Ruck, *Libel and Slander* (4th edn, 1992) pp 166–177. For a comparison, see McFadden (1994) 39 JLSS 24.

traditionally, assessed in Scotland at a modest level[1], though patrimonial loss may be far more substantial[2].

Aggravation of damages

The circumstances in which the defamation or verbal injury occurs may lead either to the aggravation or the mitigation of the sum awarded as solatium: this reflects the position that damages are compensatory, and a factor will be regarded as aggravating when it appears to make the pursuer's loss worse. So for example a defender who deliberately publishes a defamatory statement far and wide will normally be subjected to greater damages than a defender who communicates the statement to the pursuer alone[3]. A peak-time broadcast is likely to attract more damages than one at a less popular time for this reason, that more people will have heard or seen the defamatory broadcast. Likewise, it will aggravate the damages that the defenders falsely represented that others concurred in the view of the pursuer's character that they slanderously stated[4]. And the pursuer's reaction may aggravate damages: so a pursuer who can show much distress and even damage to health (as in *Winter v News Scotland Ltd*[5]) might expect a larger sum than the more robust pursuer who shakes off the allegation with a healthy 'sticks and stones' attitude.

The more scurrilous the allegation, the greater would be the insult likely to be felt and the greater, therefore, the damages[6]. It has been suggested that the more eminent the pursuer the higher the damages will be[7], this presumably on the view that a person with a greater reputation suffers more loss when it is attacked than a private person with no public reputation[8]. This approach has a certain logic to it, but it should not be assumed that an entirely private person has no public reputation to be harmed. An unknown individual who becomes

---

1 In 1986, when a policeman sued for defamation that caused no patrimonial loss Lord McDonald described the sum sued for (£10,000) as 'utterly ridiculous' and he awarded £200: *Anderson v Palombo* 1986 SLT 46.
2 See *Henderson v George Outram & Co Ltd* 1993 SLT 824 at 825–826. The decision there concerned the amount appropriate for an arrestment on dependence in an action for defamation and Lord Abernethy pointed out that the pursuer was, before the alleged defamation, a successful Queen's Counsel practising principally in criminal defence work. 'In that situation it is perfectly possible that any patrimonial loss which resulted from the alleged defamation could be very substantial'. In *Shanks v BBC* 1993 SLT 326 a self-employed accountant whose business was allegedly ruined by a television programme sued for £900,000.
3 *Morrison v Ritchie & Co* (1902) 4 F 645 at 652 per Lord Moncreiff. See also *Winter v News Scotland Ltd* 1991 SLT 828 at 830A.
4 *Cunningham v Duncan & Jamieson* (1889) 16 R 383 at 387 per Lord President Inglis.
5 1991 SLT 828.
6 *Winter v News Scotland Ltd* 1991 SLT 828 at 829J.
7 *Cooper* p 250.
8 In *McCluskie v Summers* 1988 SLT 55 a trade union official sued successfully for defamation and Lord Murray said: 'I consider it to be a particularly damaging defamation of a trade union official, who depends on the trust of his members and of the employers' side of industry, to make a false allegation of perjury against him . . . The offence is compounded where the official is of high public standing'.

notorious through scurrilous accusations has lost a reputation no less personally valuable than the public figure, and may well feel as insulted. Walker puts the matter correctly when he points out[1] that some classes of person are specially concerned with their reputations in particular respects and that particular kinds of imputations may be especially harmful to such individuals. Thus a minister is particularly susceptible to harm through allegations of sexual impropriety, and a solicitor or accountant is particularly susceptible to harm through allegations of financial impropriety. Care must be taken here, however, because the circumstances may be relevant both to the question of whether there is defamation at all, and the effect these circumstances have on the level of damages awarded under the heading of solatium. It is unlikely to be defamatory to say that an ordinary person had sexual intercourse (even, today, outwith marriage[2]); it could well be defamatory to say so of a Roman Catholic priest; the Roman Catholic bishop may well be able to claim more damages than the parish priest accused, but innocent, of the same sin.

The existence of malice on the part of the defender was at one time regarded as an aggravating (and its absence a mitigating) feature[3], but this is no longer the case today. In *Stein v Beaverbrook Newspapers*[4] it was held that the measure of damages in defamation cases as in other delict cases is the loss suffered by the pursuer and that loss is not increased by the fact that the defamation was inspired by the defender's previous malice. Damages are aggravated only by factors that aggravate the loss. Lord Justice-Clerk Grant said:

'The fact . . . that the defender maliciously or malevolently persists in his libel, or reprints it or refuses to withdraw it is in each case highly relevant to the question of damages, because in the circumstances envisaged the damage suffered by the pursuer may well be increased . . . None of this, however, has any bearing on the question whether a defamatory statement, because it is actuated by malice, entitles a pursuer, for that reason alone, to greater damages – without an averment or proof of greater injury – than he would have obtained had there been no malice.'[5]

It followed that the averments of malice in the case, which was not one of privilege, were irrelevant.

Mitigation of damages

Questions of mitigation of patrimonial loss are not apt. Such loss is either suffered, in which case damages are due to the extent that it can be proved, or not suffered, in which case damages are not due; and there is no room for increasing or decreasing an award because of the circumstances in which the defamation

---

1 *Civil Remedies* p 993.
2 See above at p 20.
3 See Walker, *Civil Remedies* p 994; *Cooper* pp 250 and 258; *Hamilton v Hope* (1827) 5 S 569 at 586 per Lord Glenlee.
4 1968 SC 272.
5 1968 SC 272 at 278–279.

occurred, unless these circumstances increase or decrease the loss suffered[1]. Solatium is, however, different and it is appropriate in assessing the award under this head to examine the whole circumstances in order to determine the just and proper amount to be awarded. The defender is allowed to lead evidence of facts and circumstances which could be used to mitigate the amount referable to solatium awarded against him. So for example an immediate retraction of the defamation and an offer of apology will mitigate the damages awarded[2], as will the circumstances of privacy in which the statement was made[3], or the fact that the defender has innocently published the words of others[4]. In *McCluskie v Summers*[5] Lord Murray held that it was appropriate to reduce damages from £10,000 to £7,500 because of the limited circulation given to the defamation in that case.

Provocation

The fact that the pursuer has provoked the statement complained of is a mitigating factor[6], though what amounts to provocation has never been laid down clearly[7]. The basis of provocation seems to be that the pursuer is to some extent to blame for calling down upon himself the defamatory allegation, rather than that his character is less injured, and is, therefore, analogous to contributory negligence[8]. In *Ogilvie v Scott*[9] Lord Justice-Clerk Boyle explained provocation as an example of the principle that when a party seeks reparation in a court of law he must come into court with clean hands. A good example is found in the case of *Bryson v Inglis*[10]. There the defender had slandered the pursuer in a letter, but claimed to have written the letter in response to disparaging remarks the pursuer had made about him to a third party. Evidence of these disparaging remarks was held to be competent[11]. Similarly, where the pursuer has laid himself open by his own conduct to a charge short of that complained of, and this has to some extent influenced the defender in writing or publishing the alleged defamation, evidence may be led

---

1 Section 10 of the Administration of Justice Act 1982 provides that certain matters, such as unemployment benefit, are to be taken into account in determining the level of damages awarded in personal injury cases (including actions for defamation and verbal injury: s 13(1)). It is only very rarely that this provision will be applicable here and it is in any case more a question of set-off than mitigation.
2 *Symmond v Williamson* (1752) Mor 3435; *Sproll v Walker* (1899) 2 F 73; *Morrison v Ritchie & Co* (1902) 4 F 645.
3 *Tytler v Macintosh* (1823) 3 Mur 236; *White v Clough* (1847) 10 D 332 at 335 per Lord President Boyle. *Cooper* p 256 comments as follows: 'probably the more correct view to take is that the privacy of the statement does not tend towards mitigation of damages, but the publicity of it towards aggravation'.
4 *Morrison v Ritchie & Co* (1902) 4 F 645 at 652 per Lord Moncreiff.
5 1988 SLT 55.
6 *Tullis v Crichton* (1850) 12 D 867; *Paul v Jackson* (1884) 11 R 460.
7 See Walker, *Delict* (2nd edn, 1981) pp 788–789.
8 See *Cooper* pp 254–255.
9 (1835) 14 S 729.
10 (1844) 6 D 363.
11 See also the defence of fair retort, discussed above at pp 155–156.

of this in mitigation of damages[1]. So for example to call a person a rapist who has not committed that crime is defamatory, but the damages might be less if the accusation was made in response, say, to a boast by the pursuer of brutal sexual conquest. Evidence of provocation in mitigation of damages will not be allowed to be led without a counter-issue of *veritas*[2] (which, of course, is an absolute defence rather than merely mitigation) if the evidence amounts, in essence, to a plea that the defamatory allegation is true[3].

Similar to provocation is the plea, commonly used in the older cases, of *compensatio injuriarum*, whereby the pursuer's slander of the defender is of similar harmfulness as the defender's slander of the pursuer, and the two wrongs cancel each other out. If the compensation is exact no damages are due, and if inexact but still in the pursuer's favour, damages can be mitigated.

Lack of good character

That the pursuer has little or no character or reputation to harm is also a mitigating factor, since damages are given in compensation for injury to reputation that exists. So it is competent for the defender to lead evidence as to the pursuer's general character or reputation in order to show that the defamatory statement would have less effect than it might otherwise have had[4]. In *C v M*[5] Lord President Clyde pointed out that whenever a pursuer asks for damages in respect of the harm done to his character by a slanderous statement he necessarily puts his own character in issue, and that it is therefore a relevant defence to a claim for damages to aver and prove that the pursuer's character is such that it could not have suffered any damage by the statement complained of[6]. This does not mean that the action for defamation completely fails, because even a person of no character will still be presumed to have suffered hurt feelings which entitles him or her to solatium (nominal or otherwise): rather it simply means that the value or otherwise of the reputation averred to have been lost will be reflected in the award made for loss of that reputation. Similarly, the fact that the defamatory statements complained of are repetition of a current rumour may be relevant to mitigate damages if the pursuer's character has already been damaged and the further damage by repetition is not so great as the original damage. In *MacCullochs v Litt*[7] it was held competent to ask a witness whether there was a prevailing rumour of the pursuer's guilt of the impropriety alleged in the defamation, and it was observed that the answer could be founded on, not as an answer to the action,

---

1 *Browne v McFarlane* (1889) 16 R 368 at 372 per Lord Shand. See also *Winter v News Scotland Ltd* 1991 SLT 828 at 830F-G.
2 On which, see above at pp 133–134.
3 *McNeill v Rorison* (1847) 10 D 15; *Craig v Jex-Blake* (1871) 9 M 973; *Paul v Jackson* (1884) 11 R 460.
4 *Kingan v Watson* (1828) 4 Mur 485 at 490; *McDonald v Begg* (1862) 24 D 685.
5 1923 SC 1.
6 1923 SC 1 at 4.
7 (1851) 13 D 960.

but merely as enabling the jury to assess the amount of damages[1]. This case is inconsistent with the earlier one of *Brodies v Blair*[2] in which the court held a defender not entitled to prove that the statement complained of was repetition of what had been previously current rumours in the country[3]. There has been no modern case directly raising the point, but it has to be said that there is a logic in giving less damages to a person whose character has previously been destroyed, however unjustly, than to the person whose reputation was previously unsullied. Repetition of defamatory remarks is clearly defamation itself[4], but reparation is due only for the harm actually caused by the legal wrong[5], and if a defender adds to a loss that he or she did not cause it is the addition rather than the initial loss that is properly the measure of damages awarded against the defender. The initial loss may well, of course, give a right of action against another person.

Statutory mitigation

The defender may give evidence in mitigation of damages that the pursuer has recovered damages or brought actions for damages for defamation in respect of the publication of words to the same effect as the words on which the present action is founded, or has received or agreed to receive compensation in respect of any such publication[6].

Remoteness of damage

The test for remoteness

Defamation and verbal injury are intentional forms of delict, and while in general 'the intention to injure the [pursuer] disposes of any question of remoteness'[7] it does not follow that questions of remoteness are always irrelevant in such actions. Both intent to injure and loss in the shape of hurt feelings are presumed in defamation and that loss cannot, therefore, ever be regarded as too remote; but they are not presumed in verbal injury, and in both actions a pursuer may claim damages beyond the injuries presumed to occur such as, typically, economic losses. If the pursuer does so then he must prove not only that they were caused by the defamation[8] or verbal injury but also that they are not too remote from the wrong to found the claim for damages.

---

1 (1851) 13 D 960 at 961 per Lord Wood.
2 (1834) 12 S 941.
3 See also *McNeill v Rorison* (1847) 10 D 15 in which the defender was held not entitled to prove a rumour since in effect he was claiming the rumour true without a counter-issue of veritas.
4 See above at pp 29–31.
5 See below at p 173.
6 Defamation Act 1952, s 12.
7 *Quinn v Leathem* [1901] AC 495 at 537 per Lord Lindley.
8 *Wallace v Bremner* (1900) 16 Sh Ct Rep 308.

The test for remoteness of damage in delict has been subject to much analysis in the law of negligence[1] where some confusion is apparent. With intentional delicts such as defamation the issue has received far less attention, but it has been held in England that actions for defamation are to be treated no differently on the question of remoteness from other actions and that the principles developed primarily in relation to negligence apply equally here[2]. Certain conclusions can be drawn. First, intended consequences are never too remote. If a person intends to cause a certain type of loss by defaming the pursuer, and that precise loss is caused, no issue of remoteness will arise. Secondly, the direct and natural consequences of a deliberately inflicted harm will not be too remote even although these consequences were not themselves intended[3]. So for example if a direct and natural consequence of uttering a defamatory remark is that it will be repeated, the original defamer will be liable for the repetition as well as the original utterance[4]. It is a question of fact to be determined on a case to case basis whether repetition of a defamatory comment is a direct and natural consequence of making the original comment, though prima facie if the repetition is unauthorised it will not be regarded as a direct and natural consequence[5]. Another way of describing direct and natural consequences may well be to say that they are foreseeable consequences[6]. Thirdly, an unforeseeable event in the chain of causation will amount to a *novus actus interveniens* and subsequent losses will be regarded as too remote. In *Slipper v BBC*[7] the defendants had broadcast a programme in which the plaintiff, a senior police officer charged with the task of returning a famous fugitive from justice[8] back to England from Brazil, was allegedly portrayed as an incompetent buffoon, and had previewed the programme to the national press for the sake of publicity. The press repeated the alleged defamation in reviews of the programme and the plaintiff sought damages from the defendants for the repetitions as well as the original broadcast. The defendants pleaded that the repetitions amounted to a *novus actus interveniens*. It was held that whether or not the chain of causation was breached by the press repeating the allegations depended upon whether the defendants invited them to do so or could foresee that they would do so. Though an English case, the approach is likely to reflect Scots law also[9].

---

1 See particularly *Walker* pp 242–283 and authorities cited therein; Thomson *Delictual Liability* pp 225–229.
2 *Slipper v BBC* [1991] 1 QB 283 at 296 per Stocker LJ, and at 299 per Bingham LJ.
3 See Lord Ardwell in *Finburgh v Moss' Empires Ltd* (1908) 16 SLT 61 (p 116) at 121.
4 *Weld-Blundell v Stephens* [1920] AC 956; *Basse v Toronto Star Newspapers Ltd* (1983) 4 DLR (4th) 381.
5 *Slipper v BBC* [1991] 1 QB 283 at 301 per Slade LJ.
6 Ibid. The logic of this suggestion has been challenged by *Thomson* p 226.
7 [1991] 1 QB 283.
8 Biggs, the 'Great Train Robber'.
9 In *Wallace v Bremner* (1900) 16 Sh Ct Rep 308 the pursuer alleged that he had been suspended from his post as minister because of the defender's letter to him claiming that he was not, in fact, a minister of a particular church. The claim was dismissed because the pursuer's suspension had been caused by his own act of publishing the letter rather than the defender's act in writing it.

Heads of damages claimable

Both defamation and verbal injury can cause various forms of harm to the pursuer. Primarily of course, and this indeed is presumed with defamation, the pursuer will suffer affront, which attracts compensation by way of solatium. Further losses have to be averred and proved. These might include other emotional hurts such as anxiety and depression which are a direct and probable cause of the defamation[1], or economic losses. There are various forms of economic loss such as lost profits, lost earnings, and more speculative heads such as loss of employment prospects. Damages have been awarded in England for loss of marital prospects[2] and a claim would be competent in Scotland for that or for the breakup of a marriage[3] so long as that was a direct and natural consequence of the wrong. Probably loss of amenities such as the loss of friendship would also be a competent element in the damages awarded.

Physical injury can be claimed also, so long as the pursuer can prove that this is a direct and natural consequence of the defamation: there may be situations in which this is possible. Emotional upset may have physical bodily manifestations. Or the defamatory allegations may result in the pursuer being physically attacked. If for example a pursuer is wrongly accused of child sex abuse and is, as a consequence, beaten up by an outraged mob, there is little doubt that this would found a competent claim for the physical injury[4]. Similarly, if such defamation resulted in the pursuer's wrongful imprisonment then that deprivation of liberty would found a claim[5]. Claims for verbal injury, such as malicious falsehood, though normally limited to economic losses[6], are not necessarily so and are subject to the same principles.

Reviewing awards of damages

It is no longer the case (if, in truth, it ever was the case) that an appeal court will only interfere with an award of damages if it is more than double or less than half of what the appeal court itself would have awarded[7]. In the case cited this was said to be so 'except perhaps in relation to awards of pure solatium and awards for defamation', but the objection behind such a working rule is as

---

1 *Winter v News Scotland Ltd* 1991 SLT 828.
2 *Lynch v Knight* (1861) 9 HL Cas 577; *Speight v Gosney* (1891) 60 LJ QB 231 (CA).
3 Cf *Brodies v Blair* (1834) 12 S 941.
4 In *Al-Kandari v JR Brown & Co* [1988] 2 WLR 671 a solicitor was negligent in looking after the passport of a client's estranged husband. The husband obtained the passport, removed the client's children from her and beat her up. The Court of Appeal held that both the woman's physical injuries and her emotional upset at losing her children were natural and probable consequences of the solicitor's negligence.
5 Indeed, suing for the direct and probable consequences of the defamation in that situation rather than the wrongful imprisonment itself would have the advantage that the pursuer would not have to prove, as he would to establish liability for wrongful imprisonment, want of probable cause.
6 See above at p 48.
7 *McGinley v Pacitti* 1950 SC 364.

applicable to these awards as to any other and the qualification simply reflects the court's unwillingness to interfere with awards in areas in which any assessment is necessarily speculative. Probably the most that can be said is that 'the court should be even more reluctant to interfere with a jury's award [in cases of defamation] than it is in cases of physical injury'[1]. Likewise, an appeal court is less likely to interfere with the award made by a jury than by a sheriff or judge[2] who, in any case, is obliged to explain the basis of his assessment[3].

In cases tried before a jury any party who is dissatisfied with the verdict may apply to the Inner House for a new trial on various grounds, specified in section 29(1) of the Court of Session Act 1988, including that of excess or inadequacy of damages. Where the court is of the opinion, in an application under section 29, that the only ground for granting a new trial is either excess of damages or such inadequacy of damages as to show that a new trial is essential to the justice of the case, it may grant a new trial restricted to the question of the amount of the damages[4]. The wording of this provision suggests that it will be easier to persuade the court to grant a new trial on grounds of excess than on grounds of inadequacy of damages, because the reference to the justice of the case could be taken to be limited to the ground of inadequacy. It is however likely that this qualification is implicit in the ground of excess also. There is appeal to the House of Lords against an interlocutor granting or refusing a new trial on the grounds of excess or inadequacy of damages[5].

In *Winter v News Scotland Ltd*[6] the Inner House said that in determining whether to order a new trial limited to the question of damages,

'the general test is well settled although it has been expressed in different ways in a number of different cases. The principle to be applied is that the court should only interfere if the excess is "such as to raise on the part of the Court, the moral conviction that the jury . . . have committed gross injustice, and have given higher damages than any jury of ordinary men fairly and without gross mistake exercising their functions, could have awarded": *Landell v Landell*[7]. It has been consistently emphasised in that and subsequent cases that the mere fact that an award is more, and even a great deal more, than a court would have awarded does not provide sufficient justification for holding it to be excessive'[8].

In this case a female prison officer was awarded £50,000 damages against a newspaper which had alleged that she had committed an act of sexual intercourse with a prisoner. The defenders sought a new trial restricted to the issue of damages, arguing that the amount awarded was excessive, but this was refused. The Inner House held that the jury's award in the case was, 'much

---

1 *Winter v News Scotland Ltd* 1991 SLT 828 at 831A per Lord Morison.
2 *Houlden v Couper* (1871) 9 SLR 169; *Casey v United Collieries Ltd* 1907 SC 690.
3 *Walker* p 479.
4 Court of Session Act 1988, s 30(3). The decision is to be made by a majority of the judges, and in cases of equal division judgment shall be given in conformity with the verdict (s 30(4)).
5 Court of Session Act 1988, s 40(2). The proviso to s 6 of the Jury Trials (Scotland) Act 1815 disallowing such appeals is repealed by Sch 2 to the 1988 Act.
6 1991 SLT 828.
7 (1841) 3 D 819 at 825.
8 1991 SLT 828 at 830I-J per Lord Morison.

larger than this court would have awarded on the basis of the information before us. But it is not in our opinion an award which in all the circumstances can properly be regarded as one which a reasonable jury could not make'[1].

The Inner House cannot, itself, substitute an award that it considers reasonable for that awarded in the lower court[2] (unless this is done with the consent of the parties[3]). In this respect the law of Scotland now differs from that of England, for due to the bizarrely high levels of damages awarded in that jurisdiction – on very different principles from those applicable in Scotland – Parliament gave the English Court of Appeal power to vary the award itself rather than, as is still the case in Scotland, grant a new trial limited to the question of damages[4]. Such variation can be made if the Court of Appeal considers the award to be excessive or inadequate, and the principles to be applied were discussed in the case of *Rantzen v Mirror Group Newspapers*[5], in which a jury award of £250,000 was reduced by the court to £110,000.

Damages for patrimonial loss, being less speculative, are less likely to be challenged. If the award is challenged the appeal court will interfere only if 'the assessment has been reached through the use of wrong facts or the application of wrong principles or a manifestly unfair assessment has been reached'[6].

Interdict

For essentially practical reasons, damages is the main remedy available to a pursuer seeking a remedy for defamation or verbal injury. A pursuer is seldom aware of the threat to his or her reputation until it has eventuated, and the retrospective remedy of damages is usually all that is practically available. However, a pursuer who knows that either defamation or verbal injury is about to be committed against him or her will have title to seek an interdict to prevent the threatened harm. In addition a person whose reputation has already been impugned may seek interdict against the repetition thereof. However the court can only interdict against specific remarks and will not interdict someone from publishing 'defamatory statements' in general[7]. The right to petition for interdict is important because often damages will not be a satisfactory or sufficient remedy: loss of reputation may be irreparable, even by damages; and in many cases a person may prefer his reputation to remain unsullied than to receive compensation for its impugning. There has been much discussion of when interdict (injunction) should be available in English

---

1 1991 SLT 828 at 831J.
2 *Boal v Scottish Catholic Printing Co* 1908 SC 667.
3 As for example in *Ritchie & Son v Barton* (1883) 10R 813.
4 Courts and Legal Services Act 1990, s 8(2) and RSC Ord 59, r 11(4).
5 [1993] 3 WLR 953.
6 *Blair v FJC Lilley (Marine) Ltd* 1981 SLT 90 at 92.
7 *Shinwell v National Sailors' and Firemen's Union* 1913 2 SLT 83 at 85 per Lord Cullen.

law[1], and the position there seems to be that interim injunction will be granted only in the clearest of cases, that is when there is little or no doubt that the threatened wrong will take place and will amount to defamation. Due to basic procedural differences from Scots law[2], English authority is of little assistance here and the strict test in that jurisdiction will not be applied in the Scottish court, but there is a similar feeling in both jurisdictions that the court ought not to assume that the wrong will be committed by a proposed publication. The matter was put succinctly by Lord Ross in *Fairbairn v SNP*[3]:

'It is well settled that once a slander has been published, the court may grant interdict against its repetition. The court, however, is slow to grant interim interdict of slander because to do so is to some extent to take the jurisdiction away from the jury. Nevertheless, interim interdict can be granted in clear cases of slander'.

When Lord Ross talks of 'clear cases of slander', he means no more than situations in which a prima facie case of slander can be made out: 'In the present case I have held that the words complained of are prima facie defamatory, and subject to considering the balance of convenience, that might justify the granting of interim interdict'[4]. Interim interdict is unlikely ever to be granted when the pursuer is relying on innuendo, for then the case is, by definition, not clear[5]. The furthest one can take any reluctance to grant interim interdict is as specified by Sheriff Principal Bryden in *Boyd v BBC*[6], when he said:

'I imagine no court would be likely to grant interim interdict or to allow interim interdict previously granted to continue, if it was, for any reason, clear that the pursuer's case would be bound to fail. But I think the matter must be judged from the point of view of whether there is a prima facie case alleged, and, if there is, then the question can be resolved by the test of the balance of convenience'.

A case may be 'bound to fail' if, for example, the statements were made in a situation of absolute privilege, or in a situation of qualified privilege when there is no or insufficient averment of malice[7], or when the words are not on the face of them defamatory and no innuendo is pleaded. If the pursuer can make a case which the defender is bound to answer then interim interdict will be available to prevent publication or repetition of the harmful communication.

The balance of convenience

Once the test for the availability of interdict has been satisfied, the question of whether or not interim interdict will be granted turns on the balance of

---

1 See *Carter-Ruck* pp 177–181.
2 Adverted to by Lord Justice-Clerk Wheatley in *Waddell v BBC* 1973 SLT 246 at 252.
3 1980 SLT 149 at 151.
4 1980 SLT 149 at 152.
5 And indeed was refused for that reason in *Sangster v Catto* (1893) 9 Sh Ct Rep 153.
6 1969 SLT (Sh Ct) 17. In this case the Sheriff Principal rejected the English approach as being part of the law of Scotland.
7 See the decision of Sheriff Middleton in *Waddell v BBC* 1973 SLT 246 at 248.

convenience. Each case must be looked at on its own facts in order to determine in whose favour that balance lies, but previous cases can provide illustrations of the sorts of factors that the courts have considered relevant to striking the balance. It is always a matter of the court's discretion whether or not to grant interim interdict, or whether to recall interim interdict that has already been granted.

In *McMurdo v Ferguson*[1] a sporting agent sought interdict against a news-paper seeking to prevent the publication of an article accusing him of improperly depriving a footballer and his family of various assets. Lord Murray balanced the public interest in rows between prominent figures in the sporting world with the fact that the loss to the petitioner's professional reputation could be immediate, and irreparable even by damages: he held that the balance of convenience in these circumstances, though very even, favoured the petitioner and interim interdict was granted. In *Fairbairn v SNP*[2] a petition was presented for the recall of an interim interdict previously granted. Lord Ross identified the respective losses that each party would suffer if they lost their case and concluded that the possible prejudice to the respondent would be less than the possible prejudice to the petitioner. The case involved alleged defamatory statements about a member of Parliament contained in election leaflets distributed by the respondents. Lord Ross held that the risk that the petitioner would be defamed in the eyes of the electors was a greater prejudice than the risk that the respondents would be wrongly stopped from circulating a statement which was *ex hypothesi* true. He concluded that 'any inconvenience or loss which [the respondents] do sustain will be a direct consequence of their having included in the pamphlet a statement which is prima facie defamatory of the petitioner and as to which the respondents are unable to put forward a prima facie case of justification'[3] and he therefore refused the motion for recall of the interim interdict against the SNP[4].

In other cases the balance has been held to be in favour of refusing or recalling the interdict. In *Kwik-Fit-Euro Ltd v Scottish Daily Record & Sunday Mail Ltd*[5] the petitioners sought to interdict a newspaper from repeating an allegation in an article to the effect that they persuaded their customers to have shock absorbers fitted to their motor vehicles when this was not necessary. Lord Mackay of Clashfern identified the factors to be put into the balance: (1) that since there had already been publication, interim interdict against repetition could not fully protect the petitioners in any case, (2) that the petitioners had held a news conference to put their own side of the story, and (3) that to grant interdict would be to prevent the respondents from discussing a topic of public interest which was a central part of their business. In these circumstances the

1 1993 SLT 193.
2 1980 SLT 149.
3 1980 SLT 149 at 153. 'Justification', of course, means *veritas*.
4 See also *Cameron v Scottish Daily Record and Sunday Mail* (1987) GWD 29–1119.
5 1987 SLT 226.

balance of convenience was against issuing interim interdict. Lord Mackay also pointed out that the refusal did not deprive the petitioners of a remedy since damages would be available for any defamation, even although the award would be difficult to quantify exactly. The fact that the remedy of damages is always available if the wrong can be proved was also held to be a significant element of the balance in *Waddell v BBC*[1], and this was considered so notwithstanding that the non-availability of legal aid might often make that remedy impractical. Interim interdict against a television programme accusing the petitioner of murder was recalled in this case on the ground that the matter the respondents wished to publish would quickly lose its current interest: this, together with the availability of damages if the petitioner could prove his case, suggested that the balance was in favour of refusing the appeal against recall of the interim interdict. Interim interdict cannot be used to prevent fair and accurate reporting[2]: so it was refused in *Cameron v Scottish Daily Record and Sunday Mail*[3] when the petitioner sought to prevent a newspaper reporting a complaint that had been made against him to the Law Society of Scotland, because freedom of the press was an important consideration and interdict would have prevented any article on the complaint and its disposal, however fair and accurate. And in *Gecas v Scottish Television*[4], which concerned a television programme accusing the petitioner of war crimes, an important consideration was the potential prejudice to future court actions involving the petitioner (though interdict would be available to prevent such prejudice in any case irrespective of the defamatory content of the statements being interdicted). It was also argued there that parliamentary consideration of the War Crimes Inquiry Report would be prejudiced if the programme were broadcast but Lord Coulsfield held that interim interdict could not be granted for that reason alone:

'I do not think that it is any part of the function of the Court to control what material is to be put before Parliament, even if the material includes matters defamatory of the petitioner. The only remedy for the petitioner in these circumstances seems to me to be an action of defamation'.

Other relevant factors in the balance of convenience include the ease of removing the defamatory content from the proposed publication, the effect allowing publication would have on the petitioner, the effect disallowing publication would have on the principle of freedom of expression, how speculative these effects are, whether the facts the petitioner wants suppressed are common knowledge or not, whether there is a prima facie defence of *veritas*, whether the defender would be in a position to pay any damages awarded against him, and whether the decision on interim interdict effectively ends the case.

1 1973 SLT 246.
2 *Riddell v Clydesdale Horse Society* (1885) 12 R 976.
3 1987 GWD 29–1119.
4 1991 GWD 5–276.

Declarator

Any person with interest can seek a declarator from the Court of Session or the sheriff court[1]. Though there is no reported instance of a case in which the pursuer has sought nothing more than a declarator that a statement made about him or her is false and defamatory there is nothing in principle against the competency of such a crave. Seeking declarator rather than damages might be considered appropriate when no patrimonial loss has been caused and the pursuer's intent is solely to restore his or her reputation, and in this respect declarator would serve the same function as the ancient remedy of palinode, which was a public recantation by the defender of the accusation made. Declarator might also be a useful precursor to the seeking of interim interdict which, as we have seen, is granted only in 'clear cases of defamation'.

---

1 See Walker, *Civil Remedies* pp 105–119.

CHAPTER THIRTEEN

International issues

Introduction

Defamation and verbal injury are wrongs that are peculiarly susceptible to giving rise to international problems, for the essence of both is communication[1] and modern means of communication more and more frequently involve and are dependent upon international methods. A defamatory or injurious allegation that is printed in a book, magazine or newspaper will almost invariably have the potential for involving more than one legal system: national newspapers published in this country are circulated in at least the three domestic legal systems and indeed are widely available throughout the world. Even local newspapers are circulated further than their own locality and many Scottish local daily newspapers are available in London. Television and radio broadcasts originating here can frequently be received abroad, and foreign broadcasts can, by means of cable and satellite, easily be received in Scotland. Letters and telexes and FAXes and E-mail and notices on computer systems cross jurisdictional borders far more easily than people do and the 'information highway' is an international network. If a defamatory allegation is made by any means that transmit the allegation from one jurisdiction to another then at least two questions may arise (though, it has to be admitted, they seldom have done in practice[2]): (1) when will the Scottish court have jurisdiction to hear the action, and (2) which law will be applied to that action?

Jurisdiction of the Scottish court

Prior to the coming into force of the Civil Jurisdiction and Judgments Act 1982, the jurisdiction of the Scottish courts in delict was governed by the Law Reform (Jurisdiction in Delict) Act 1971 under which (very basically) the Scottish court would have jurisdiction if the delict had been committed within Scotland. In *Russell v FW Woolworth & Co*[3] the Lord Ordinary (Lord Murray), in interpreting the provisions of that Act, held that so long as a 'material element' of the delict occurred in Scotland the delict would have a locus here

---

1 See above at p 28.
2 Though the increasing reliance on electronic information processing and delivery may well result in these questions becoming more frequently raised.
3 1982 SLT 428.

and the Scottish courts would therefore have jurisdiction. In relation to defamation (though the issue never arose in that context under the 1971 Act) this probably meant that the Scottish court had jurisdiction either when the allegedly defamatory statement originated in Scotland or when the hurt was suffered in Scotland, for both the defender's act and the pursuer's loss are clearly 'material elements' in the delict of defamation.

The law was, however, substantially altered by the Civil Jurisdiction and Judgments Act 1982, which came into force on 1 January 1987. This Act was passed in order to give effect to the Brussels Convention on Jurisdiction and the Enforcement of Judgments in Civil and Commercial Matters 1968 and certain related conventions emanating from the European Union[1]. It is important to note that while the change of law was motivated by the need to fulfil European requirements, the rules relating to delict in the 1982 Act apply generally and are not limited to cases involving other jurisdictions in the European Union.

The general rule of jurisdiction under the 1982 Act is based upon the domicile of the defender[2], with the result that the Scottish court can now hear an action for defamation whenever the defender thereto is domiciled in Scotland. 'Domicile' is not, however, accorded its usual Scottish meaning but is given a new definition, to be applied only for the purposes of the 1982 Act, based upon the defender's residence in and 'substantive connection' with a jurisdiction[3]. If the defender is a corporation or association then its domicile is where it has its 'seat', that is the country either (a) under the law of which it was incorporated or formed and where it has its registered office or some other official address or (b) where its central management and control is exercised[4]. Under this provision the Scottish court will have jurisdiction to hear any defamation action brought against a company which has its 'seat', as so defined, in Scotland. In addition to this general rule there are a number of special jurisdictional rules, one of which applies to actions for delict. Under article 5(3) of the 1968 Convention a person may be sued 'in matters relating to delict, or quasi-delict, in the courts for the place where the harmful event occurred'[5]. This formula is somewhat ambiguous in that 'the harmful event' might refer either to the breach of duty or to the resultant loss, or to both. The European Court of Justice[6] resolved the matter in Case 21/76 (commonly called the *Reinwater* case)[7] in which Dutch pursuers sought damages from a French company for loss caused to their business by the poisoning of the river

---

1 For a detailed description of these conventions and the 1982 Act, see Anton, *Civil Jurisdiction in Scotland* (1984) and Anton & Beaumont, *Civil Jurisdiction in Scotland: Supplement* (1987).
2 1968 Convention, art 2; 1982 Act, s 2 and Sch 1 (for defenders domiciled in a country of the European Union other than the United Kingdom); s 16 and Sch 4 (for defenders domiciled in a part of the United Kingdom other than Scotland); and s 20 and Sch 8 (for defenders domiciled in any country outwith the European Union).
3 See Anton & Beaumont, *Private International Law* (2nd edn, 1990) pp 179–180 for details.
4 Civil Jurisdiction and Judgments Act 1982, s 42.
5 1982 Act, Sch 8, rule 2(3).
6 The principles laid down which a British court must have regard to: 1982 Act, s 20(5).
7 *Handelswerkerij GJ Bier v Mines de Potasse d'Alsace* (21/76) [1976] ECR 1735.

Rhine, for which the defenders were responsible. The case was raised in the Netherlands and the defenders argued that the Dutch court had no jurisdiction since the 'place where the harmful event occurred' was France. The European Court of Justice was asked by the Dutch court to interpret the contentious phrase and in doing so it pointed out that article 5(3) was intended to cover a wide variety of different forms of liability. For that reason,

'the expression "place where the harmful event occurred" . . . must be understood as being intended to cover both the place where the damage occurred or the place of the event giving rise to it. The result is that the defendant may be sued, at the option of the plaintiff, either in the courts for the place where the damage occurred or in the courts for the place of the event which gives rise to and is at the origin of that damage'[1].

The result of the ruling in the *Reinwater* case is not essentially different from the approach of Lord Murray in *Russell*, described above. Its application to defamation is illustrated in the English case of *Shevill v Presse Alliance SA*[2]. Here, the Court of Appeal accepted that an action for defamation could be raised in England against the proprietors of a French newspaper which had a small circulation in England but who were 'domiciled' in France, where the main circulation of the newspaper occurred[3]. The defendants had argued that no harm could be said to have occurred in England since the substantial loss had occurred in France and that 'harm' occurred in England only in the sense that English law presumed harm[4]: presumed harm did not, it was argued, come within the phrase 'the harmful event' as used in article 5(3). This argument was rejected and the Court of Appeal confirmed that, on a question of jurisdiction, a presumed harmful event was sufficient, with the result that the plaintiff had the option of suing in the courts of the defendants' domicile or in the courts of the place where the wrongful act was committed or in the courts of the place where the damage occurred or was presumed to occur[5]. There is no doubt that this represents Scots law also.

Choice of law: general

It is of the nature of international private law that questions of jurisdiction will determine whether a case can be heard in a particular forum but will not

---

1 [1976] ECR 1735 at 1748–1749. It should be noted that, technically, decisions of the European Court of Justice are binding only in cases relating to actions involving member states of the European Union and would not be binding if the harmful event had occurred elsewhere (Beaumont 'Jurisdiction in Delict in Scotland' (1983) 28 JLSS 528 at 530). There is no doubt, however, that the Scottish court will not adopt a different approach depending upon whether the place of harm is within or without Europe. To do so would be to go against the clear intention of Parliament in passing the Civil Jurisdiction and Judgments Act 1982 and applying the same law whichever country is involved.
2 [1992] 1 All ER 409.
3 Out of a circulation of over 200,000, approximately 230 were said to be sold in England.
4 As, of course, does Scots law.
5 See also *Foxen v Scotsman Publications Ltd* (1994) Times, 17 February, in which a plea of *forum non conveniens* was rejected by the English court hearing a case in which the alleged defamation had been published mainly in Scotland.

determine the issue of what law applies to the case once the forum has been settled. The latter is a question of choice of law and a Scottish court with jurisdiction over a particular case will not necessarily decide the issue according to Scots domestic law. There are few areas in the conflict of laws that have attracted so much criticism but for which the rules are so settled (at least in Scotland) as choice of law in delict. If the international private law rules have a tendency to limit actionability, then this is no criticism in relation to defamation with which actions can usually be argued from a purely domestic point of view in any case. Nevertheless it is a curious feature of the rules for choice of law in delict that they were developed in Scotland primarily in relation to two sorts of claims: actions by relatives of Scotsmen killed in England (usually on the railways), and actions for defamation. The rules in relation to defamation are those to be applied in the general law of delict, subject to the specialties to be noted below.

Development of the law

Originally, in both Scotland and England, the judicial tendency in relation to actions for damages in delict was to see the matter in purely domestic terms, so that if an action were raised in Scotland it would be Scots law that applied, and if it were raised in England, English law would apply. This can be seen, for example, in the case of *Callendar v Milligan*[1] which was an action raised in Scotland for defamation and wrongful imprisonment that had occurred in England. The judges held that notwithstanding that the events leading to the case had occurred in England, Scots law would apply in this Scottish case. Though it is difficult to extract a common *ratio* from the reported opinions, most of the judges appear to fail to distinguish between the right of action and the remedy sought[2]. The feeling clearly was that a remedy could be granted by the court only if the domestic law of the forum recognised that remedy. This may well be correct but it does not follow that a right of action can be recognised only if the domestic law of the forum recognises the action, otherwise there would be no need for international private law at all. However, interestingly, one of the judges in *Callendar*, though concurring in the result, expressed some reservations as to how far the predominance of the law of the forum could be taken, and in particular he felt that if a defence were available under the law of England, this would also have the effect of a defence in a case tried in Scotland. Lord Mackenzie said: 'I cannot say that I am so clear [as my brethren] that this case must be ruled by Scotch law. If it were made out that what was done, did not amount to an injury by the law of England, I would not say that we could sustain the action, under the law of Scotland'[3]. Though none of the other judges in *Callendar* adopted this approach (which was *obiter*)

1 (1849) 11 D 1174.
2 See also *Horn v North British Railway Co* (1878) 5 R 1055.
3 (1849) 11 D 1174 at 1176.

it does contain the seeds of the recognition of the relevance of the *lex loci delicti*, or the place where the delict occurred, in addition to the *lex fori*, or the place where the action is raised. There are clear justifications for taking account of both. The *lex loci* is relevant because delict concerns conduct and the place where the conduct occurs has a natural interest in classifying and controlling that conduct and determining whether or not it is acceptable[1]. And if only the *lex fori* were applied then the forum would in some cases be providing remedies for acts which were not wrong where – and therefore when – they were done, and the movement of the defender to another jurisdiction could have the effect of rendering wrongful an act previously innocuous. On the other hand, to claim damages is to claim a remedy and the *lex fori* has an interest not only in defining its own remedies but also in specifying when these remedies are available. How the balance between the two systems is to be struck has been the subject of much dispute, in both Scotland and England.

In *Phillips v Eyre*[2] the defendant was accused by the plaintiff of having falsely imprisoned him while the former was Governor of Jamaica, and the defendant pleaded in defence that the Jamaican legislature had passed an act of indemnity in his favour. Willes J laid down a two stage test for liability in tort where the wrong is committed abroad: 'First, the wrong must be of such a character that it would have been actionable, if committed in England [the *lex fori*] . . . Secondly, the act must not have been justifiable by the law of the place where it was done [the *lex loci delicti*]'[3]. It may well be that Willes J used the ambiguous term 'not justifiable' because of the fact that the defendant's acts in the present case were only made valid retrospectively, or had been subsequently justified, rather than having been legally innocuous from the start but the words were unfortunately chosen and led in England to many years of doubt and difficulty. Until *Boys v Chaplin*[4] it was assumed that the 'not justifiable' test was satisfied if the act could be characterised as wrongful, even although not civilly so. Though *Phillips* was not mentioned by the judges, it was cited in argument by counsel in the Scottish case of *McLarty v Steele*[5], which evinces such an approach. Here, a verbal slander was allegedly committed by one Scotsman against another while the former was in Penang (which at that time was subject to English law). The action was raised in Scotland after both parties had returned here and the defender pleaded that the action was incompetent in so far as the pursuer had not averred special damage, which required to be proved by Penang/English law before damages could be given for a verbal slander. In other words, while the wrong was actionable in Scots law it was not actionable according to Penang/English law and therefore, it was argued, could not found a claim in

1   The same reasoning lies behind the approach of the criminal law, which has little international private law content since it is almost entirely jurisdictional.
2   (1870) LR 6 QB 1.
3   (1870) LR 6 QB 1 at 28–29.
4   [1971] AC 356, discussed above at pp 189–191.
5   (1881) 8 R 435.

Scotland. It was held that the averments in relation to Penang/English law were irrelevant. Lord Justice-Clerk Moncreiff said:

'It may be the case that by English law redress will not be given for verbal slander unless special damage can be proved, but it is certainly not the case that therefore verbal slander is lawful. We have thus here an admitted wrong, which is a wrong both by the law of the place where it was committed and of the country where the action for redress is raised.'

This suggests that, while the act complained of must be a 'wrong' in both jurisdictions it need not be a 'wrong' in precisely the same way: rather, to be actionable a delict such as defamation need not be actionable on its own terms according to the *lex loci delicti*, so long as in some way it can be characterised as a wrong by that law. This approach is made the basis of the decision in the later English libel case of *Machado v Fontes*[1] in which the act complained of was actionable as libel in England and was a criminal wrong in Brazil: the libel was held actionable before an English court since the act was 'wrongful' by the *lex fori* and 'not justifiable' (because criminal) by the *lex loci*.

However, the approach exemplified by *McLarty* and *Machado* did not take root in Scotland[2]. In *Goodman v L & NW Railway Co*[3] an action was raised by a widow against a railway company for the death of her husband in England. Lord Shand in the Outer House considered the proposition 'extravagant' that a person could claim damages in the Scottish court for an accident in England when the English court would give no civil remedy in damages and he dismissed the action. In the defamation case of *Evans & Sons v Stein & Co*[4] Lord Kinnear ignored *McLarty* and interpreted *Phillips v Eyre* to mean that the act complained of must be civilly actionable (rather than simply wrongful) by the *lex loci delicti* as well as the *lex fori* and concluded,

'The law . . . as I think it is settled by modern decisions, is that in order to maintain an action *ex delicto* in the courts of this country, when the wrong is committed in another country, the wrong must be one for which an action can be maintained both by the law of this country and by the law of the country in which it is said to have been done . . . If there is no obligation *ex delicto* by the law of the place where the alleged wrong is done . . . there is no action anywhere'[5].

The later case of *Naftalin v LMS Railway Co*[6] clearly suggests that to be actionable in Scotland a delict that occurs abroad must be currently actionable in similar terms both in Scotland and in the country where the delict occurs. And finally the law was put beyond doubt by the Whole Court decision in

---

1 [1897] 2 QB 231.
2 And indeed was later held in England not to represent the law. In *Boys v Chaplin* [1971] AC 356 the House of Lords held that 'not justifiable' was synonymous with 'civilly actionable' and they overruled *Machado*. *McLarty* was formally overruled by the Whole Court decision of *McElroy v McAllister* 1949 SC 110.
3 (1877) 14 SLR 449.
4 (1904) 7 F 65.
5 (1904) 7 F 65 at 70–71.
6 1933 SC 259.

McElroy v McAllister[1], which affirms *Naftalin*, disapproves *Machado v Fontes* and overrules *McLarty v Steele* and *Horn v North British Railway Co*.

The current law

It has been clear since *McElroy v McAllister* that both the *lex fori* and the *lex loci delicti* are of relevance. Lord Justice-Clerk Thomson allows a role to both systems. He says that the *lex fori* must be satisfied because 'it would be too much to expect the Court of the forum to entertain an action for what is not a wrong by the law of the forum. The Court of the forum must in fundamentals be true to its own law'[2]. And the rules of the *lex loci delicti* must be satisfied because 'otherwise a quite unjustifiable emphasis is given to the *lex fori*'[3]. The Scots law since *McElroy v McAllister* has been stated to be to the effect that 'an action for reparation based on a delict committed outside Scotland will fail unless the pursuer can show that the specific *jus actionis* which he invokes is available and available to him both by Scots law and by the *lex loci delicti*'[4]. This is known as the 'double actionability' rule, and will apply to defamation cases as to other claims in delict. The effect is that a pursuer can claim damages for defamation in a Scottish court only if by both Scots law and the internal[5] law of the country in which the wrong occurs[6] he has the right to sue for defamation, in the capacity in which he sues[7]. Further, both legal systems must recognise the type of damages (ie the remedy) that the pursuer is seeking. So, for example, while written slander is actionable in both Scotland and England a pursuer cannot come to a Scottish court complaining of slander written in England and claim exemplary damages. That is a remedy that is not available in Scots law and the Scottish court cannot give effect to a head of damage recognised by the *lex loci delicti* but not the *lex fori*[8]. Nor can a plaintiff

---

1　1949 SC 110.

2　1949 SC 110 at 117.

3　1949 SC 110 at 118.

4　*Anton & Beaumont* p 401, approved by Lord Coulsfield in *James Burrough Distillers plc v Speymalt Whisky Distillers Ltd* 1989 SLT 561 at 564–565. As will be seen, below at pp 187–188 this formula is inaccurate in so far as it concerns the pursuer's onus of proof.

5　*Renvoi* is not appropriate: see Lord Russell in *McElroy v McAllister* 1949 SC 110 at 126.

6　That is, where the loss occurs: see below at pp 191–192.

7　So if he sues as a representative, this must be permitted and appropriate in both systems.

8　*Mitchell v McCulloch* 1976 SC 1. This decision was criticised by Professor JM Thomson in 'Delictual Liability in Scottish Private International Law' (1976) 25 ICLQ 873 on the ground that the decision asserts the primacy of the *lex fori* and leaves to the *lex loci* merely the subsidiary role of cutting down the pursuer's rights. However, both on the facts of the case and in principle the decision is surely correct. A Scottish court cannot give a remedy that is not within its own armoury of remedies. It is rather like going to an Irish court and asking for the matrimonial remedy of divorce: that cannot be had there, even by parties domiciled in Scotland, for while the Irish courts may recognise foreign divorces, it is not within their competence to grant what they do not have. And besides, as will be explained in the text, the role of the *lex loci* is precisely the subsidiary role of providing a possible defence to the pursuer's claim.

go to the English court complaining of a defamatory statement in Scotland and claim solatium for the affront, because English law does not recognise that head of damages. Conversely a pursuer cannot come to a Scottish court and claim solatium for an affront suffered in England, for affront is not a loss recognised in that jurisdiction[1]. To sue in Scotland for defamation which occurred in England the pursuer could claim only economic loss (which is recognised in both systems) and general damages (which we may call solatium) for loss of reputation. It is to be remembered that quantification of damages, and all other matters of procedure, are questions solely for the *lex fori*[2] and that the double actionability rule applies only to matters of substance such as actionability, heads of damage claimable and remoteness of damages[3].

It may seem harsh to impose an obligation on pursuers to satisfy two legal systems rather than one, but that harshness is mitigated by two important considerations. First, founding jurisdiction in the *lex loci delicti* will usually and especially since the coming into force of the Civil Jurisdiction and Judgments Act 1982 be relatively easy[4] and if the action is taken in the place where the harm occurred[5] the double actionability rule is elided. We need waste little sympathy on the pursuer who wishes to go elsewhere simply in the hope of obtaining higher damages.

Secondly and more significantly, it is quite wrong to say[6] that the pursuer has an obligation positively to satisfy two legal systems, thereby suggesting that the onus lies on the pursuer to establish actionability under both systems. For it is a principle of Scots law that, unless the contrary be averred and proved, foreign law is presumed to be the same as Scots law[7] and the pursuer in an action for defamation that occurs abroad is entitled to rely upon this presumption. The pursuer is not, therefore, obliged to prove that his claim is actionable by the foreign law (though he ought certainly to plead that he has a good claim according to the law of the place of the delict): rather, in relying on Scots law he is also relying on the same rules being applied in the *lex loci* and the result of this is that the onus lies on the defender to establish not only that a foreign legal system is applicable in addition to Scots law but also that the foreign legal system is different and that it denies actionability. In other words, in applying the double actionability rule, the pursuer has the onus only of establishing actionability by the *lex fori*, while the defender has the onus of proving (as a matter of fact) non-actionability by the *lex loci delicti*. Non-

---

1 *Naftalin v LMS Railway* 1933 SC 259; *McElroy v McAllister* 1949 SC 110. Both these cases involved a type of solatium not at that time recognised in England, being damages awarded to a surviving relative for the death of a person due to the negligence of a defender.
2 *Evans & Sons v Stein & Co* (1904) 7 F 65 at 71 per Lord Kinnear; *Mitchell v McCulloch* 1976 SC 1.
3 *McKinnon v Iberia Shipping Co* 1955 SC 20; *McElroy v McAllister* 1949 SC 110.
4 See above at pp 180–182.
5 This being, for the purposes of actionability, the place of the delict: see below at pp 191–192.
6 As, for example, Anton & Beaumont say in the quotation above at p 186.
7 *Stuart v Potter, Choate & Prentice* 1911 1 SLT 377 at 382 per Lord Salvesen; *Bonnor v Balfour Kilpatrick Ltd* 1974 SLT 187 per Lord Kincraig (upheld 1975 SLT (Notes) 3).

actionability by the *lex loci* is properly to be seen as a defence rather than actionability being seen as part of the claim[1].

Double actionability and prescription and limitation

Since the claim must be currently actionable by the particular pursuer against the particular defender on the same or substantially similar terms in both the law of the forum and the law of the country in which the harm is suffered, it follows that it is a defence that the claim has prescribed or is subject to limitation at the end of the period adopted by either legal system, whichever is the lesser. The action must be extant in both systems at the time it is raised and if it can be shown by the defender to have prescribed in one then the action will fail notwithstanding that it would still be available in the domestic law of the other[2]. The wording of section 23A of the Prescription and Limitation (Scotland) Act 1973[3] does not detract from this, for that section provides for the application of the foreign limitation period only when the matter is governed by the foreign law: under the double actionability rule the matter is governed by Scots law subject, as explained above, to there being a defence of non-actionability under the foreign law.

Double actionability and privilege

There is no doubt that if an action is raised in the Scottish court in circumstances in which, in the domestic situation, the statement complained of would not be actionable as being absolutely privileged by Scots law, then that conclusion will not be altered by the fact that the harmful effect of the defamation occurred in a country in which the statement would not be absolutely

---

1 See the decision to this effect of Popplewell J in the English cases of *University of Glasgow v Economist* and *University of Edinburgh v Economist* (1990) Times, 1 March. The correct approach was taken by the defender in *McLarty v Steele* (1881) 8 R 435 in which he proposed a counter-issue to the effect that the law of the place of the delict did not recognise actionability. The court disallowed that counter-issue but, of course, that decision was overruled in *McElroy v McAllister* 1949 SC 110. In *Bonnor v Balfour Kilpatrick Ltd* 1974 SLT 187, 1975 SLT (Notes) 3 the pursuer claimed damages for an accident that had occurred in Oman but made no averments as to whether the law of Oman recognised a right of action. The claim was held relevant on the basis that the foreign law was presumed to be the same as Scots law and therefore if Scots law allowed the action it was presumed, until the contrary was proved, that the foreign system allowed the action also. The pursuer could rely on the presumption and did not need to aver and prove the content of the foreign law. See *Armour v Thyssen* 1986 SLT 452, 1989 SLT 182 for the difficulties a defender will face in proving foreign law.

2 *McElroy v McAllister* 1949 SC 110. See especially at 125–128 per Lord Russell. Lord Keith dissents on this point, but does so on the basis that a wrongful act beyond the limitation period is 'not justifiable' and therefore applies an interpretation of *Phillips v Eyre* that is not accepted by the majority in the case and was indeed later disapproved by the House of Lords in *Boys v Chaplin* [1971] AC 356.

3 As inserted by s 4 of the Prescription and Limitation (Scotland) Act 1984: 'Where the substantive law of a country other than Scotland falls to be applied by a Scottish court as the law governing an obligation, the court shall apply any relevant rules of law of that country relating to the extinction of the obligation or the limitation of time within which proceedings may be brought to enforce the obligation to the exclusion of any corresponding rule of Scots law'.

privileged. So for example a defamatory remark made by an MP in the House of Commons would not found an action in Scotland even if the statement causes harm in a foreign country where absolute privilege is not granted to statements in the British Parliament. Not only would the double actionability rule not be satisfied since the law of Scotland as the forum does not recognise, because of privilege, the actionability of the statement[1], but the nature of privilege requires that the forum applies, even in the international setting, its own public policy, upon which the whole notion of privilege is based. The matter is rather less obvious if the privilege is granted not by Scots law but by the law of the place of the delict. Absolute privilege is based upon the forum's own policy and it can be argued that it is no place of the forum to further the policies of other fora or to protect freedom of speech in other countries: yet to apply the double actionability rule without qualification would have this effect. If, for example, one party in a civil action raised and conducted in England sues the other party for defamation during the litigation, the claim in Scotland would be allowed if malice is averred and proved while the claim in England would be absolutely barred. To accept that the claim should be barred in Scotland too, by applying the double actionability rule, is to further an English policy that is the reverse of the Scottish policy[2]. However, to ignore the absolute privilege granted by the *lex loci delicti* would have the result that the action in Scotland would be on the basis of an act done in England which would not found an action there: it ought not therefore to found an action here, for the very reason that the *lex loci* is of any relevance at all. This is not, in truth, the Scottish courts taking upon themselves the task of protecting English policy, but merely the recognition that it is a defence that no actionable act has been committed according to the law where the act is done. There is no authority, nor indeed reason in principle, why the double actionability rule should be qualified if the ground for non-actionability abroad is absolute privilege or any other principle based upon public policy.

Possible exception to the double actionability rule?

In England the strict application of the double actionability rule has for some time been felt to lead to injustice, particularly in cases in which the *lex loci delicti* is purely accidental and the parties are effectively isolated from it. In *Boys v Chaplin*[3] the plaintiff sued the defendant for injuries caused in a motor accident in Malta due to the latter's admitted negligence. Both parties were temporarily based in Malta as serving members of the British armed forces. Under Maltese law only damages for economic loss could be claimed, while under English law general damages for pain and suffering could also be claimed. A strict application of the double actionability rule would have meant that only economic losses could be compensated for, as being the only

---

1 See above at pp 91–92.
2 See above at p 108.
3 [1971] AC 356.

element recognised by both Maltese and English law. However the House of Lords held unanimously that the general damages recognised only in English law could be awarded and that their non-actionability in Maltese law would not provide a defence in the unusual circumstances of this case. Basically, the court was attempting to introduce some degree of flexibility into the law to allow for cases in which the *lex loci delicti* is purely accidental and has no real connection with the parties or the facts. How that flexibility was to be achieved was the subject of much dispute between the judges, and there is no real majority for any approach other than the recognition that flexibility may sometimes be necessary[1]. A House of Lords decision in an English case is of course highly persuasive in Scotland, but even if *Boys* had possessed an ace in the form of a single approach to the problem adopted by a majority, it would still be trumped by the Whole Court decision in *McElroy v McAllister*[2], in which there is no qualification to the double actionability rule there affirmed. Scots law comes from the Scottish case, which would have to be overruled before any of the approaches in *Boys v Chaplin* were followed.

And it is submitted that *McElroy* ought not to be overruled. While one can, just, accept that in a personal injuries case raised in negligence justice might sometimes only be done by departing from the double actionability rule, the same conclusion is not so readily reached in relation to defamation, or indeed any of the intentional delicts which have a greater analogy to crime than to negligence (and therefore a greater attachment to the place of the wrongful act). If, say, a Scottish-domiciled couple go to England for a weekend break and while there, enclosed in their motor car, one takes the opportunity verbally to defame the other with no-one else present, there is no good reason why the Scottish court should give a remedy – at the end of the day what was done was not wrongful where and when it was done and it is no reply to that to say that had it been done elsewhere it would have given rise to damages. Again, if a Scotsman writes to another Scotsman in Scotland, but the latter takes the letter to England and, while temporarily there, opens and reads the letter and is affronted by a defamatory comment contained therein, there is little obvious connection with the law of England. Or if a Scottish newspaper published, distributed and sold only in Scotland is purchased at Glasgow Airport and read on the London shuttle by a person defamed therein and affronted thereby, the law of England seems irrelevant. Why should the defender have a defence in both these situations to the effect that affront is not civilly actionable in England? The answer is, quite simply, that no wrong has been committed – the delict is committed where the harm occurs[3] and in that place there is no recognisable harm. The rule that the delict is committed where the harm occurs gives that place a say in the characterisation of the harm. It is submitted that the strict application of the double actionability rule, as described above, is entirely appropriate in cases of defamation and

1 See *Anton and Beaumont* pp 401–405, and the voluminous literature generated by the case cited therein.
2 1949 SC 110.
3 See below at p 181.

verbal injury and that the temptation to follow *Boys v Chaplin* in an attempt to introduce more flexibility into the law should be resisted. In this area at least such flexibility would be misconceived.

The place of the delict

To apply the double actionability rule it is, of course, necessary to know where the delict is located. With many forms of delict the place where it actually occurs can prove awkward to establish if different elements of the wrong occur in different countries[1]. Defamation may be stated in one country and have effect in another. So for example a person may publish a statement in Scotland which another person reads in England, causing economic loss in Canada. Where is the place of the delict for the purpose of the double actionability rule? The answer to this question is, in relation to the Scots law of defamation, relatively clear. The delict occurs where the loss occurs[2]. This rule was established in the following two cases.

In *Longworth v Hope*[3] an action was raised in the Court of Session concerning allegedly defamatory matter that had been published in a newspaper in London. The wrong was held to have been committed in Scotland where the harm (hurt to the pursuer's reputation and feelings) resulted, rather than in England where the defenders had acted. In the words of Lord Deas[4], 'the reputation can only be taken away where the reputation exists; and the character and credit can only be injured or taken away where the character and credit exist . . . The injury is done where the publication takes place'.

Similarly, in *Evans & Sons v Stein & Co*[5] a letter which was allegedly defamatory had been written and posted in Scotland and received and read in England. In an action in Scotland the First Division held (overruling the Lord Ordinary) that the loss had occurred in England and therefore the delict had been committed there: as a result the claim had to be actionable in England as the *lex loci delicti* on the same terms as it would be actionable in Scotland as the *lex fori* (and since that requirement was not met the action was dismissed). Lord Kinnear said:

---

1 See *Anton & Beaumont* pp 412–414. In for example *Soutar v Peters* 1912 1 SLT 111, in an action for seduction and breach of promise of marriage, the promise had allegedly occurred in Scotland and the sexual intercourse thereupon had allegedly occurred in England. It was held that the essence of the wrong, being the 'preliminary steps . . . where [the defender] practises the arts and wiles whereby he fraudulently captured the woman's affections' had taken place in Scotland which was, therefore, the *lex loci delicti*.
2 A different approach is evident in *John Walker & Sons v Douglas McGibbon & Co* 1972 SLT 128 in which a wrong was held to have occurred in the place where the defenders acted, but this decision can be explained by the fact that the case was one of interdict, where the defender's actions are more clearly of the essence than the pursuer's loss.
3 (1865) 3 M 1049.
4 (1865) 3 M 1049 at 1058.
5 (1904) 7 F 65.

'I quite agree with Lord McLaren that the injury which the pursuer alleges must be held to have been done in Wolverhampton when he opened and read the letter which contains injurious imputations. So long as the letter was not opened and read by anyone except the person who wrote it, no harm was done, and . . . the injury, if there was injury, was done only when the pursuer opened and read the letter'[1].

It may follow from this, of course, that a defamatory attack can result in there being a number of *loci delicti*. Newspaper and book publishing and radio and television broadcasting can, in particular, result in the spreading of defamatory attacks far and wide as can, even more potently, electronic and computer-driven methods of communication[2]. The rule is not to the effect that there is a defence to an action in Scotland when the defender can show non-actionability in any country in which the attack is published. Rather, the pursuer will be able to claim damages for losses caused abroad only if these losses result from wrongs civilly actionable in the place where they occur[3] and the defence is that there is no liability in that place. So it would be a defence to an action in Scotland that the losses suffered in England were not actionable there (because, for example, affront is not actionable) even although the libel is also published in, say, South Africa where affront does give a good cause of action. If the affront was actually felt in England, it is that law that can be used to provide a defence through the double actionability rule.

It also follows that actions may be available in a number of different countries. So long as the pursuer seeks damages for the losses separately incurred in these different countries a plea of *res judicata* will not be available to the defender since each claim will be for different losses. However, in any action for defamation brought in Scotland the defender may give evidence in mitigation of damages that the pursuer has recovered damages, or has brought actions for damages, for defamation in respect of the publication of words to the same effect as the words on which the action is founded, or has received or agreed to receive compensation in respect of such publication[4]. This would cover damages obtained in other countries.

---

1 (1904) 7 F 65 at 69–70.
2 In *University of Glasgow v Economist* and *University of Edinburgh v Economist* (1990) Times, 1 March two Scottish plaintiffs sued in England for a defamation that was allegedly published in over 40 jurisdictions.
3 *Longworth v Hope* (1865) 3 M 1049 at 1057 per Lord Deas.
4 Defamation Act 1952, s 12.

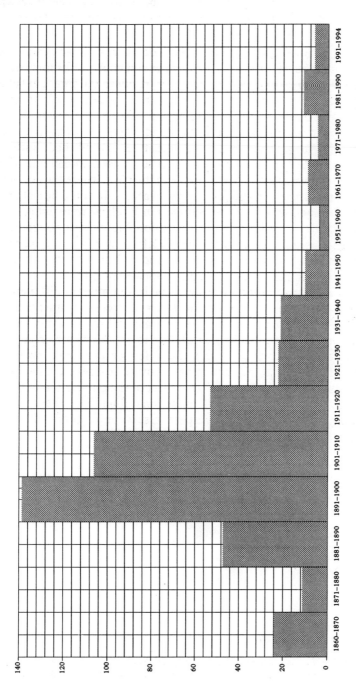

Number of defamation and verbal injury cases appearing in the Scottish law reports 1860–1994.

Index

r